IRELAND AND THE FICTION
OF IMPROVEMENT

Ireland and the Fiction of Improvement

HELEN O'CONNELL

OXFORD
UNIVERSITY PRESS

OXFORD
UNIVERSITY PRESS

Great Clarendon Street, Oxford OX2 6DP

Oxford University Press is a department of the University of Oxford.
It furthers the University's objective of excellence in research, scholarship,
and education by publishing worldwide in

Oxford New York

Auckland Cape Town Dar es Salaam Hong Kong Karachi
Kuala Lumpur Madrid Melbourne Mexico City Nairobi
New Delhi Shanghai Taipei Toronto

With offices in

Argentina Austria Brazil Chile Czech Republic France Greece
Guatemala Hungary Italy Japan Poland Portugal Singapore
South Korea Switzerland Thailand Turkey Ukraine Vietnam

Oxford is a registered trade mark of Oxford University Press
in the UK and in certain other countries

Published in the United States
by Oxford University Press Inc., New York

British Library Cataloguing in Publication Data
Data available

Library of Congress Cataloging in Publication Data
Data available

Typeset by Laserwords Private Limited, Chennai, India
Printed in Great Britain
on acid-free paper by
Biddles Ltd., King's Lynn, Norfolk

ISBN 0–19–928646–9   978–0–19–928646–1

1 3 5 7 9 10 8 6 4 2

For John and James

Acknowledgements

I am enormously grateful to the staff of the National Library of Ireland for assistance over many years with the research for this book. Thanks to the staff of both the Representative Church Body Library, Dublin and the Library of University College Dublin.

This book has been much improved by the reports of the two readers for Oxford University Press and I am very grateful to them for their support. The earlier feedback from Seamus Deane and Declan Kiberd on the original PhD thesis has been invaluable. In addition, I am indebted to them both for assistance over the last few years. Tadgh O'Sullivan and Emer Nolan very kindly read chapters of this book and I have benefited from their comments. The following deserve thanks for help on points of research at various stages: John Kelly, Harold Hislop, P. J. Mathews, Niall Ó Ciosáin, and Joanna Wydenbach; Glenn Hooper obligingly sent me a copy of the typescript of his book, *Travellers in Ireland, 1750–1850*. The inaccuracies and gaps that remain here are solely my responsibility.

I would like to thank the following: my family, Charlotte Bourke, Steven Bourke, Janet Clare, Brian Donnelly, Aileen Douglas, Darryl Jones, Jarlath Killeen, Norman Kelvin, Anne Mulhall, Michelle O'Connell, Nickolas Pappas, Margaret Robson, and Joshua Wilner.

The completion of this book was made possible by the financial assistance of the Department of English Studies at the University of Durham. Special thanks to Catherine Davidson, Stephen Regan, and Patricia Waugh. Thanks also to Dermot Seymour and Kevin Kavanagh for permission to reproduce the painting, *Consumed Unit of Silver*, on the cover.

Andrew McNeillie, Veronica Ions, Tom Perridge, Valerie Shelley, and Eva Nyika at Oxford University Press have all been hugely helpful and patient and I am very grateful to them for lessening the trials of publication.

My greatest debt is to John Nash for supporting this project from the outset and for so much else besides. This book would have been unimaginable without him.

Contents

Abbreviations

The following abbreviations of works by William Carleton are used throughout this book. Full publication details are provided in the Bibliography.

Art Maguire	*Art Maguire, or The Broken Pledge* (Dublin, 1845).
Autobiography	*The Autobiography*, vol. i. First published London, 1896. Reprinted with a Foreword by Benedict Kiely (Belfast: White Row Press, 1996).
Emigrants of Ahadarra	*The Emigrants of Ahadarra: A Tale of Irish Life* (London and Belfast, 1848).
Parra Sastha	*Parra Sastha, or The History of Paddy-Go-Easy and his Wife Nancy* (Dublin, 1845).
The Red-Haired Man's Wife	*The Red-Haired Man's Wife* (Dublin and London, 1889).
Rody the Rover	*Rody the Rover, or The Ribbonman* (Dublin, 1845).
The Squanders of Castle Squander	*The Squanders of Castle Squander* (London, 1852).
The Tithe Proctor	*The Tithe Proctor: A Novel, Being a Tale of the Tithe Rebellion in Ireland* (London and Belfast, 1849).
TSIP	*Traits and Stories of the Irish Peasantry, with an Autobiographical Introduction* (Dublin 1842–4). Facsimile Edition, 2 vols. (Gerrards Cross, Bucks: Colin Smythe, 1990).
Valentine M'Clutchy	*Valentine M'Clutchy, the Irish Agent, or The Chronicles of Castle Cumber* (Dublin, London, and Edinburgh, 1845).
Willy Reilly	*Willy Reilly and his Dear Colleen Bawn: A Tale Founded upon Fact* (London, 1855).

The first person who, having enclosed a plot of land, took it into his head to say *this is mine* and found people simple enough to believe him, was the true founder of civil society.

Jean-Jacques Rousseau

Introduction: The Aesthetics of Plainness

A STORY commonly told about Irish writing is that it failed to produce realist fiction at a time when realism was flourishing in the European mainstream. Rather than narrating fictions of social harmony, Irish writers were supposedly more drawn to the imaginative excesses of fantasy and supernaturalism. According to this version of literary history, weird, imaginative, and, at times, incoherent tales are prevalent in Irish writing while stories of thriving, stable communities united by a shared rhetoric and frame of reference are notably absent. Irish history can be drawn upon to confirm this account of the literature of the nineteenth century: the instability of the post-Union period, the absence of a strong middle class, and absenteeism are all thought to work against the production of realism but to provide fertile ground for works of wild literary experimentation.[1] Hence, Irish writing has been characterized as either Romantic or modernist, lacking the stable, disciplining middle ground of a liberal realism. The following study seeks to undermine that description of Irish literary history by exploring a tradition of writing that was neither Romantic nor modernist, but which sought instead to ensure that such literary modes would be rendered entirely redundant.

This book accordingly examines a particular strain of realism that found expression in the 'improvement' fiction of post-Union Ireland. Strongly didactic and assertively realistic, Irish improvement fiction laboured to address the squalid condition of post-Union Ireland by instructing both peasants and landowners in a range of practical matters such as agricultural modernization and the effective administration of estates. In these tracts, instruction is conveyed in fictional narratives

---

[1] See Terry Eagleton, *Heathcliff and the Great Hunger: Studies in Irish Culture* (London: Verso, 1995), 145–225; Joep Leerssen, *Remembrance and Imagination: Patterns in the Literary and Historical Representation of Ireland in the Nineteenth Century* (Cork: Field Day/Cork University Press, 1996); Ina Ferris, *The Romantic National Tale and the Question of Ireland* (Cambridge: Cambridge University Press, 2002).

and dialogues, which are simultaneously fantasies of harmony and stability. This material was intended to appeal to a peasant readership by being packaged in the guise of the popular chapbooks of the period. Improvement tracts were distributed within the channels of popular literature or delivered directly to the doorstep of peasant readers by landowners, clergy, and, on occasion, improvement writers themselves. The tracts were, in the first instance, supposed to counter the demand for popular literature, diverting attention away from the political propaganda and 'immoral' chapbooks that were in circulation in Ireland from the late eighteenth century onwards. These texts were supposed to eradicate the very ground of popular literature, transforming those social conditions that gave rise to such material as *Valentine and Orson* and even Thomas Paine's *The Rights of Man*. This reforming impulse did not stop at political tracts and popular chapbooks, but was also directed more generally towards literary discourses such as Romantic poetry and the novel.

Improvement fiction was addressed to landowners and the upper classes as well as the peasantry in a sustained effort to create a shared textual frame of reference in post-Union Ireland. As such, it was an attempt to re-define the textual culture of the period, displacing aestheticism, fantasy, romance, and political extremism with a strongly practical and realistic body of writing. This realism was itself entwined in a larger project to formulate a liberalism that would provide the necessary conditions for modernization in Ireland.

Unlike other terms such as utilitarianism or Marxism, 'improvement' is more amorphous and less associated with a distinct, definable body of thought as articulated by, say, a Bentham or a Marx. It tends to connote a historical period and set of events (such as the enclosure acts) more readily than a series of intellectual arguments or positions. The modern usage of improvement—'to make things better'—does not indicate the economic or intellectual history that lies behind this seemingly banal term. As a discourse, 'improvement' tends to exist at the margins of intellectual life—in so far as it is even seen to comprise a facet of intellectual history—in pamphlets, magazines, and the practical manuals of agriculturalists rather than in the mainstream of the history of thought. Through a focus on the improving fiction distributed as pamphlets to the peasantry and landowners throughout Ireland in the late eighteenth and early nineteenth centuries, this book shows how improvement can be understood in intellectual terms. The 'calmly practical' rhetoric of improvement, which sought to eschew any theoretical inquiry, was nonetheless produced by a range of events and occurrences in intellectual, political, and literary history.[2]

Campaigns to create an orderly and sanitized public realm were common throughout England from the late medieval period onwards. Correction facilities and workhouses were established and intolerance of idle, lewd, and drunken behaviour was expressed. While 'improvement' clearly stemmed from these various crusades, which were mostly urban in origin, the term is particularly associated with technological developments in agriculture in the seventeenth and eighteenth centuries. A process of rationalization, agricultural improvement transformed rural life in Britain in that period, enclosing common land and shifting the focus of production from local markets to larger commercial economies.[3]

Defining 'improvement', Paul Slack recounts how 'in the seventeenth century the word was just beginning to move by analogy beyond its initial association with the land.'[4] Additionally, Raymond Williams notes 'the complex underlying connection' between improvement and the extraction of profit.[5] In the pamphlet literature explored in this book, economic improvement was always tied at a rhetorical level to a code of frugality, sobriety, and restraint. The articulation of this set of values was central to the project of modernization. Profitable agricultural methods are presented as an essential component of the moral and properly fulfilled life, while an economy of hand-to-mouth production and consumption is shown to be debased, as well as the source of countless delusions and untruths.

Improvement was a stabilizing discourse, seeking consensus and coherence in the public sphere in order to prepare the ground for modernization and progress. In the post-revolutionary period, this discourse shaped the counter-revolutionary polemic of many British and Irish writers, including those analysed here. Irish improvement discourse laboured to represent the modernization of agricultural production by

---

[2] The phrase is Raymond Williams's characterization of improvement discourse in the eighteenth century. Williams, *The Country and the City* (London: Chatto and Windus, 1973), 65.

[3] For an account of improvement, ibid.; Paul Slack, *From Reformation to Improvement* (Oxford: Clarendon Press, 1999); and Richard Drayton, *Nature's Government: Science, Imperial Britain and the 'Improvement' of the World* (New Haven: Yale University Press, 2000).

[4] Slack, *From Reformation to Improvement*, 73.

[5] Raymond Williams, *Keywords: A Vocabulary of Culture and Society* (rev. and expanded edn., London: Fontana, 1983), 133.

recourse to 'tradition', emphasizing how improvement was a process of reform and certainly not one of revolution. The work of Mary Leadbeater, Charles Bardin, William Carleton, and Martin Doyle is rooted in a liberal tradition of counter-revolutionary discourse. For these writers, modernization was a process of clarification, the ridding of extremism, obscurity, and confusion from public discourse. Improvement modernization purports to reveal the harmony that, it claims, really does exist underneath the needless obfuscation of contemporary discourses. In making such a claim, improvement writers created a representation of a traditional, organic past that was nonetheless shaped by a range of novelistic and poetic conventions of the eighteenth and nineteenth centuries. As such, improvement tradition is a literary trope, which expresses discomfort with modern conditions—such as an expanded print culture and novelistic representation—while being itself both modernizing and a product of modernization.

Clearly, improvement discourse in Ireland was produced in the shadow of a set of troubling historical events, such as the French Revolution, the 1798 Rebellion, and the Act of Union of 1801. There were, however, other, less overtly historical, developments that impelled the writing of these fictions. Irish improvement fiction can be taken as exemplary of a particular mode of reaction, perceived by these writers as a crisis, in eighteenth- and nineteenth-century culture, which then stimulates the literary and cultural Revival at the end of the century. This reaction was produced by literary as well as political developments. Raymond Williams has described 'the retreat from society' which was signified by the novels of Samuel Richardson (particularly *Clarissa*) and by 'the later phases of Puritanism and still later of Romanticism'.[6] This retreat was sparked, in Williams's mind, by distress at the 'rootless order' of early capitalist society, which encouraged a brooding inwardness that shaped the later work of Richardson and the Romantic poetry of Blake, Wordsworth, and Shelley. This chronic situation was exemplified for improvement writers by a perceived breakdown of traditional and, supposedly, once reliable modes of representation. According to these writers, this predicament was rife in the novel and Romanticism, but also, in a more archaic mode, in the (apparently) incoherent ravings of the poor. Improvement fiction was an attempt to rescue experience from this chaos and anarchy, all of which could potentially lead into dangerous political experimentation. Connections were continually forged

---

6 Williams, *The Country and the City*, 65.

in improvement tracts between a reluctance to accept the conventional, prevailing social modes and politicization.

The writers of improvement fiction in Ireland were primarily secular liberals whose liberalism was principally formed in response to events such as the French Revolution, but, as will be shown here, that response was also determined by literary developments. These writers were keen to differentiate their fiction from both the novel and Romantic poetry, insisting that the didactic tract exemplified a form of writing that was free from the delusions and difficulties that characterized other genres as well as particular political and social situations. Writers of improvement fiction prided themselves on possessing a disciplined focus on the state of things in the empirical world and of prescribing a practical and logical means of addressing the endemic problems of post-Union life. The language of these tracts is, of course, supposed to embody this discipline by a commitment to a strict plainness and simplicity. Improvement prose seeks to liberate itself from the ambiguities and confusions that allegedly characterize 'literary' writing; as such the didactic tract sets itself against the 'literary', aspiring to surmount the representational void of so much contemporary writing. Improvement writers were made deeply nervous by the 'retreat' described by Williams—for them an abyss from which their pamphlets were supposed to mark a return.

The writers examined in this book were perturbed by the democratization of literary forms which supposedly lay at the root of both the popular novel and a thriving market in chapbooks and pamphlets. However, improvement fiction was itself made possible by that democratization: many writers of didactic tracts were women, who both instigated and benefited from this democratized literary culture. Improvement writers nonetheless sought to regulate this literary environment by pleading for a strongly plain and unmediated form of representation (which was also supposed to characterize their realist fictions). Plain language was itself, of course, a product of literary discourse and, as this book shows, was a stock convention of didactic fiction. It is notable that clarity was such a preoccupation in the work of women writers (as in that of Hannah More, Maria Edgeworth, and Mary Leadbeater). Women writers asserted plainness against a perceived obscurity (deemed to be rampant in poetry) in order to distance themselves from feminized and, thus, supposedly convoluted genres.

This book does not purport to offer a comprehensive history of improvement discourse in Ireland in the late eighteenth and early nineteenth centuries. That project would be too enormous an undertaking for a single study and beyond the scope of the literary analysis undertaken here. Instead, the focus of this study is the improvement fiction that was distributed directly to the peasantry as pamphlets or disseminated through pedlars packaged in the format of popular chapbooks.[7] Explicitly, the improvement material discussed here was written in reaction to popular literature. Both J. R. R. Adams and Niall Ó Ciosáin have written of the place of Irish improvement fiction in the context of general histories of the popular literature and culture of this period. They both recount the manner in which improvers attempted to assert control over popular print culture. Adams emphasizes how improvement writers succeeded in shaping popular reading in the early nineteenth century whereas Ó Ciosáin claims that these tracts and pamphlets did not permeate the popular culture of the period in any truly significant way.[8] This study will show that it was not simply disgust with popular literature that motivated improvement writers, but that the presumed aestheticism of 'high' literary culture also compelled them to produce their self-consciously materialist fictions. For these writers, both high and low culture presented a similar, and profoundly disconcerting, spectacle of meaninglessness and social breakdown that had to be overcome.

The project of improvement in Ireland in the nineteenth century was an attempt to curb the alleged excesses and hedonism associated with the rural peasantry—impoverished yet, paradoxically, given to excess—and those political discourses (particularly Republicanism) that seemed to be endlessly seductive to the Irish masses. Indeed, the Irish Revival of the late nineteenth and early twentieth centuries should be understood against this broader context: the aestheticism of Revival writers such as Yeats, Synge, and Hyde was both a product of improvement modernization and a deeply felt reaction against it. Revivalism, in its celebration of excess, supernaturalism, and rural poverty, can be understood as a retort to the rationalizing project of improvement in Ireland in the nineteenth century.

---

[7] The writings of both Mrs S. C. Hall and Harriet Martineau are excluded from this book on the grounds that they were not distributed to the peasantry as pamphlets or chapbooks. On Martineau, see Harriet Martineau, *Letters from Ireland*, ed. Glenn Hooper (Dublin: Irish Academic Press, 2001), and on Hall, see Maureen Keane, *Mrs S. C. Hall: A Literary Biography* (Gerrards Cross, Bucks.: Colin Smythe, 1997).

[8] J. R. R. Adams, *The Printed Word and the Common Man: Popular Culture in Ulster 1700–1900* (Belfast: Institute of Irish Studies, 1987), 43–61; and Niall Ó Ciosáin, *Print and Popular Culture in Ireland, 1750–1850* (Basingstoke: Macmillan, 1997), 132–53.

The starting point for this study is the distribution throughout Ireland of the Cheap Repository Tracts of the English evangelical and counter-revolutionary writer Hannah More. More's tracts were distributed by the Association for Discountenancing Vice (ADV) in an attempt to counteract the prominence of immoral chapbooks and seditious literature.[9] The tracts were disseminated by a variety of means, so that they might instil practicality and organization in a society that was perceived to be wildly impractical and overly imaginative. Hannah More was herself a member of the ADV, an organization which had directly supported the establishment of her Cheap Repository Tracts in 1795.[10] The ADV was founded as an educational and evangelical agency within the Church of Ireland in 1792. In this capacity, it administered educational grants and attempted to formulate an educational model for schools under its jurisdiction. These evangelical societies in Ireland were modelled on similar organizations in Britain, which established Sunday schools and printing presses for the publication of tracts and pamphlets.

More sought to intervene in the development of literacy by shaping reading and writing practices in accordance with a rigid social code. According to Susan Pederson, More's Cheap Repository Tracts 'consciously' adopted 'the forms, writing styles, and even distribution channels of popular literature'.[11] The circulation of cheap editions of *The Rights of Man* was of particular concern for More, who countered Paine's republicanism in all of her tracts with a strident evangelicalism. More pioneered the practice of distributing the pamphlets through pedlars at prices competitive with popular chapbooks, which was to be imitated later in Ireland by the Society for Promoting the Education of the Poor of Ireland (also known as the Kildare Place Society). Tracts advising on moral and economic improvement were set to compete directly with the chapbooks and pamphlets of popular distribution and indirectly with discourses of republicanism. The Cheap Repository Tracts were also a response to the alleged aestheticism of Romanticism as well as to popular literature—More pitting a strictly empirical ideology against Romantic idealism (seen, of course, to be complicit with revolutionary France).

---

[9] The very title of that organization expresses the rhetorical origins of 'improvement' in the reforming projects of early modern Britain. See Slack, *From Reformation to Improvement*.

[10] Ó Ciosáin, *Print and Popular Culture in Ireland*, 136.

[11] Susan Pedersen, 'Hannah More Meets Simple Simon: Tracts, Chapbooks and Popular Culture in Late Eighteenth Century England', *Journal of British Studies*, 25/1 (Jan. 1986), 88.

The restraint and frugality called for in More's tracts were an attempt to subsume idealism in an assertive practicality and to warn against any tendency to disengage from the material world through politics, aesthetics, or any behaviour, such as drinking or idleness, that skewed one's rational grasp of reality. Writers such as More were greatly perturbed by the Republican rationality expressed by revolutionary figures such as Paine, but their entire counter-revolutionary project relied on the very rational codes exemplified by texts such as *The Rights of Man*. The Cheap Repository Tracts were enormously influential in shaping improvement fiction in Ireland, but—given their evangelical excess—were generally acknowledged by writers such as Leadbeater to be inappropriate reading material in a context of religious and political tensions.

At a certain level, More's tracts complemented a project that was already under way in Ireland in the late eighteenth century and which was exemplified by the literary and administrative labours of the Edgeworths. The novels of Maria Edgeworth were a component of the various experiments in agricultural improvement, pedagogy, and estate management conducted on the Edgeworthstown estate. These experiments were all pursued with strictly utilitarian ends in mind (not that this was always necessarily the outcome). Edgeworth used the genre of the novel to imagine the possibility of a post-Union community that would be harmonized by work and productivity rather than divided by religion and politics. As such, Ireland would become safely 'British', ceasing to be a colonial oddity and irritation.

R. L. Edgeworth's interest in educational issues and role as commissioner for a series of inquiries into Irish education make him a central figure in the history of educational policy in Ireland and therefore of importance to any analysis of improvement education. Both Edgeworths should be understood within a particular counter-revolutionary tradition, which, secular-liberal rather than conservative-evangelical in nature, articulates profound nervousness regarding republicanism, Romantic aesthetics, and revolution; as such their work seeks to mark a sharp distinction between theory and practice, discounting the former in order to ensure the possibility of the latter (a gesture that was seen to be absolutely necessary in Irish conditions). This is particularly evident in all of Maria Edgeworth's Irish fiction. It is in this intellectual (or anti-intellectual) sense that the Edgeworths were to make their hugely significant contribution to the history of Irish writing. The literary repercussions of the Edgeworthian project were immense: Maria Edgeworth's novels all seek to 'improve' novelistic representation, rendering the novel a responsible and engaged literary genre that was fully immersed in, rather than disengaged from, actual conditions. Crucially for the history of both Irish writing and the novel, Edgeworth's fiction appeared to provide a means of narrativizing a way out of both novelistic and Romantic impasse. Her 'national tale' is resolutely counter-Romantic, preparing the ground for the nationalizing, Scottish novels of Walter Scott. In this respect, Edgeworth's writing needs to be read in terms of its sustained critique of Romanticism, which, in turn, determined the Irish literary mainstream through to the Revival. Recent scholarship has placed Edgeworth and Sydney Owenson (Lady Morgan) within the context of Romanticism, categorizing the 'national tale' as a 'Romantic' genre. The work of both Edgeworth and—if less coherently—Owenson was written in reaction to Romanticism. That reaction also underwrote improvement discourse and, indeed, the literary fiction of the nineteenth century. Whatever their source, the rhetorical excesses of *The Wild Irish Girl* are not rooted in Romanticism. Her national tale, *The Wild Irish Girl,* is strongly practical, berating Irish peasants for laziness and the remnants of the Gaelic aristocracy for a debilitating nostalgia. To Owenson, post-Union Ireland presented itself as an impasse, which she sought to resolve by subsuming the perceived excesses of 'Gaelic' culture by translation, novelistic narrative, and a marriage plot of Saxon and Celt.

Given their commitment to improvement in Ireland, it is unsurprising that the Edgeworths became involved in the production and distribution of Mary Leadbeater's *Cottage Dialogues* throughout 1809. Both Edgeworths advised Leadbeater on a range of matters regarding her fictional tract and arranged for its publication in London. The English edition was accompanied by a preface and glossary, the former written by Maria Edgeworth and the latter composed by R. L. Edgeworth (in the mode of his annotations for *Castle Rackrent*). Edgeworth's novels feed into Leadbeater's tracts, where scenes from *Ennui* and *The Absentee* are reworked (or translated perhaps) for more assertively didactic ends. While Leadbeater directly followed the example of Hannah More by presenting her pamphlets in the form of popular chapbooks, Edgeworth's fiction served as a model of a didactic realism that was secularizing rather than proselytizing. This didacticism was aggressively materialist, claiming that its representations of rural life were all grounded in the actual conditions of post-Union Ireland and were free of any embellishment or distortion. Leadbeater insisted on the authenticity of the fiction in all of her pamphlets, claiming that 'I told nothing that I have not seen or known.'[12] Anxiety regarding popular chapbooks and the novel forced Leadbeater to distinguish her tracts from these vulgar and, in her mind, deceitful genres. Clearly, tracts that warned steadily against superstition and irrationality felt obliged to present themselves as resolutely truthful and realistic.

Leadbeater's fiction addressed both peasants and landowners in a sustained effort to reform the rural agricultural economy. As a member of the Society of Friends, Leadbeater articulated a liberal ideology of moderation and inclusiveness (as compared with the evangelicalism of More or the members of the ADV). She was firmly opposed to all proselytizing, which, in her mind, only worked to antagonize the very rural Catholic class she wanted to reform. Traditional political and religious disputes in Ireland were, for Leadbeater, an obstacle to necessary economic development, which in turn depended upon the education and improvement of the Catholic lower classes. Central to Leadbeater's writing was the conviction that modernization was not political and was, indeed, transcendent of political disputes, differences, and traditions. However, as this book argues, her fiction repeatedly points to the political basis of improvement discourse, demonstrating how notions of difference—between the pre-modern and the modern, orality and literacy, and Irish and English—were central to the articulation of improvement modernization.

Leadbeater attempted to define a middle ground between colonialism and republicanism, one which would be governed by the rationality of markets and profits and unburdened by claims of memory and difference. In addition, she sought to break with the despotic colonialism of the eighteenth century, advocating instead a liberal discourse which would provide the proper conditions (and terms of rhetoric) for the achievement of economic modernization. Writers such as Leadbeater laboured to represent an utterly ordinary existence, which thrived in the absence of all political and religious tensions and had no need whatsoever for 'thought' or reflection. Her tracts were an attempt to represent a version of community which would be distinguished by coherence and order and united in a highly rational manner by a shared commitment to the market. This fiction seeks to recount and enact

---

[12] Mary Leadbeater, Preface, *Anecdotes Taken from Real Life, for the Improvement of Children* (Dublin, 1809), p. vi.

a narrative of progress from squalid conditions, riven by politics and difference, to harmonious civility.

Leadbeater's non-denominationalism was the stock rhetoric of Irish improvement discourse as well as being a policy of most educational institutions in the post-Union period (particularly those in receipt of government grants). A teacher-training college and publishing house, the Society for Promoting the Education of the Poor of Ireland (more commonly known as the Kildare Place Society) was the first organiza-tion to institutionalize non-denominationalism.[13] In 1811, it received a government grant for its teacher-training college, which educated teachers from all religious backgrounds in an attempt to create an edu-cational culture in Ireland that would be free of the religious prejudices that paralysed Irish society. The Kildare Place Society was supposed to provide an alternative to both hedge schools and proselytizing society schools, displacing both the political extremism of the former and the religious fervour of the latter.

Throughout the nineteenth century, a variety of institutions and organizations, such as the National Schools and Young Ireland, also proclaimed a non-denominational ethos. So too did cultural societies of the Revival period, such as the Irish Literary Society in London and Dublin and the Gaelic League. This non-denominational rhetoric was not, of course, welcomed by all constituencies. By mid-century, the Catholic Church declared its frustration and refused to back the new so-called 'godless' Queen's colleges. The Catholic hierarchy equated non-denominationalism with Protestantism whereas for liberal improvers it signified the necessary conditions for progress. The Catholic Church withdrew its support of Kildare Place education in 1825 amidst reports that many of the schools in its jurisdiction were engaged in proselytizing. In part, the educational debates of the mid- and late nineteenth century, such as Newman's appointment as Rector of the Catholic University in 1854, the establishment of the Queen's Colleges and the Royal University, are better understood against the background of these experiments in improvement education at the beginning of the century. While these educational debates are beyond the scope of this study, the analysis of improvement discourse in this book does provide a neglected

[13] For an account of the Kildare Place training college by a former pupil, see Harry Whitney, Philomath [Patrick Kennedy], *Legends of Mount Leinster: Tales and Sketches* (Dublin, 1855), 214–34.

context for the controversies surrounding the provision of education in Ireland up to the foundation of the state in 1922.

The Kildare Place Society exemplified and, in many ways, perpetuated the non-denominational rhetoric of the early nineteenth century. The Society initially distributed reprints of English textbooks to schools and pedlars, but, following the example of More and Leadbeater, produced its own series of school texts and improving pamphlets from 1816 until the Society was dissolved in 1831. As well as the standard primers and mathematical texts, the Kildare Place list included travel narratives, improvement fiction, and studies of natural history.[14] Two Kildare Place Society tracts will be examined in detail in this book: Leadbeater's *The Pedlars* (1826) and the Revd Charles Bardin's *Cottage Fireside* (1826). Many of the Kildare Place pamphlets were adapted or written by Bardin in his capacity as literary secretary to the Society from 1817. Bardin's task was to produce improving literature and to excise any evangelical or anti-Catholic material from the Kildare Place reprints. Yet, it so happens that Bardin was also an active member of the proselytizing ADV. Bardin clearly felt at home within both organizations, singularly embodying the ideological complexity of Anglican culture and Irish liberalism throughout this period. It is striking that he was working by day to ensure the absence of religious polemic in Kildare Place texts whilst faithfully attending meetings of the Association for Discountenancing Vice of an evening.[15]

In *Voyage of the Amber*, a Kildare Place travel text adapted by Bardin, the civilizing nature of both empire and improvement is emphasized:

What a blessing is navigation, when it thus affords the means of imparting to the ignorant savage the arts and improvements of civilization. Indeed, it may be remarked, that this makes the distinction between the maritime discoveries of the present and former ages; the main object of the present being the extension of science, and the good of the human race, whilst those of earlier times, however enterprising the persons engaged in them, were undertaken solely from the spirit of conquest, or of personal gain.[16]

[14] Harold Hislop, 'The Kildare Place, 1811–1831: An Irish Experiment in Popular Education', PhD thesis, University of Dublin, 1990, 118.

[15] Bardin's presence at ADV meetings is clearly noted in the Minutes for the Proceedings of the ADV, 1820 (Representative Church Body Library: MS 174).

[16] [Charles Bardin], *Voyage of the Amber* (Dublin, 1831), 7.

Like 'navigation', improvement literature was a component of the former kind of exploration, devoted to 'progress' and phrased precisely to signify assistance for the poor and 'savage' rather than the imperial conquest of peoples and territories. Bardin's improving project portrayed itself as enlightening rather than conquering (or colonial), committed to gentle persuasion and example, not coercion or force. There is no doubt that such narratives were intended to convince the Irish peasant of the utter necessity of imperialism in the guise of both exploratory navigation and improving pamphlets and institutions. These narratives also worked to instil factuality, an awareness of life as a material, physical experience in place of what was perceived to be a prevailing immaterialism.

In keeping with this, 'scientific' and broadly 'factual' analysis of natural resources was already under way in the early nineteenth century by means of statistical surveys, agricultural improving societies, and travel literature.[17] Improvement fiction was in part written in response to the conventionalized representation of the backward Ireland of travel narratives.[18] The fiction discussed here sought to remedy that representation by imagining, and bringing into being, a coherent and orderly post-Union society. This tract literature was part of a project to assimilate Ireland fully within a broader British polity by erasing those residues of a supposedly eccentric and anachronistic social order. Irish improvement discourse was an attempt to enact the process of rationalization called for by travellers to Ireland throughout this period. The distribution of travel texts to schools and homes throughout Ireland by the Kildare Place Society is itself an indication of the common ground between the discourse of travel and that of improvement. As travel literature was entwined in enlightenment discourses of progress, it is to be expected that the genre should lurk in the background of

[17] In his study of Irish travel literature in the post-Union period, Glenn Hooper notes how British writers repeatedly pointed to the absence of comprehensive facts and figures regarding the country's resources. These writers argue endlessly that Ireland could not be properly absorbed within Britain until the country was properly analysed and classified. One of the implications of Hooper's study is that the establishment of fact and, indeed, the institutionalization of 'information' were themselves forms of improvement. See Glenn Hooper, *Travel Writing and Ireland, 1760–1860: Culture, History, Politics* (Basingstoke and London: Palgrave, 2005).

[18] For a discussion of the relationship between travel literature and nineteenth-century Irish writing, see Ferris, *The Romantic National Tale and the Question of Ireland*, and for an analysis of travel writing in an enlightenment context, see Seamus Deane, 'Virtue, Travel and the Engligtenment', *Foreign Affections: Essays on Edmund Burke* (Cork: Cork University Press/Field Day, 2005), 47–56.

improvement discourse in Ireland (the country itself the subject of a vast archive of travel literature).

Like many improvement pamphlets, the Kildare Place readers eagerly asserted facts (or rationality), in the form of scientific and geographic knowledge, over fiction, as expressed in the oral narratives and superstitions of the poor. Even the titles of these publications are notable in this respect: *Animal Sagacity: Exemplified by Facts* (1824) and *The Entertaining Medley, Being a Collection of True Histories and Anecdotes* (1826). These narratives were all presumed to be safely educational, conveying 'matter' about the physical world rather than perpetuating superstitious delusions or political fictions.

The establishment of agricultural fact was of particular concern for the Revd William Hickey, who established a non-denominational agricultural seminary on the estate of Mr Samuel Boyce at Bannow, Co. Wexford.[19] The school was in existence from 1821 to 1826 and was even the subject of discussion by a House of Commons select committee in 1823.[20] After closing the seminary, Hickey produced many pamphlets under the pseudonym Martin Doyle, and was awarded a literary pension by Queen Victoria in the 1860s.[21] Doyle's writing—which ranges from plain instruction on farming methods to didactic fiction extolling the civility of an improved rural life—is discussed in detail in the following chapters. His most important contribution to agricultural improvement was *Hints to the Small Farmers of Ireland*, which—according to *Dublin University Magazine's* portrait of Doyle in January 1840—was 'successful beyond his most sanguine expectation', with 'edition after edition rapidly disappearing, and such was the sale that the "Hints" were stereotyped in order to meet the demand.'[22] All of Doyle's tracts attempted to instil a scientific understanding of agriculture in place of the traditional, barbarous methods of the rural poor.

The improvement pamphlets discussed in this study are analysed in particular relation to the stories and novels of William Carleton,

[19] An interesting description of the Bannow school is to be found in Leadbeater's *The Pedlars* (Dublin, 1826). Leadbeater was effectively advertising the school on Hickey's behalf.

[20] Revd P. A. Doyle, OSA, 'Bannow School (1821–1826)', *The Past: The Organ of the Uí Ceinnsealaigh Historical Society* (Nov. 1920), 126.

[21] The Scrapbook of Mrs William Hickey, National Library of Ireland: MS 407. As with most of the contents in the Scrapbook, the material relating to Doyle's pension is all undated.

[22] [Unsigned], 'Our Portrait Gallery—Martin Doyle', *Dublin University Magazine*, 15/7 (Apr. 1840), 374.

exploring the ways in which both tract and literary fiction constituted a discourse of improvement in Ireland in the early nineteenth century. In so doing, this book questions the claim in Joep Leerssen's study of nineteenth-century Ireland that 'there was very little caring, paternalistic improvement attempted' in the early nineteenth century 'apart from the quixotic bible missions and the interesting case of the national school system, which was treated with some mistrust in the very quarters it was supposed to benefit.'[23] However, the national schools were themselves a product of years of educational experimentation by liberal improvers who were opposed to the proselytizing bible organizations. According to Leerssen, 'many aspects of nineteenth-century cultural history in Europe have been studied by social historians in terms of a civilizing offensive' but 'there is very little of that sort of thing happening in Ireland.' The research put forth in this study necessarily challenges this claim, demonstrating the prevalence of liberal improvement discourse in Ireland in this period, all of which was strongly civilizing in intent. Carleton's career particularly exemplifies the manner in which 'a civilizing offensive' operated in nineteenth-century Ireland, one which had a lasting impact on the literary culture of the period.

Many commentators have noted the influence of Caesar Otway and the New Reformation on Carleton's early career and writing, and yet the hugely important influence of improvement tracts and institutions on his work has not been noted, let alone explored.[24] Carleton worked in the offices of the Sunday School society in Dublin in the early 1820s and, later, as a schoolmaster in parochial institutions administered by the ADV in Mullingar and Carlow.[25] The Church of Ireland records note that More's Cheap Repository Tracts and Leadbeater's *Cottage Dialogues* were used as class texts in the parochial school in Carlow throughout Carleton's employment in that institution.[26] Carleton's fiction was first published by Otway when he served as editor of the evangelical

---

[23] Leerssen, *Remembrance and Imagination*, 160.

[24] The exception is Rolf and Magda Loeber, who note that Carleton published three improving tracts in 1845, but they do not discuss his writing in relation to improvement discourse. See 'Fiction Written to and for Cottagers' in Bernadette Cunningham and Máire Kennedy, eds., *The Experience of Reading: Irish Historical Perspectives* (Dublin: Rare Books Group of the Library Association of Ireland and Economic Social History of Ireland, 1999).

[25] Unfortunately, the records of the Mullingar school no longer exist. For Carleton's own account of his employment in Mullingar and Carlow, see *Autobiography*, 218–37.

[26] 25 May 1823, Carlow Parish School Minutes, Oct. 1818– Mar. 1839 (Representative Church Body Library P. 317–313).

Christian Examiner. For Otway, Carleton's fiction was of importance because of its strongly improving character. Carleton's representation of a backward, oral Catholicism was, in his thinking, itself a form of improvement. Otway published Carleton's fiction in order to initiate a process of reform that should culminate eventually in improvement civility. Carleton's writing consistently imported the didactic tract into the stories and novels he produced throughout his literary career. I argue in what follows that Carleton's famous representations of peasant Ireland were grounded in the fictional world of the improvement tracts of the early nineteenth century and were not, as is still often assumed, faithful accounts of pre-Famine peasant life.

Doyle and Carleton were close contemporaries, contributing simultaneously to the improving *Irish Penny Journal* throughout its short existence from 1840 to 1841. Their fiction is so similar that Doyle was urged by his publishers to insert a preface into *Irish Cottagers* claiming that he had not read any of Carleton's stories prior to composing his own peasant narratives. In 1845 Carleton appended Doyle's *Hints to the Small Farmers of Ireland* to an edition of his own strikingly titled tract on agricultural improvement, *Parra Sastha, or The History of Paddy-Go-Easy and his Wife Nancy*, explicitly calling attention to the common ground between his fiction and the manuals produced by improvement writers at the time.

A story by Carleton entitled 'The Brothers: A Narrative' appeared in the evangelical *Christian Examiner* in 1830. Ten years previously, the Kildare Place Society had published a tract with the similar—if lengthier—title, *The Brothers, or Consequences: A Story of What Happens Every Day;* and, going further back, one of Hannah More's Cheap Repository Tracts of 1795 had also been entitled *The Brothers.* The fates of two brothers are contrasted in all three narratives: one is improving and predictably successful while the other meets with the unpleasant consequences of those who refuse to internalize the 'truths' of improvement. As is typical of all Carleton's *Christian Examiner* fiction, his characterization is explicitly sectarian: improvement is Protestant and failure is Catholic. Unlike his improving contemporaries in Ireland, Carleton freely espoused anti-Catholicism in his writing, but it is possible that such sectarianism was more acceptable in work which did not strictly obey generic distinctions and which was expressed by a Catholic rather than Church of Ireland or Presbyterian writer.

Like all improvement writers, Carleton sought to justify his own writing in terms of a need to displace the popular literature that had been the standard reading material in Irish schools and homes and which he himself claims to have read in his hedge school.[27] He explicitly denounced popular reading material such as *Freney the Robber* and *Valentine and Orson*, which he wanted to replace with his own morally and nationally improving texts. Carleton is important in this respect as he explicitly connects the discourse of improvement with that of a national literature, the latter a fulfilment of the practicality of the former. Carleton replicated improvement tracts in his writing in order to achieve a national literature, which would signify that Ireland had become 'a reading, and consequently a thinking, country' (*TSIP*, vol. i, p.vii). Like improvement writers, Carleton equated the act of reading with becoming a rational subject; if the people could read, it should only be a matter of time before they become rational, modern, and, indeed, enlightened citizens.

Carleton's importance as a writer lies in the manner in which he articulates the particular generic—and hence social and political—tensions of nineteenth-century writing within his fiction. From the nineteenth century onwards, however, his writing has been presented as an authentic representation of the vanishing peasant Ireland of the pre-Famine period. This interpretation of Carleton was famously expressed by Yeats when he described how in Carleton's writing 'the true peasant was at last speaking, stammeringly, illogically, bitterly, but nonetheless with the deep and mournful accent of the people.'[28] In Yeats's account, Carleton's stories are pervaded by the 'accent' of spoken language rather than the inflections of literary convention. For Yeats, still mindful of the creation of a national literature, Carleton was 'the historian of his class', providing a truthful representation of peasant orality.[29] While contemporary critics do not share Yeats's particular concerns, recent work has for the most part reiterated this interpretation of Carleton as an archivist of oral, peasant Ireland.[30] Carleton has been described as a 'seanachai' and oral storyteller by critics who proclaim the existence

[27] See Carleton, *Autobiography*, 73.
[28] W. B. Yeats, 'Introduction', *Representative Irish Tales*, 1891 (Gerrards Cross, Bucks: Colin Smythe, 1991), 28.
[29] Ibid. 28.
[30] See Robert Lee Woolf, *William Carleton, Irish Peasant Novelist: A Preface to his Fiction* (New York and London: Garland Publishing, 1979); Eileen Sullivan, *William*

of an authentic peasant 'voice' in his fiction.[31] By placing Carleton's fiction within the history of Irish improvement discourse, this book argues that Carleton's writing emanates from the written conventions of improvement discourse and does *not* provide an authentic representation of pre-Famine oral culture. When Carleton claims to be offering his readers truthful and accurate representations of rural life, he is invoking a standard convention of the improvement and novelistic fiction of the period. Furthermore, Carleton sought to expose the irrationality and barbarity of oral culture by attempting to represent its practices on the written page. By so doing, he places his work within the context of the improvement tracts and pamphlets distributed throughout Ireland in the early nineteenth century. I argue that his peasant characters and settings are more shaped by the improvement fiction of writers such as More and Leadbeater than by his own memories of rural life in Co. Tyrone.[32]

In 1845, James Duffy published three improvement tracts written by Carleton as part of Charles Gavan Duffy's Library of Ireland—*Parra Sastha, Art Maguire,* and *Rody the Rover*—but the earlier and more famous fiction was also shaped by the conventions of the didactic pamphlet: stories such as 'Larry M'Farland's Wake' (1830) and 'The Landlord and Tenant, An Authentic Story' (1830)—later called 'Lha Dhu'—were clearly written within the conventions of improvement fiction, espousing at a generic level the codes of rationalization while imparting advice on a range of practical matters. Carleton sought to position himself and his writing within a process of modernization rather than as the voice of a culture which was supposedly about to disappear. It was Carleton's understanding that he could improve Ireland

---

Carleton (Boston: Twayne, 1983); and David Krause, *William Carleton the Novelist: His Carnival and Pastoral World of Tragicomedy* (Washington, DC : University Press of America, 2000).

31 See H. J. O'Brien, 'The Poor Scholar: The Oral Style of William Carleton', *Aquarius,* 4 (1971), 74–82 and Eileen Sullivan, 'William Carleton: Artist of Reality', *Éire-Ireland,* 12/1 (Spring 1977), 130–40.

32 The more insightful readings of Carleton's work are those conducted within the broader context of the history of Irish writing. See Thomas Flanagan, *The Irish Novelists 1800-1850* (New York: Columbia University Press, 1959); Seamus Deane, *A Short History of Irish Literature* (London: Hutchinson, 1986), 107–14; John Cronin, *The Anglo-Irish Novel: The Nineteenth Century* (Belfast: Appletree Press, 1980); Barry Sloan, *The Pioneers of Anglo-Irish Fiction, 1800–1850* (Gerrards Cross, Bucks.: Colin Smythe, 1986); Norman Vance, *Irish Literature, A Social History: Tradition, Identity and Difference* (Oxford: Blackwell, 1990); Christopher Morash, *Writing the Irish Famine* (Oxford: Clarendon Press, 1995); Declan Kiberd, *Irish Classics* (London: Granta, 2000), 265–86.

by comprehensively representing it in writing and that 'improvement' would ultimately manifest itself in the development of a national literature. By showing the failure of Carleton to achieve this aim, I demonstrate how his writing contributes to the *fiction* of improvement.

Improvement liberalism, as a discourse of modernization, was predictably anxious to distinguish itself from both sectarianism and despotism but not within the terms of republicanism or by means of any kind of speculative or theoretical engagement. Irish liberal improvement sought a programme of reform rather than revolution and, in order to achieve this, committed itself to solely practical matters while explicitly refraining from all political and religious discussion. It would appear from the material examined in this study that liberal improvement discourse was itself articulated by means of a critique of republicanism. This suppression of politics expresses a desire to move beyond the political realm entirely, of which 'literature' had become a particularly disconcerting expression. For improvement writers the achievement of modernization would herald an end to politics, rendering the fraught tensions of post-Union Ireland an anachronism. Improvement liberalism sought to achieve liberation from the weight of colonial despotism, religious authoritarianism, political oppression (and literary authority?) by insisting on the necessity of practical action in the present. However, this focus on practicality, or the rationalization of everyday life, was, as this book will demonstrate, also the principal limitation of the project. Practical action is variously defined as physical labour, administration, commerce, and the writing of instructional manuals and didactic fiction. Inevitably, a rigorously realistic fiction is the only acceptable literary mode. As such, improvement practicality is always distinguished from those pursuits or activities deemed to be impractical: lyric poetry, classical education, popular literature, revolution, and 'thought'. In this respect, action is the work of modernized progress, which ought to render unnecessary all pointless and oftentimes dangerous speculation.

Improvement realism prided itself on providing an utterly truthful account of social conditions. For improvement writers, this truth could only be attained by an 'aesthetics of plainness'. Improvement tracts attempted to present themselves as models of transparency, as having overcome the delusions of contemporary political and literary discourses. For writers such as More, Leadbeater, and Bardin, plainness would both exemplify and embody the clarity of a modernized social order. At the level of narrative, the plain realism of improvement discourse was supposed to displace the fireside storytelling of rural Ireland.

Chapter 1 examines how improvement plainness was intended to offset the convoluted utterances of both oral and high literary cultures. The lengthy stories of oral tradition were to give way to the educational and enlightening narratives of improvement. The reforming tracts of Bardin, Leadbeater, and Carleton represented fireside storytelling in order to supplant it. In the process, this chapter argues that the textual device of the fireside in the fiction of the period calls attention to the conventionality and novelistic nature of improvement discourse itself. This long chapter, which establishes the literary and cultural context of Irish improvement fiction, shows how an emphasis on plainness was central to the articulation of modernization and progress in these tracts, but argues that the 'plain' was itself an utterly generic and conventionalized response.

While improvement could be diffused around the hearth of the peasant cottage, a more comprehensive programme of reform was envisaged for education in Ireland prior to the eventual establishment of the National Schools in 1831. Chapter 2 demonstrates how improvement education was defined against the example of the hedge school and accordingly sought to instil an 'ordinary', vocational education—attuned to the needs of a developing market economy—instead of the 'high-minded' academic instruction in Latin and Greek provided in many hedge schools. Educational debates in Ireland in the post-Union period were beset by revolutionary anxieties. Hence, the provision of education in Ireland in this period was largely determined by a counter-revolutionary liberalism, which was decidedly anti-intellectual in emphasis. The focus on useful and vocational instruction in improved schools was meant to counter the lure of revolutionary idealism as well as aestheticism (the latter bound up for improvers in the study of classical languages).

Despite his explicit condemnation of the hedge school in his stories and novels, depicting it as mired in oral backwardness, Carleton was nonetheless troubled by the ideology of improvement education. A nostalgic note exists alongside Carleton's espousal of improvement modernization, one which hints at a possible regret for the mediocrity produced by the very modernizing processes he himself advocated.

Carleton's improving sensibility is particularly manifest in his representations of the Irish language. In his writing, the Irish language is characterized as overly figurative and irrational. Chapter 3 shows how the irrationality of Irish is exemplified by its invocation as a metaphor for sentimentality and pathos in 'Hibernian' idioms such as 'asthore' and 'machree'. Improvement pamphlets are generally silent on the issue of the Irish language, the assumption being that the language could not withstand the processes of modernization. The Irish language and modernization are simply assumed to be antithetical. In the process, the language is represented as static, indeed paralytic, and so incapable of linguistic, let alone economic, production. This chapter argues that Irish was conventionally seen in this manner in the early nineteenth century and questions the historical, not to mention linguistic, basis for a claim which came to be accepted as a 'truth' in the travel writing and literature of the period.

In the literature examined in this book, the Irish language was cast as figurative and emotional and, therefore, incapable of communicating the rational truths of modernization. Similarly, the perceived passion and extremism of the peasantry were considered to be obstacles to the achievement of economic progress. In improvement pamphlets, the excesses of the peasantry are shown to reflect those of landlords. Chapter 4 explores how improvement writers attributed agrarian unrest in rural Ireland to the absenteeism, decadence, and irresponsibility of landlords as well as to the difficulty of civilizing the peasantry. Carleton's stories and novels represent the plight of a small farming class throughout the economic depression of the post-Napoleonic wars. In his fiction, the sufferings of a hard-working, improving peasantry are depicted against the context of absenteeism and the anarchy of agrarian unrest. Improvement writers attempted to counter all extremism—of religion, politics, language, and temperament—with a 'rhetoric of moderation'.

Chapter 4 argues that this rhetoric of moderation shaped the nationalist discourse of Young Ireland. In keeping with his project to mould a disciplined and orderly citizenry for the eventual creation of a nation state, the essays of Thomas Davis are steeped in the tropes of improvement. In part, Davis and Charles Gavan Duffy sought to achieve national consensus by means of the *Nation* and the Library of Ireland. Despite being directed at ostensibly nationalist ends, the Library of Ireland was clearly grounded in the improvement discourse that shaped the publication schemes of the Kildare Place Society as well as the tracts of Leadbeater and Doyle. This chapter argues that Young Ireland nationalism was a component of improvement discourse in Ireland. Strongly utilitarian, both Davis and Gavan Duffy articulate a nationalism that is less inspired by European Romanticism (as is assumed in the cultural and literary histories of the period) than it is by counter-Romantic traditions of liberal improvement and utilitarianism.

Young Ireland rhetoric dominated Irish cultural institutions from the 1840s through to the Revival period. In the early 1890s, a young Yeats was embarking on his project to instil aesthetic revivalism in Ireland, a project that was in part a response to the rationalizing ideologies of improvement modernization. For Yeats, those ideologies were literary as well as social and political in nature, achieving their most coherent expression in the nineteenth-century tradition of English realism. Chapter 5 explores how Yeats's Revival was directed against those discourses of progress, counteracting realist assertions of linearity and causality with supernaturalism and 'orality'. It is thus unsurprising that Yeats was to find himself at odds with the Young Ireland orthodoxies of the period. Mainstream nationalism was strongly modernizing, striving to replace peasant orality with a literate, nationalist domesticity. Predictably, Yeats found himself in a bitter dispute with the elderly Young Irelander Charles Gavan Duffy over an early Revival experiment, The New Irish Library. This dispute brought to light yet again those tensions between improvement utilitarianism and aestheticism, the one implicit in the domesticating impulses of a modern nation state and the other an expression of disenchantment with improvement modernization. Chapter 5 speculates that the Revival writings of Yeats, Hyde, and Synge were a product of the inevitable failures of both improvement discourse and Young Ireland nationalism.

The following chapters argue that improvement literature in Ireland was a counter-revolutionary discourse, which set itself in opposition both to the perceived idealism of republicanism and to the alleged aestheticism of Romanticism. The didactic fiction of writers such as Edgeworth and Leadbeater is steeped in a revolutionary anxiety that manifests itself in a striking nervousness surrounding matters of representation. For these writers, superstition and Catholicism combined in Ireland to make the lower classes susceptible to revolutionary persuasion and, it seems, utterly impractical and incapable of bearing the forces of modernization. Impracticality resulted from a commitment to the (perceived) political fictions of revolution or rebellion and avoidance of economic, material reality. Central to improvement discourse is the representation of the satisfaction achieved through physical work and an ordinary plain life (free of all excess and embellishment). Improvement fiction was an attempt to instil that practicality, to promote a life lived at a solidly empirical level. A preoccupation of this book is the manner in which improvement discourse manifests itself in literary terms in an attempt to engender a solidly didactic and realist, rather than gothic or idealist, mode of representation.

Throughout, I show that improvement discourse in Ireland was an attempt to assert the values and 'order' of tradition within a broader context of modernization and change. Improvement writers articulated a discourse of modernization which was embedded in a nostalgia for a particular 'past'. Crucially, however, this past was recalled not from a historical reality but from a particular literary, textual tradition of the late eighteenth and early nineteenth centuries. In effect, improvement was a literary discourse which was engaged in a debate regarding genre and representation. In the course of the following study, I call attention to the manner in which improvement discourse was ironically entwined in the written conventions that it sought to escape. It so happens that in seeking to convey instruction on domestic and agricultural economy, improvement writers were forced to draw upon a range of fictional tropes, which often undermined the supposedly practical rhetoric of their discourse. Carleton's writing is of particular interest for this study because it repeatedly highlights the 'literary' nature of improvement discourse. In this respect, the material under discussion in this book is crucial to an understanding of the literary culture of the nineteenth century and Revival period.

1

'False Refinement', Plain Speech and Improved Writing

IN Irish improvement fiction, improved characters all dress, speak, and comport themselves in a highly restrained and practical manner. Decoration, ornamentation, and embellishment are shunned in an effort to achieve transparency in physical bearing, language, and the social and political order as a whole. Value is placed in the ordinary world of work, housekeeping, and commerce and readers are strongly discouraged from preoccupying themselves with unreasonable political or social expectations. An insistence on literalism is perceived to be necessary for an improved society to be imagined and, if possible, brought into existence. This chapter explores how these themes are articulated in the fiction of More, Leadbeater, Bardin, and Carleton, demonstrating the relationship between improvement discourse and an aesthetics of the plain.

That plainness was opposed to the perceived rampant 'orality' of the rural poor. Improvement writers were disdainful of the intensely 'oral' habits of the peasantry, from storytelling and smoking to the idle 'talk' and drinking of both whiskey and tea that were supposedly indulged around the fireside of Irish cabins. The fireside—or cottage interior—was seen to enforce the destructive habits and prejudices of the peasantry, deepening the repetitive and monotonous patterns of the pre-modern. In these fictions, the peasant cabin has been re-formed from a place of compulsive, debased orality into a focal point for work and enlightened (in this instance, technical) reading. The improved cottage would be shaped by the clock on the wall, instilling the necessary order and rationality of a modern economy.

An improved social order would require a strict disciplinary and linguistic code in order to protect against all potential disruption. Improvement writers repeatedly claim that adhering to this code would rid experience of those indeterminacies that were the source of immense distress and unhappiness. This representational code had to be applied to all facets of behaviour such as speech, public demeanour, and choice of clothing. Hannah More was not only wary of the mass circulation of popular chapbooks and Paine's republican pamphlets in the 1790s, but was equally perturbed by the clothing favoured by the poor.[1] Factory-produced clothing, popular chapbooks, and political radicalism all somehow combined to represent an apparent revolutionary threat to a particular social order in both England and Ireland.[2] These anxieties were shared by many of More's Irish contemporaries, most notably Maria Edgeworth, Mary Leadbeater, and the membership of the Association for Discountenancing Vice (ADV). More's fiction—as well as that of Irish writers—exemplifies a particular anxiety of the period regarding both popular literacy and the 'rise' of the novel whilst nonetheless espousing the ability to read and write in standard English as an absolutely necessary component of the civilizing process. In More's mind, popular literature, which most certainly included the novel, was fully entwined with the perceived development of mass consumerism. Hence, the Cheap Repository Tracts strive to maintain integrity in this environment, presenting improvement as a solution to the proliferation of discourses in an age of industrial (and textual) reproduction. Paradoxically, all of More's pamphlets and tracts were produced and reproduced on an industrial scale. Niall Ó Ciosáin notes that her pamphlets were 'short and cheap ... costing a penny' and that she 'claimed to have circulated two million copies' of the tracts in 1795 when the project was started.[3]

More's tracts were modelled on the popular chapbooks of the period and it was by appropriating the genres of popular chapbooks that she

---

[1] Niall Ó Ciosáin discusses these chivalric romances, claiming that they 'were strongly condemned by elite commentators on popular culture': *Print and Popular Culture in Ireland, 1750–1850* (Basingstoke: Macmillan, 1997), 74. On this popular material in a broader European context, see Peter Burke, *Popular Culture in Early Modern Europe* (London: Temple Smith, 1978), 244–84.

[2] On Hannah More, see Mary Alden Hopkins, *Hannah More and her Circle* (New York: Longmans, Green and Co., 1947); M. G. Jones, *Hannah More* (Cambridge: Cambridge University Press, 1952); Susan Pedersen, 'Hannah More Meets Simple Simon: Tracts, Chapbooks and Popular Culture in Late Eighteenth-Century England', *Journal of British Studies*, 25/1 (Jan. 1986), 84–113; Angela Keane, *Women Writers and the English Nation in the 1790s* (Cambridge: Cambridge University Press, 2000); Seamus Deane, *Strange Country: Modernity and Nationhood in Irish Writing since 1790* (Oxford: Clarendon Press, 1997), 28–31; Anne Stott, *Hannah More: The First Victorian* (Oxford: Oxford University Press, 2003).

[3] Ó Ciosáin, *Print and Popular Culture in Ireland*, 137.

hoped to dominate the market. Readers were to be lured into reading her tracts by provocative titles such as *Path to Richness and Happiness*. The tracts themselves provide advice on matters from frugal domestic economy to the importance of choosing a 'plain' wife. *The History of Tom White, the Postillion*, recounts how 'Tom knew that a tawdry, vain, dressy girl was not likely to make cheese and butter, and that a worldly and ungodly woman would make a sad wife and mistress of a family.' In time, this character is united with a woman whose 'neat, modest, and plain appearance at church ... was an example to all persons in her station'.[4] Readers were urged to esteem neatness, modesty, and plainness as values rooted in tradition and stability and as comprising the only workable code in an industrializing age. Improvement is characterized by orderliness while its absence is steeped in relativity and confusion. The Cheap Repository Tracts not only encourage men to value plain and ordinary women, but they seek such (stabilizing) value in language, literary discourse, and society itself. These tracts were an attempt to protect all representation from the supposedly 'worldly' language and discourse of both popular and high culture (a threat posed especially by the novel). As such, More's tracts were trying to safeguard a particular patriarchal and logocentric code while having to accommodate the inevitability of both women and the poor working, consuming, and reading.

The French historian Daniel Roche has argued that in eighteenth-century France the 'bourgeois critique' of fashion was conducted 'in the name of the thrift and austerity necessary to the accumulation of capital'.[5] In More's writings, commercial success is carefully linked to an inevitable plainness in clothing and appearance. For More, fashionable dress was an unwelcome substitution for the supposedly plain, honest, and, it would appear, transparent clothing of domestic manufacture. In addition, fashion signified a lower-class disrespect of traditional class divisions, suggesting the increasing fragility of such boundaries within society as a whole. One of More's biographers notes how she 'disapproved of French fashions, cookery, literature, and politics',[6] all of which presumably signified, at once, aestheticism, *ancien régime* decadence, Republican politics, and a culture of consumption, which then get condensed into an image of debased femininity. More

---

[4] Hannah More, *The History of Tom White, the Postillion*, Cheap Repository Tracts [n.d.], 15–16. For More, the term 'worldly' connotes commodification and consumerism.
[5] Daniel Roche, *The Culture of Clothing: Dress and Fashion in the Ancien Regime*, 1989, trans. Jean Birrell (Cambridge: Cambridge University Press, 1994), 57.
[6] Hopkins, *Hannah More and her Circle*, 15.

instinctively disliked luxury, in the form of aristocratic ostentation, the lower-class predilection for 'dressy' clothing, and textual (or literary) excess. Luxury implied an arbitrary social signification that greatly disconcerted More: the possibility that representation did not coincide with the social hierarchy as she perceived it.

Restraint was, in More's mind, the only means by which satisfaction could ever be achieved in actual daily life itself. An unrestrained life was one caught up in endless complications and difficulties, which effectively worked against the ability to function in the world. By contrast, More's disciplinary code was an attempt to articulate how action towards a particular future might be possible, one in which representation and experience would be fully reconciled. More was disconcerted by contemporary literary discourses as they appeared to encourage a retreat from work into fantasy, self-obsessiveness, or pure 'thought' (speculation), disallowing the possibility of progression in a spiritual or, indeed, material sense. In her mind, alienation from work also entailed alienation from religion (which, in the rhetoric of the Cheap Repository Tracts, was seen in strongly material terms). The evangelicalism espoused in these tracts considered itself to be at one with work in the form of manual labour or benevolent administration of schools, factories, and estates. The fact of More's evangelicism should not deflect from the strongly utilitarian nature of her project. It is this latter component which makes More an important figure in the history of improvement discourse and which renders her tracts—which were essentially utilitarian fictions (or fantasies?)—of importance to the history of both narrative and the novel.[7]

The preservation of moral, linguistic, and aesthetic integrity depended on the assertion of simplicity and practicality within a culture that had veered increasingly towards embellishment and, in More's mind, debilitating speculation. To this end, More urged her readers, ideally encompassing all social groups, to speak (and write) in a resolutely plain mode. She warned her upper-class readers of the necessity of instructing servants—a class susceptible to revolutionary persuasion and decadent excess—in a strictly plain manner. For More, the upper classes had themselves become alienated from those essential truths of language which the Cheap Repository Tracts were working to reinstate. In its

---

[7] For a further discussion of Hannah More in the context of the history of the novel, see Emily Rena-Dozier, 'Hannah More and the Invention of Narrative Authority', *ELH*, 71/1 (Spring 2004), 209–27.

depiction of an encounter between a shepherd and landlord, More's *The Shepherd of Salisbury Plain* attempts to represent the possibility of a transparent language and, thus, a stable social order. The landlord of the tract is especially struck by 'the plain, humble way in which this honest' shepherd 'taught his family'.[8] This landlord had experienced difficulty in communicating with his servants who failed to comprehend his overly convoluted speech. The assumption is, of course, that language can be representational when used in a strictly plain manner in the mode of More's shepherd. This narrative is about the meeting of two extremes of language: the one plain and supposedly representational and the other intricate and heavily mediated by a range of discourses. The humility of the shepherd's occupation—and his supreme contentment in that social role—should confirm for the reader the existence of a fixed social hierarchy, which has merely been obscured by the rhetorical excess of the period. This figure of the shepherd is supposed to demonstrate how satisfaction can be achieved by returning to a relatively raw state, stripping away the literary in order to arrive at a space in which things can both be said and acted upon. Though More claims that this story was based entirely on actual observation, her use of the shepherd—a figure rooted in biblical and literary discourses—discloses the strongly figurative, indeed literary, components of her project. The shepherd signifies a symbolic return to an integrated and self-contained system of meaning, which is symbolized by an evangelical reading of the Bible.

More's evangelical excess—as such it is—should not obscure the utilitarian objectives of her writings. The religious overtones of the Cheap Repository Tracts do not contradict their modernizing objectives. These tracts assert that the Bible ought to be the principal model for individual and public morality as well as written discourse, canceling the influence of revolutionary pamphlets, indecent chapbooks, and popular novels. It is by such means that modernization would be most effectively achieved.

In *The Two Wealthy Farmers*, More expresses her anxiety over the very existence of lower-class literacy and the consequent need to intervene and control it. She imagines the worrying possibility of chapbooks being read aloud in factories to groups of women (some of whom would probably have been illiterate), suggesting that such printed material could be readily absorbed within the essentially oral environment of the modern

[8] Hannah More, *The Shepherd of Salisbury Plain*, Cheap Repository Tracts [n.d], pt I, 14.

factory. This prospect was made all the more disconcerting by the fact that women, in however limited a capacity, were entering into the public sphere and were both producing and consuming printed material. Print could supposedly pollute 'by scenes and descriptions' in a manner not possible within either traditional oral storytelling or manuscripts, thus enhancing, rather than displacing, an already debased orality.[9] There was an imperative to intervene in the development of literacy and to substitute this immoral printed material with virtuous narratives, which could be as effective in the dissemination of improvement as 'corrupt reading' was in the spread of dissent and immorality.[10] The equating of orality and popular literacy with women, republicanism, and industrial reproduction was integral to More's improvement project, itself paradoxically availing itself of all the resources of an expanded and democratized print culture at every opportunity.

Like More, Irish writers such as Mary Leadbeater were anxious to reach the precise social class that was perceived to be receptive to radical politics. Irish improvement writers were particularly preoccupied by the impoverished condition of the rural poor, and had become alarmed by the explosion in population in the post-Union period.[11] Improvement discourse in Ireland presents itself as a mode of restraint, curbing by narrative and linguistic means the perceived extremes of the post-Union period. However, wary of More's evangelicalism, Irish improvement writers steered clear of all religious polemic and discourse in favour of a more liberal, indeed secularizing, rhetoric. Leadbeater's writing generally sought to persuade and encourage rather than indoctrinate or threaten, asserting a liberalism which, in its emphasis on moderation, was eager to distinguish itself from the oppressive discourses of the past. Leadbeater was keen to keep her writing free from all extremism, be it evangelicalism, revolutionary discourse, or, even, 'literary' language. As such, her pamphlets articulate a desire to create a liberal public sphere. However, as this book will demonstrate, Leadbeater's improving rhetoric was itself the product of an extreme response to orality, superstition,

---

[9] Hannah More, *The Two Wealthy Farmers*, Cheap Repository Tracts [n.d.], 21.
[10] Ibid.
[11] S. J. Connolly states that this surge in population was accommodated by an agricultural boom during the Napoleonic Wars as well as the buoyant linen industry. The ending of war, however, resulted in an agricultural depression and the linen industry declined markedly outside of Ulster. 'Population', however, 'continued remorselessly to expand, rising from 6.8 million in 1821 to 7.8 million in 1831 and to 8.2 million in 1841.' *Priests and People in Pre-Famine Ireland, 1780–1845*, 1982 (Dublin: Four Courts Press, 2001), 47.

the Irish peasantry, agrarian unrest, and other literary genres. It can even be claimed that Leadbeater's improvement pamphlets were made possible by a fictionalization of excess, her liberalism dependent upon the fictional construction of extremism.

Leadbeater wrote from within a culture already shaped by improvement and enlightenment discourses: she was a member of the Society of Friends and her grandfather had educated Edmund Burke in his famous school in Ballitore in County Kildare.[12] She had read Edmund Burke, William Godwin, Mary Wollstonecraft, and William Wordsworth, and maintained a steady correspondence with the poet, George Crabbe.[13] Leadbeater was immersed in the educational theory of Locke and was a committed and devoted reader of Maria Edgeworth's writing. In the tradition of More and, indeed, Edgeworth, Leadbeater claimed that her fiction was written in a resolutely truthful rather than fictionalized form. Accordingly, instruction is always conveyed in a realistic mode in her tracts, which seek to impart the ease with which improvement and cultivation can be carried into effect. This form was also intended as a model of writing and discourse generally, which should be unmediated and free of figuration, striving for complete clarity in order to communicate unambiguously the necessary skills and tools for modernization. The aesthetic code of Leadbeater's improvement writing is encapsulated by her choice of epigraph from George Crabbe for *The Cottage Biography* (1814)—'No muse I ask before my view to bring, | The humble actions of the swains I sing.' Leadbeater sought to reiterate the anti-conventionalism of Crabbe, suggesting that her peasants will be drawn from reality and not the artificial conventions of English pastoral poetry.[14] No muse is required to create characters she can freely copy from her own authentic, pastoral experience. Interestingly, Leadbeater initiated her correspondence with Crabbe by enquiring if the subjects of his poetry were invented or based on actual observation.[15] In his reply,

---

[12] For an analysis of Leadbeater's Quaker background and politics in the 1790s, see Kevin O'Neill, 'Mary Shackleton Leadbeater: Peaceful Rebel', in Nicholas Furlong and Dáire Keogh, eds., *Women of 1798* (Dublin: Four Courts Press, 1998), 137–63.

[13] Ibid. 147.

[14] On Crabbe's ultimately conventional pastoralism, see Raymond Williams, *The Country and the City* (London: Chatto and Windus, 1973), 87–95.

[15] Letter from Mary Leadbeater to George Crabbe, 7 Nov. 1816. Reprinted in Mary Leadbeater, *Papers: The Annals of Ballitore with a Memoir of the Author; Letters from Edmund Burke Heretofore Unpublished and the Correspondence of Mrs. R. Trench and Rev. George Crabbe with Mary Leadbeater* (London: Bell and Daldy, 1862), ii. 336. Hereafter cited as *Papers*.

Crabbe stated that he endeavoured 'to paint as nearly as I could and dare ... but I was obliged in most instances to take them from their real situations, and in one or two instances even to change the sex'. While conceding that his representations are removed from directly observed experience, Crabbe nonetheless seeks to reassure Leadbeater of the ultimate authenticity of the figures contained in his verse by stating that

Indeed, I do not know what I could paint from my own fancy and there is no cause why I should. Is there not diversity sufficient in society? And who can go even but a little into the assemblies of our fellow-wanderers from the way of perfect rectitude, and not find characters so varied and so pointed that he need not call upon his imagination.[16]

Leadbeater's writing had already been shaped in part by Crabbe's realistic pastoralism before they ever started to correspond. In this rhetoric, imagination is entirely redundant in the process of representation; figures from nature—already sufficiently diverse and varied—can pass directly onto the written page without significant mediation or embellishment on the part of the author. However, Leadbeater's characters are of course more indebted to Crabbe's verse, the Cheap Repository Tracts, and *Castle Rackrent* than her neighbours in Ballitore. Indeed, in this letter, Crabbe articulates a rhetoric of pastoral realism which was integral to the improvement discourse of Leadbeater and, later, Doyle and Carleton as well. This realism felt a strong need to characterize itself by opposition to both Romanticism and revolution.

Leadbeater was keen to reach as wide a readership as possible among the literate peasantry in order to establish the common moral, social, and domestic codes that were, for her, definitive of modernization. The instilling of desire for a better standard of living through fictional representation was to be the principal means of achieving improvement. The assumption was that the Irish peasantry were alienated from the English-speaking, literate, and Anglican economy of post-Union Ireland. Leadbeater's texts were explicitly engaged in an effort to create a standardized public sphere in which a specific code of values would acquire universal and unambiguous acceptance amongst all constituencies. Her particular dialogue form only allows for an overt relationship between narrative and instruction, suggesting that meaning should be explicit rather than implicit in language. Interestingly,

[16] Letter from George Crabbe to Mary Leadbeater, 1 Dec. 1816, in Leadbeater, *Papers*, ii. 340–1.

Leadbeater adopted the 'oral' mode of the dialogue in order to convey an assertively literate project, invoking the perceived immediacy, presence, and literalism of speech to convey the value of improvement literacy.

Leadbeater strives to maintain a strict narrative as well as linguistic economy in her improvement writing in order to avoid the possibility of being drawn into a more novelistic and, to her mind, duplicitous discourse in which meaning lurks ambiguously behind rather than unambiguously on the surface of things. Moral instruction within Leadbeater's *Cottage Dialogues* (1811) is thus efficiently communicated through an emphasis on household and agricultural matters, seeking to confirm itself as a resolutely materialist programme of social reform. The assertion—intrinsic to the ideology of improvement—that language, narrative, and social practice can be fully and harmoniously united is always embedded in representations of fulfilled action in the present in the form of modern agricultural methods producing abundant crops or the enlightened administration of estates creating a contented and productive tenantry. The internalization of improving rhetoric never fails to produce material reward. A scrupulously moral and disciplined life is shown at all times to result in palpable material and, indeed, spiritual fulfilment. The expedience of maintaining an improved economic and moral existence is always in evidence in descriptions of neat, abundant gardens, clean children, a pig-free home, and savings (the profit gleaned from various enterprising activities, such as hygienic butter-making, that can be put aside). An emphasis on hard work is echoed throughout the *Dialogues*: in fact, there is no room for idleness (or idle reflection) and leisure time is only usefully spent in the reading of instructional literature or engaging in some 'light' work, such as 'straw-plait'. The necessity of combining pleasure and utility is always stressed: one character glances out the window at her garden as she sews, thus keeping her hands busy while enjoying the flowers outside. It would appear, then, that all (aesthetic) pleasure has to be fully grounded in material, physical experience, united with the raw world of work rather than separated from it.

Leadbeater was particularly keen to encourage peasants to cultivate their way out of a hand-to-mouth existence and thereby liberate themselves from entrapment in a dark, hungry, and backward environment. In this modernizing vein, Leadbeater's *Cottage Dialogues* encourages the reader to avail of various facilities newly established in rural Ireland, such as dispensaries, hospitals, and psychiatric institutions.[17] The reader is assured that these institutions will alleviate the miseries of rural life, the weight of superstition (allied also to a form of feudal or colonial oppression) lifted by the introduction of medical and agricultural knowledge. Leadbeater's pamphlets all sought to instil a form of rational individualism, repeatedly insisting on the necessity for individual responsibility: time and again, these tracts illustrate how controlling one's situation in a rational manner and taking appropriate action always has predictably positive consequences. In an improved life, the outcome is never arbitrary. However, the refusal to assume responsibility over given circumstances invariably condemned one to the deterministic forces of nature and to the arbitrariness of culture. Improvement is supposed to be free of all arbitrariness, safely returning experience to the stability it once possessed.

Leadbeater's reader, ostensibly poor and peasant, is shown how to cope and even thrive—by no means merely survive—within seemingly tightened circumstances: a small patch of ground can feed a family and create sufficient profit to purchase various necessities, such as bedding, clothing, or other 'conveniences for the cabin'.[18] Many of the dialogues seek to show that everything necessary for a relatively comfortable, satisfying existence—one even enlivened by the occasional commodity—is available within the cramped space of a cottage and small piece of land. Rose and Tim embody a model cottage economy and the possibility of extracting profit and comfort for themselves on the same terms as their poor and hungry neighbours. Needless to say, they also experience immense satisfaction by fully inhabiting the material world without giving into dangerous distractions such as politics or alcohol. In order to demonstrate the feasibility of improvement, situations are presented in the dialogues as exemplary micro-economies, instances of good management, calculation, and orderliness within the means given. All that is required is that perception be altered, traditional (oral, Catholic, and thus entirely impractical) modes of perceiving the world displaced by rationalized and enlightened observation.

In *The Cottage Fireside* (1826), Charles Bardin carefully counsels against all characteristic oral vices from tea- and whiskey-drinking to

---

[17] On these developments, see Oliver MacDonagh, *Ireland: The Union and its Aftermath* (London: George Allen and Unwin, 1977), 37.
[18] Leadbeater, *Cottage Dialogues*, expanded edition (Dublin, 1811–13), 131.

idle talk and gossip. In general, Bardin's pamphlet urges a restrained orality in all matters and suggests that 'we ought to keep our tongues under some sort of government.'[19] It was necessary to govern the tongue from engagement in gossip and idle talk as well as from the compulsive activity of drinking.[20] A particular neighbour is censured for her gossiping tendencies and endless 'running about from house to house spreading tales.'[21] Bardin is clearly disconcerted by the presumed existence of an orality which is energetic and diffuse and which could be readily deployed for political ends. Like all improvement pamphlets, *The Cottage Fireside* is an attempt to classify the peasantry as a class and, in the process, shape a form of acceptable lower-class behaviour that will allow for rather than impede economic development.

Improved narratives were supposed to impart the values of rationalization, organizing experience into a tight organic form. By contrast, the traditional oral story recounted at the cottage fireside was prolonged, drawn out, and constructed to fill the ample time of the pre-modern. The supposedly undisciplined, digressive quality of these stories could not be facilitated within the context of a modernizing economy. Improvement tracts were designed to be read and comprehended speedily, catering to busy, disciplined peasants with only a specified amount of time to spare for reading. Improvement narratives would not labour the reader with any redundant, 'literary', or digressive material. An example is *The Entertaining Medley, Being a Collection of True Histories and Anecdotes Calculated for the Cottage Fireside*, which was distributed by the Kildare Place Society in 1826. This pamphlet contained a mixture of travel and natural history, forms of narrative which were deemed alien to the oral storytelling that supposedly characterized the standard fireside. These narratives provided information on geography and natural history, educating the reader on matters beyond the reach of the rural cottage and immediate local environment.

The fireside of the traditional Irish cabin was, according to improvers, strongly communal, suffused by the careless, relaxed atmosphere of a hand-to-mouth economy. There was no need to rush as there was no shortage of time in the scarce, idle world of the rural poor. Wakes could last for several days and storytelling sessions endure through

---

[19] Bardin, *The Cottage Fireside* (Dublin, 1826), 12.
[20] For a fascinating representation of women and tea-drinking, see Carleton's story 'Barney Brady's Goose; or Dark Doings at Slathbeg', *Dublin University Magazine*, 11/65 (May 1838), 604–24.
[21] Bardin, *The Cottage Fireside*, 13.

the night without disturbing the peculiar rhythms of the pre-modern. Improvement writers sought to replace this 'carelessness' with the regulation and order necessary for economic progress. Leadbeater encouraged her readers to forsake the meaningless (and decadent) pleasures of the fireside for more beneficial and profitable activities such as reading, spinning, and gardening. A prize-winning cottager in *The Landlord's Friend* (1813) has shunned the attractions of the fireside to sit out in her cultivated garden with her knitting and spinning wheel, claiming that the delights of her garden do 'not hinder us out of our work, and because I don't smoke I am not so fond of the chimney corner as they are'.[22] By sitting in her garden rather than at the fireside, this character can exist openly in the linear time of progress beyond the entrapment and concealed 'dead time' of a pre-modern economy.

Leadbeater attempted to displace the insularity of rural backwardness by instilling a consciousness of time in her readers. In *The Pedlars* (1826), the exemplary English cottage is described as containing 'bright windows', 'well-scrubbed furniture', and 'the clock, with the warming pan hanging by it'.[23] Irish readers are accordingly encouraged to emulate this precise domestic model by transforming their shabby, dark, and timeless interiors into bright, clean, and regulated environments. The perceived darkness of rural cabins greatly disturbed improvement writers, a lack of light invariably suggesting the absence of rationality and enlightenment. The Irish cabin had to be radiated by light and time, integrated within the broader national economy rather than isolated from it.

In the same pamphlet, a character, Rose, is praised for having 'accomplished a great deal by her regularity, diligence, and patience'; having timed 'her business', she 'was never unemployed, nor ever in a hurry'.[24] As Rose was capable of maintaining perfect discipline in her work patterns—never rushing and never idling—she was consistently orderly and free of those destructive extremes of temper or mood. Rose's understanding of the importance of time ensures that she achieves the perfect stability, indeed subjectivity, necessary for material gain. An understanding of the materiality and finality of time is emphasized in an attempt both to encourage discipline and to discourage the prevailing rhetoric of prophecy and millenarianism ingrained in popular culture and literature.[25]

---

[22] Mary Leadbeater, *The Landlord's Friend* (Dublin, 1813), 79.
[23] Mary Leadbeater, *The Pedlars* (Dublin, 1826), 125.   [24] Ibid. 27.
[25] The issue of millenarianism will be explored in greater detail in Ch.5. See James S. Donnelly, Jr., 'Pastorini and Captain Rock: Millenarianism and Sectarianism in the

Bardin likewise educated readers in the economics of time and cautioned that the leisureliness of a pre-modern economy had to be replaced with the relentless activity of improvement. In *The Cottage Fireside*, Bardin even entitled a dialogue 'The Economy of Time': a young girl is instructed by her grandmother as to how time, like money, can be saved and managed.[26] Jenny's knitting ability is improving every day and her grandmother assures her that she will soon be able to knit in the dark, thereby filling what may have appeared to be the empty, wasted time of night with activity and potential material gain. Time is presented as a material entity which needs to be understood and managed for profit. As Jenny's grandmother states: 'The value of time ... what a little of it, well applied, can do.'[27]

The wasted time of the pre-modern greatly irritated all improvement writers. In *Hints for the Small Farmers of Ireland* (1830), Martin Doyle comments crossly on the 'idle hands' of the rural poor in the midst of the numerous undrained fields that existed throughout the countryside. An idle peasant, according to Doyle, deserved 'to be poor and miserable'.[28] Rural impoverishment was largely attributed to the idleness of the poor (and landowners) rather than to the economic mismanagement of the government. Hence, improvement created busy, industrious peasants who plan their days in meticulous detail and are receptive to change and progress. These improved peasants are liberated from the hungry, struggling past of wakes and oral storytelling into economic prosperity, information, and technology.

It could be suggested that improvement dialogues and narratives embody the generic tensions between 'story', 'novel', and 'information' famously described by Walter Benjamin. Benjamin defines the story as 'experience which is passed on from mouth to mouth' and is thus characterized by 'companionship' between storyteller and listener and,

---

Rockite Movement of 1821- 4', in Samuel Clark and James S. Donnelly, Jr., eds., *Irish Peasants: Violence and Political Unrest 1789–1914* (Manchester: Manchester University Press, 1983).

[26] Bardin's pamphlet undoubtedly drew upon an earlier Scottish improving tract of 1815 by Henry Duncan entitled *The Cottage Fireside, or The Parish Schoolmaster*. On Duncan, see Penny Fielding, *Writing and Orality: Nationality, Culture, and Nineteenth-Century Scottish Fiction* (Oxford: Clarendon Press, 1996), 123–4.

[27] Bardin, *The Cottage Fireside*, 20.

[28] Martin Doyle, *Hints for the Small Farmers of Ireland* (Dublin, 1830), 9. Doyle's *Hints* was first published in 1828, but the 1830 edition is the earliest I have been able to locate.

even when transferred to the written page, between writer and reader.[29] The traditional 'storyteller' is, according to Benjamin, 'a man who has counsel for his readers', whose stories will always contain 'openly or covertly, something useful'.[30] Improvement fiction adopts the oral counsel of the story by embedding instructional advice within the relaxed anecdotal form of conversations between, say, the characters in *Cottage Dialogues*. The ordered but 'spoken' quality of *Cottage Dialogues* tries to accommodate both the possibility of oral delivery around the chimney corner and quiet reading (the latter of a very direct, indeed, oral variety).

In this respect, the improvement tract tries to pass itself off as more story than novel, which, for Benjamin, is dependent 'on the book' and 'neither comes from oral tradition nor goes into it'.[31] In Benjamin's terms, 'the birthplace of the novel is the solitary individual, who is no longer able to express himself by giving examples of his most important concerns, is himself uncounseled and cannot counsel others.'[32] Benjamin argues that the novel is produced by the breakdown of the relationship between experience and narrative (or representation) that had supposedly characterized the 'artisanal' genre of the story. The demise of the story was then epitomized by the ascendancy of both the novel and 'information'. The improvement tract is an attempt to fight against this literary fate (or abyss), asserting the possibility of communication in the terms of fictional, didactic realism. Despite itself, however, the didactic tract is not able to escape the void that is the novel. Novelistic conventions are deployed in the improvement tract, which invokes the linearity and causality of the novel for the representation of improved characters and settings (such as the thriving peasants and farm of *Cottage Dialogues*). Additionally, the clear informative mode of so many tracts is shaped by the efficiency and concision of 'information', which, according to Benjamin, is exemplified by the 'prompt verifiability' and immediate plausibility of the newspaper report.[33] In a manner most unlike the traditional story, information is 'already ... shot through with explanation' when heard or read, refusing to allow for the interpretive possibility and scope that characterized the story of old.[34] Similarly, the improvement tract tries to avoid the expansiveness (or literariness) and

[29] Walter Benjamin, 'The Storyteller', in *Illuminations: Essays and Reflections* ed. Hannah Arendt, translated by Harry Zohn (New York: Schocken Books, 1988), 84 and 100.
[30] Ibid. 86.   [31] Ibid. 87.   [32] Ibid.   [33] Ibid. 89.
[34] Ibid.

cyclical nature of the traditional story, which could only get in the way of the need to communicate clear, precise instruction. Improvement fiction could possibly be understood as a self-consciously transitional genre between the assumed orality of the fireside and popular chapbook and the literacy of the realistic novel and newspaper. Indeed, improvement discourse labours to present itself as transitional, sharply marking the end of one era (oral, pre-industrial, and religiously fanatical) in order to make way for another (literate, industrial, and secular).

In these pamphlets, improvement is achieved at a rhetorical level by means of the conventions of the domestic novel: an orderly kitchen presided over by an organized, thrifty woman, humanizing the space of cottage, farm, and, in time, that of the state as well.[35] These tropes are all clearly rooted in the domestic novels of writers such as Richardson and Burney, which were themselves shaped by the conduct literature of the seventeenth and eighteenth centuries. However, I would suggest that conduct books, which were in J. Paul Hunter's formulation 'before novels', were themselves already novelistic.[36] The conduct book readily gave 'rise' to the novel because it was itself an inherently novelistic mode. As such, this study questions the linear, progressive literary history deployed in the work of J. Paul Hunter and, indeed, Nancy Armstrong.

The lives of improved peasants are plotted in accordance with the linearity and causality associated with the realist novel: civilized peasants measure their work against the clock, accurate cultivation produces abundant crops, and regularity in the home ensures both domestic and political stability. This can also be understood as a determination to replace one particular narrative order (millenarian and circular) with another (realist and linear) and thereby instil a realist rather than Romantic or oral temporality. The structure of a fictional improved society—transparent, homogeneous, and stable—was itself the product of a complicated reaction to the historical circumstances represented by the 'rise' of the novel. The repeated assertions in improvement fiction of the existence of stability, which existed in the past and was to be achieved again in the future, only serve all the more to emphasize its absence and to confirm the 'loss' of an 'organic community' that of course never existed. For improvement writers, this loss was exemplified by the perceived proliferation (or

[35] On the tradition of the domestic novel in England, see Nancy Armstrong, *Desire and Domestic Fiction: A Political History of the Novel* (Oxford: Oxford University Press, 1987).

[36] J. Paul Hunter, *Before Novels: Cultural Contexts of Eighteenth-Century English Fiction* (London: Norton, 1992).

democratization) of literary discourses. That proliferation was in part encapsulated by the novel. It seems to me that the improvement tract was both a product of and reaction to the novel and that the didactic tale emerged directly from novelistic discourse and was compelled, indeed fated, to engage critically with the novel. Seamus Deane has noted that the 'national novel' in Ireland 'retains its early intimacy with the didactic tale'.[37] It could be further suggested that the didactic tale never succeeded in escaping from the generic grip of the novel.

The backward peasants in Leadbeater's tracts inhabit a ghastly, gothic environment prior to the dawn of writing, medicine, and science. These characters live in dark, dirty cabins, express suspicion of authority, see ghosts, and die needlessly from disease. A character in *Cottage Dialogues* asks 'how do savages live' to which his neighbour replies:'Why, in a mud hovel without a chimney; the parents and children all pig together on the same wisp—the father goes out to look for food, and when the mother prepares it, they all fall to, and tear it with their fingers and devour it'.[38] These devouring savages represent the unimproved masses of the Irish countryside, who are ensconced in a primitive hunter-gatherer economy. Leadbeater tries to demonstrate how the dirty, squalid cabins of rural Ireland can be transformed into impeccable, radiant cottages. By means of improvement, the passage from an oral, pre-modern social order to a literate civility would be rendered complete. The chaotic conditions that prevail in the cabins of Leadbeater's backward peasants are supposed to signify the anarchistic gothicism of the pre-modern and, by extension, orality. These cabins exemplify the gothic nightmare inhabited by those who shun improvement. Leadbeater's tracts imply that a realist narrative should soon overwhelm the gothic tropes of the pre-modern: a tight social (or formal) organization subsuming the superstitions and excesses of the past.[39] At the beginning of *Cottage Dialogues*, Rose cautions Nancy to keep watch over young children at all times for fear of what may happen. Unattended children can be eaten by pigs, or worse, for, as Rose states, 'If you heard the frightful stories I did, you would never leave a child by itself.'[40] Frightening tales need

[37] Seamus Deane, *A Short History of Irish Literature* (London: Hutchinson, 1986), 94.

[38] Leadbeater, *Cottage Dialogues*, 48.

[39] For a discussion of gothic in nineteenth-century Irish writing, see Ina Ferris, *The Romantic National Tale and the Question of Ireland* (Cambridge: Cambridge University Press, 2003), 102–27, and Siobhan Kilfeather, 'Terrific Register: The Gothicization of Atrocity in Irish Romanticism', *boundary* 2, 31/1 (Spring 2004), 49–71.

[40] Leadbeater, *Cottage Dialogues*, 2.

never come into existence once a particular narrative and social code is rigorously observed.

Bardin's *The Cottage Fireside* exemplifies the generic mix of story, information, and novel that characterizes the improvement tract. The title refers explicitly to the storytelling culture that shaped the cottage fireside while the narratives themselves convey instruction on domestic improvement within the realistic setting of a conventional cottage. Bardin tries to assure the reader that his dialogues are by no means 'imaginary' creations, claiming that 'similar topics are often the subjects of discourse in the cottages of our industrious peasantry.'[41] The professed 'realism' of the cottage setting is further emphasized by a full-page illustration of a cottage fireside, radiating the order and cleanliness of domestic improvement. Advice on economic improvement was to be transmitted easily in the anecdotal form of supposedly 'ordinary' cottage speech (a device exploited by all Irish improvement writers). The narratives in Bardin's pamphlet are an attempt to reform the traditional practices of a fireside, civilizing the hearth into a place of enlightened reading and discussion.

Carleton employs the cottage fireside as the setting for a group of stories in the first volume of his *Traits and Stories of the Irish Peasantry*. These 'oral' tales, which are recounted at a cottage fireside, are presented as an authentic account of peasant storytelling. However, the fireside stories are contradictorily depicted as both oral and written, examples of unadulterated oral storytelling and literary fiction. These ostensibly oral stories are mediated by translation and annotation for the benefit of a reading public which exists far beyond the cottage chimney corner. The existence of a narrator who mediates between the 'orality' of the fireside and a reading public is made evident by the numerous annotations and translated material contained in the footnotes. By including this extraneous material, Carleton deliberately calls attention to the artificial construct of the setting. The representation of peasant orality was of course a preoccupation of many nineteenth-century writers. The use of oral narrators was common in the fiction of the Scottish writers James Hogg and Walter Scott, and in the work of Irish writers such as Edgeworth, Griffin, and Banim.[42] The fireside was thus an established improvement and literary convention before Carleton invoked it for his collection. Written 'orality' is necessarily a fiction and, of course, a contradiction in terms. The

[41] Bardin, Preface, *The Cottage Fireside*.
[42] On Hogg and oral storytelling, see Fielding, *Writing and Orality*, 124.

irony of Carleton's position as a writer is that the selling point of his work was, and continues to be, its representation of a peasant orality that he was seeking to write out of existence.[43]

The artificiality of the fireside is compounded by the inclusion of a conventional improvement narrative, 'Larry M'Farland's Wake'. This story recounts the tragic life of a poor peasant who had once been 'considhered the best labourer within a great ways of him' (*TSIP*, i. 84). In the story, the character of Larry is made to exemplify the destructiveness of a hand-to-mouth existence: he dresses above his station, indulges in drink and dancing, doesn't save, and never plans for the future. His wife, Sally, had been valued for her skill as a servant and is described as 'well-looking' but fatefully drawn to fine clothes and the decadent pleasures of the pre-modern (*TSIP*, i. 86). The story attempts to instruct those seated around the fireplace on the tragic consequences that can ensue from the conventional entertainments of traditional peasant life. The reader is warned that the tendency to live beyond one's means, which paradoxically typifies a struggling hand-to-mouth existence, can only result in devastation and tragedy of gothic proportions. As in the tracts of More and Leadbeater, Larry's fate is contrasted throughout with that of his brother, who thrives on account of his understanding of the improving values of orderliness, work, and economy despite being very much the duller and less talented of the two. Tom is described as ordinary, 'sober and industrious', characteristics he wisely sought in a wife, Biddy, whose exemplary domestic skills always serve to highlight the irregularity in the cottage of Larry and Sally. Tom and Biddy follow a well-established narrative code and form of practice, which ensured that 'they were up early and down late, improving' (*TSIP*, i. 87).

Improvement was supposed to civilize the rural poor from the primitive conditions of the pre-modern. In the process, the oral desires of the fireside that sustained the hand-to-mouth economy of the rural poor would be either regulated or eliminated. In these fictions, women are supposed to protect the household from the horrific world of the gothic by instilling rationality and order. Improvement fiction insists that the irrationality of the supernatural can be kept at bay through strict domestic and commercial organization. It is fitting that Sally should hear the banshee the night that Larry dies—her lack of domestic orderliness

---

[43] This continues to be the case in the reception of Carleton's writing. In particular, see Eileen Sullivan, 'William Carleton, Artist of Reality', *Éire-Ireland*, 12/1 (Spring 1997), 130–40.

delivering her directly to the forces of the supernatural. Carleton's writing reveals the supernaturalism that had to be suppressed in the tracts of a Leadbeater or Bardin. Gothic is the generic 'other', perhaps signifying the 'literary' and novelistic, which improvement writers cannot wholly suppress but which, at times, comes through vividly in Carleton's stories.

The conventionality of the fireside setting is epitomized by the ethnographic description of the wake that concludes the story. The discussion of the fireside group suggests that wakes were increasingly disapproved of and not practised as widely as they had been previously. Oddly, Irish oral culture is being explained around a fireside, heightening the artificiality of the 'oral' convention (and suggesting the passing of that 'orality'). In addition, the vices and excesses of orality are shown to be instructive when made the subject matter of stories. Immoral behaviour at wakes is commented on disapprovingly by the audience seated around the fireplace, and the younger people present are warned against attending such festivities ('just take a friend's advice, and never mind going to wakes', *TSIP*, i. 113). These practices all too often lead directly to the tragic course of events that comprise peasant life, such as early, improvident marriages, domestic violence, and (as Chapter 4 explores) political disturbance. As Shane Fadh, who had himself been party to a runaway match and early marriage, reminds everyone present:

sure most of the matches are planned at them, and, I may say, most of the runaways, too—poor, young, foolish crathurs, going off, and getting themselves married; then bringing small, helpless families upon their hands, without money or manes to begin the world with, and afterwards likely to eat one another out of the face for their folly; however, there's no putting ould heads upon young shoulders, and I doubt, except the wakes are stopped altogether, that it'll be the ould case still.(*TSIP*, i. 113)

It seems that practices such as wakes often lie at the root of the rampant violence of pre-Famine life. Carleton tries to present his fireplace as a place of improvement where a previously barbaric orality could be rehabilitated and imbued with the values and rhetoric of improvement and nationality. The fireside of Ned and Nancy is presented as an expression of the improved morality of an increasingly reformed national character, signalling an abandonment of the superstitious and irrational practices of the past. As in Leadbeater's *Cottage Dialogues*, the conventionality of the fireside is an attempt to demonstrate the evolution of both fictional and social forms, as the gothic world of the rural poor is transformed into the realism of improvement.

The fireside is abruptly dismissed at the end of 'The Battle of the Factions' and the remaining stories in the collection are all third-person narratives. A note at the end of that story explains that the 'oral' narrative voice was destined to become tedious and would have been impossible to sustain over the entire collection. In abandoning the original scheme, Carleton emphasizes the inauthenticity of his 'oral' fireside narratives. However, the artificiality of the fireside section had already been made abundantly clear by the inclusion of the improvement narrative 'Larry M'Farland's Wake'. The fireside device supposedly made Carleton realize the expediency of containing 'Irish dialogue and its peculiarities of expression' within an explicitly written rather than 'oral' framework. In adopting a written framework, he would, presumably, bring orality and dialect within the order of text and, in a manner, exemplify the improved national culture he was seeking to convey in his writing. In dismissing the fireside setting, he was swapping one literary device for another. It has been claimed that the manner in which he abandons the fireside trope is a serious flaw in his presentation of the collection as a whole and that he should not have brought 'the mechanics of writing' too closely to the reader's attention.[44] However, this declaration to the reader should be understood as a significant cultural fact rather than an unfortunate aesthetic weakness. It is precisely through foregrounding 'the mechanics of writing' in this way that Carleton's work is important. The manner in which Carleton rejects the oral storytelling convention emphasizes the conventionality of the professed realism and authenticity of the entire collection. His uncertainty regarding literary convention and form emphasizes the arbitrary manner in which Irish 'voice' and character were constructed in nineteenth-century writing. Far from depicting an authentic Irish accent, dialect, and character, the representations of writers such as Carleton were inscribed in a textual rather than oral culture. Carleton was not striving for authenticity in representation. His repeated claim that his representations of peasant orality are authentic is itself a mere convention of improvement fiction and, indeed, of the early development of the novel as a genre. Carleton's oral storytelling was always already written.

Carleton invoked the fireside trope in a later narrative in order to signify, at once, peasant orality and the discourse of improvement. In the Preface to his 1845 Library of Ireland temperance tract *Art*

---

[44] Barbara Hayley, *Carleton's Traits and Stories and the Nineteenth-Century Anglo-Irish Tradition* (Gerrards Cross, Bucks.: Colin Smythe, 1983), 279.

Maguire, which chronicles the fate of a talented, 'gifted' young man whose unsteady character leads him inexorably into alcoholism and destitution, he states that his objective was

to send to the poor man's fireside, through the medium of tales that will teach his heart and purify his affections, those simple lessons which may enable him to understand his own value—that will generate self-respect, independence, industry, love of truth, hatred of deceit and falsehood, habits of cleanliness, order, and punctuality—together with all those lesser virtues which help to create a proper sense of personal and domestic comfort—to assist in working out these healthful purposes is the Author's anxious wish—a task in which any man may feel proud to engage. (*Art Maguire*, pp. vi–vii)

The place to begin the process of improvement is, it seems, at the fireside of the 'poor man's' cabin where most oral vices are nurtured. Like More and Leadbeater, Carleton claims that his strategy is 'to make amusement the hand-maiden of instruction', which will in turn allow him to smuggle his tract into 'the cabin, the farm-house, and even the landlord's drawing-room' (Preface, *Art Maguire*, p. vi). By such means, his tract would imbue his readers with 'a light by which each and all of them may read many beneficial lessons' (ibid.). The tract was written for a series entitled, 'Tales for the Irish People' in Charles Gavan Duffy's Library of Ireland, which indicates that these 'tales' were primarily intended to improve an Irish reading public rather than to provide entertainment for an English readership.

Carleton implies that written representation is an integral part of the process of improvement and that his writing is engaged in this very project:

the darker page of Irish life shall be laid open before them—in which they will be taught, by examples that they can easily understand, the fearful details of misery, destitution, banishment, and death, which the commission of a single crime may draw down, not only upon the criminal himself, but upon those innocent and beloved connections whom he actually punishes by his guilt. (Preface, *Art Maguire*, p. vii.)

Oral storytelling would not have been able to achieve the same improving effects made possible by the 'page' of writing. Carleton can create 'examples' in his pamphlet which can be easily comprehended by the reader and, therefore, become readily instructive. Art Maguire loses his business, reduces his family to complete impoverishment, and almost kills his young child on account of his alcoholism. In Carleton's tract, these improving 'examples' of tragedy and despair are both sensationalized and sentimentalized, as though such a representational mode would make the dangers of excessive alcohol consumption all the more explicit. The life depicted in the improvement tract provided the reader with only two possibilities: salvation into domestic comfort or damnation into impoverished misery. The former was gained by means of an ordinary improved life and the latter was the inevitable consequence of idleness and extremism. Improvement fiction was an attempt to save the poor (and, of course, the writers of tracts) from the gothic fictional fate that would most certainly ensue from a failure to be sober, punctual, and hard-working.

In keeping with the conventions of improvement fiction, Art Maguire had a brother, who happened to be mediocre, dull, and steady (in fact, he is described as possessing 'natural sobriety and slowness of intellect', *Art Maguire*, 12). As in so many improvement narratives, the reader is shown that plainness, dullness, and mediocrity are—far from holding one back in a competitive market—the qualities that guarantee success in a modernizing economy: they are the bulwark of capitalism. Frank Maguire thrives in the world of commerce, his bland sobriety ensuring that he instinctively understands the workings of business and markets. Like More, Leadbeater, and Bardin, Carleton sought to demonstrate how the sociable and talkative characters of Irish oral culture, who are always embodiments of excess, were not acceptable in an improving economy. However appealing, the particular talents of an Art Maguire are shown to be detrimental to survival in a famine-threatened Ireland and, no doubt, beyond. Carleton adopts the tropes and rhetoric of the improvement fiction of writers from More to Bardin to demonstrate how qualities such as passion, volatility, and ebullience—all associated with Irish national character—were disastrous within the context of modernization.[45]

The lively fireside of the traditional Irish cottage had to be transformed into a place of reflection and sobriety so as to instil the character 'traits' of a Frank Maguire instead of those of an Art Maguire. In his pamphlet, Carleton expresses a desire that his temperance narrative will be embraced at the cottage firesides of rural Ireland. In so doing, he was reiterating the rhetoric of his predecessors such as Leadbeater and Bardin, all of whom sought to redefine the interiors of Irish homes and, in the process, national character itself. The order and sobriety demanded in improvement discourse were supposedly essential to guard

[45] For a discussion of national character in this context, see Deane, *Strange Country*, esp. 49–69.

against the unpredictable forces of poverty which Carleton, for one, represents in gothic terms.

Carleton names his improvement genre 'truthful fiction', which is supposedly rooted 'in the plain paths of every-day life', and distinguishes it from 'the improbable creations of Romance' (Preface, *Art Maguire*, p. viii). Carleton's plain 'truthful fiction' is, of course, as 'improbable' as any romance. His tract clearly draws on the sensationalism of gothic to depict the shocking fate of Art Maguire—who abuses his children and dies young—and to demonstrate the horror that overwhelms those who refuse to improve. Despite publishing numerous novels, Carleton claimed that he was not actually writing within the genre at all. In *Squanders of Castle Squander*, he denounced 'fashionable novels' as distinct from his own peculiar productions (*The Squanders of Castle Squander*, ii. 297). However, Carleton's fiction—as with all of the tracts discussed here—drew upon novelistic, fictional conventions in its attempt to define both economic backwardness and modernization. The 'pre-modern' is gothicized so that improvement modernization can be depicted as resolutely realist.

Carleton's writing exemplifies the manner in which the discourses of improvement and literary fiction were intertwined in early nineteenth-century Ireland. The 'rise' of improvement fiction was itself a component in the development of the Irish novel in the immediate post-Union period. This is evident in the career of Mary Leadbeater, for whom improvement had been a strongly Edgeworthian project. Indeed, Maria Edgeworth's own literary work was itself divided between tracts and novels. The literary context of Carleton's fiction becomes all the more evident when understood in the framework of this literary history. As noted in the Introduction, Edgeworth personally endorsed Leadbeater's project by editing and annotating an edition of *Cottage Dialogues* for the English market in 1811. Edgeworth was commissioned by Mrs O'Beirne, the wife of the Bishop of Meath, to provide an introduction and notes for *Cottage Dialogues*.[46] In her papers, Leadbeater states that the Bishop of Meath 'presented the manuscript to R. L. Edgeworth and his gifted daughter, who not only approved of its original tendency, but recommended it to their own bookseller in London'.[47] In a later edition

[46] Marilyn Butler, *Maria Edgeworth: A Literary Biography* (Oxford: Clarendon Press, 1972), 211–12.

[47] Leadbeater, *Papers*, i. 319.

of *Cottage Dialogues*, Leadbeater claims that the purpose of preparing an English edition was to provide a 'means of introducing the dialogues to the notice of the Society for Bettering the Condition of the Poor who were pleased to extract and publish the dialogues for the use of the English cottagers'.[48] It also transpires, however, that Edgeworth's edition of *Cottage Dialogues* was not only intended to be improving, and thus utilitarian, reading material for English cottagers but to become—as Leadbeater herself noted—'a work of entertainment' for a general English reading public.[49]

The correspondence between Leadbeater and Edgeworth regarding *Cottage Dialogues* reveals the extent to which both Maria and R. L. Edgeworth were involved in the composition of the pamphlet as well as in the more practical matters of publication in London, copyright, and even the physical size of the volume. Edgeworth advised Leadbeater to enlarge *Cottage Dialogues*, 'to make it a respectable volume—a small octavo' and even to write 'a hundred pages more'.[50] It would appear that Edgeworth was actually urging Leadbeater to novelize the tract and was excited by the novelistic potential that seemed to lurk within it. A letter from R. L. Edgeworth states that he intends 'to add notes explaining the Irish idiom as in *Castle Rackrent*,' which would suggest that the glossary to *Cottage Dialogues* was co-written by both father and daughter.[51] They propose various amendments to the text, first to augment the volume and later to reduce it back to its original size and format. Leadbeater always defers to the more knowledgeable literary judgement of Maria Edgeworth—an influential and established writer at this stage—claiming that her own understanding of publishing matters was restricted by the fact that 'she has never but once spent six months out of her own village in which she was born' and that her 'situation and education prevented her from a knowledge of the world'.[52]

[48] Mary Leadbeater, Preface, *Cottage Dialogues* (Dublin, 1814), p. vii.

[49] Leadbeater, *Papers*, i. 319.

[50] Letter from Maria Edgeworth to Mary Leadbeater, 10 July 1810. Ballitore Papers, Bundle E, 1–40, Letters of Maria Edgeworth on Literary Matters, n. 1008 p. 1090 (National Library of Ireland).

[51] Letter from R. L. Edgeworth to Mary Leadbeater, 10 April 1810. Ballitore Papers, Hereafter cited as Ballitore Papers. The evidence of this letter would contradict the account in Brian Hollingworth, *Maria Edgeworth's Irish Writing, Language, History, Politics* (London: Macmillan, 1997), 149.

[52] Letter from Mary Leadbeater to Maria Edgeworth [n.d.]. Ballitore Papers. Unfortunately, Leadbeater did not date her letters.

In addition to Edgeworth's direct assistance in the preparation of *Cottage Dialogues*, her novels continually feed into Leadbeater's pamphlets, determining representations of the peasantry, Hiberno-English, and ascendancy life.

Cottage Dialogues was not for Edgeworth simply a polarized representation of two positions (rationality and superstition), but was a model of enlightened 'reasoning'.[53] Edgeworth states in her Preface that the text exhibits the possibility of creating a rational social order in Ireland: 'The characteristic of the book is good sense. Prudence and economy, morality and religion, are judiciously and liberally diffused through the whole, without touching upon peculiar tenets, without alarming party prejudice, or offending national pride'.[54] The public realm envisaged in Leadbeater's tract, was, it seems, characterized by the moderation and toleration essential for the achievement of progress. For Edgeworth, *Cottage Dialogues* exemplifies how rationalized 'good sense'—rather than sectarian tension and political polemic—could determine public debate. In Edgeworth's characterization, Leadbeater succeeds in realizing the possibility of a liberal, enlightened space within textual terms, if not its actual realization in the day-to-day workings of post-Union society itself. It is possible that for Edgeworth the value of Leadbeater's tract may have extended beyond its more obvious utilitarian role of making peasants thriftier and more useful to themselves as well as to others; *Cottage Dialogues* may have signified another form of utilitarian value which had to do with the refining of novelistic representation (into a form of realism perhaps?) which Edgeworth was herself seeking in her novels.

In passing through Edgeworth's hands, *Cottage Dialogues* becomes an aestheticized, yet supposedly 'exact', representation of Irish peasant life. Edgeworth's annotations have the effect of dissolving the 'oral' framework of the *Dialogues*, emphasizing instead the literariness of the tract. While *Cottage Dialogues* was presented as a product of strictly pragmatic rather than aesthetic considerations, both Hiberno-English and improvement are clearly shown to be 'literary' discourses in Edgeworth's edition. In her glossary, Edgeworth links the language of Leadbeater's Irish peasants with the writings of Johnson and Shakespeare and, hence, as exemplary of a natural literary diction that was no longer to be found in the mainstream of British literature. Many expressions of the Irish

---

[53] See Edgeworth, Preface to *Cottage Dialogues* (London, 1811), p. iv.
[54] Ibid., pp. iv–v.

are conveniently Shakespearian, such as the phrase 'to demean—to debase, to undervalue' which 'is used in this sense by Shakespeare'. In explicating these terms, Edgeworth seeks to emphasize the cultural as well as geographic proximity between Ireland and England and, in the process, assure English readers that there is little reason to feel estranged from the Catholic Irish. Edgeworth presents the speech of Irish peasants as authentically—rather than artificially—literary, claiming that 'the language of the lower Irish of this day is the English of Queen Elizabeth's time, often stronger, more eloquent, and more poetical, than the more polished and fashionable diction of the present time'.[55] It transpires that many Irish phrases are intrinsically literary, such as 'comes like a cloud over me', which is glossed by Edgeworth as 'a Shakespearian expression! "How is it that clouds still land on you?" Hamlet.'[56] Another line which states, 'It might drive him to the alehouse, and then we are all lost' prompts the following annotation from Edgeworth:

Lost! Lost! Lost indeed, if he went to the alehouse; lost, ruined past redemption as Johnson defines it, is used in the Irish emphatic manner by our best poets: 'Oh! Look not on so lost a thing as I am.' But the Irish familiar use of the word lost, in the common affairs of life, would surprise and alarm those who are not aware of the manner in which it is to be best understood.[57]

At one point, Rose states 'I would have you be constant and loyal' and Edgeworth declares excitedly that 'Loyal is here used as it is by Spenser, Sydney and Milton.'[58] Edgeworth claims that Hiberno-English derived its peculiar character as much—if not more—from an English literary tradition as an Irish-language, oral one. She notes many examples of Irish idiom from the text—such as 'the life was out of it'—which apparently illustrate 'the Irish poetical mode of expression'.[59] In explicating Leadbeater's language, Edgeworth strives to bring Ireland within a sphere of political and aesthetic possibility by insisting upon its relationship with the Elizabethan age, an era venerated in the early nineteenth century (and later) for embodying an organic social harmony and cultural greatness.

Edgeworth is claiming that Hiberno-English—on account of these linguistic links with Elizabethan English—cannot really be the language of primitive savages. Hiberno-English should not be seen as entirely oral and, therefore, anarchic and dangerous, but as containing the

---

[55] Ibid. 273.   [56] Ibid. 297.   [57] Ibid. 291–2.   [58] Ibid. 325.
[59] Ibid. 269.

possibility of reform, order, and civility. In the *Essay on Irish Bulls* (1802), both Edgeworths had already claimed that many phrases in common usage in Ireland were identical to the language of Shakespeare (pp. 199–200). Consequently, Irish speech can, it seems, exhibit all the civility of a modernizing and progressive Englishness as well as a dreaded Gaelic backwardness. The Edgeworths imply that Irish speech exemplifies the effectiveness rather than the failures of the English colonial project, testifying to common linguistic and cultural ground between Ireland and England. By so doing, they were also seeking to validate their own role as Anglo-Irish landowners, erasing difference on the peripheries in pursuit of more 'universalized forms' of identity.[60] The Edgeworths are more interested in demonstrating how Ireland is capable of functioning within a modernizing, progressive economy than in representing cultural idiosyncrasies and eccentric regionalisms.[61] In fact, such quirkiness (indeed orality)—be it in the form of a duplicitous Thady Quirke or a drunken Condy Rackrent—is represented only in order to demonstrate the necessity for immediate absorption of a so-called Irishness within Britain. Improvement in Ireland would not be complete until all Gaelicisms (of language as well as politics and bearing) were eradicated, subsumed entirely within the rationality of a broader British economy, itself exemplified for the Edgeworths by a unifying rather than divisive form of identity and the material, physical work of progress. The attempt to overwhelm the perceived backwardness, disloyalty, and difference of Irish culture shaped Maria Edgeworth's national tales, improvement discourse in Ireland, and, later, the fiction of Carleton and Young Ireland nationalism as well.

Edgeworth claims that Leadbeater's pamphlet was written in a form of Hiberno-English or, in Martin Doyle's terms, 'the Anglo-Hibernian, diction, phraseology and pronunciation.'[62] Rolf and Magda Loeber argue that such representations or 'accounts' of spoken speech 'could only take place because the author had been in direct contact with his/her characters and the stories were often based on real people and facts'.[63] Indeed, Martin Doyle tells us that many of the models for characters

[60] The phrase is from Mark Canuel, *Religion, Toleration, and British Writing, 1790–1830* (Cambridge: Cambridge University Press, 2002), 124.

[61] On this topic see ibid. 124–6.

[62] Martin Doyle, Preface to *Irish Cottagers* (Dublin, 1833).

[63] Rolf and Magda Loeber, 'Fiction Written to and for Cottagers', in Bernadette Cunningham and Máire Kennedy (eds.), *The Experience of Reading: Irish Historical Perspectives* (Dublin: Rare Books Group of the Library Association of Ireland and Economic Social History of Ireland, 1999), 149.

in *Irish Cottagers* were still alive when he published an edition of *Irish Cottagers* in 1833,[64] a claim which echoes Carleton's assertion that his stories were based on real characters and events.[65] Leadbeater lived in the rural community at Ballitore, Co. Kildare, throughout her life and apparently modelled her fictional characters on her actual neighbours.[66] In speaking of her shepherd of Salisbury Plain, Hannah More claimed likewise: 'This piece of frugal industry is not imaginary, but a real fact, as is the character of the Shepherd, and his uncommon knowledge of the scripture.'[67] These claims to truthfulness and authenticity must be understood as standard conventions of improvement discourse, an explicit attempt on the part of these writers to disassociate their tracts from the novel and, indeed, novelistic discourse as a whole. However much such statements were intended to convince the reader that improvement writers were familiar with peasant life, the fiction itself clearly demonstrates the extent to which these writers were alienated from the reality of the rural poor, either by class, geographic distance, or religion. It was probably that very alienation from rural Catholic Ireland that in part motivated these writers. According to the Loebers, the representation of Hiberno-English idiom in these improvement texts 'was an innovation in Irish fiction which may have been aimed at more effectively communicating improving ideas to the cottagers'.[68] This 'innovation' was, however, especially indebted to Edgeworth's *Castle Rackrent, Ennui*, and *The Absentee* and was thus rooted as much (if not more) in novels as in the actual experiences of these writers. The representation of Hiberno-English in improvement fiction points to its novelistic origins as well as laying bare the improving rhetoric embedded within so much literary fiction. Leadbeater was more than likely inspired to write in Hiberno-English by the example of *Castle Rackrent*, a novel which she seems to have read as improvement fiction (see below).

In *Tales for Cottagers* (1814), co-written by Leadbeater with Elizabeth Shackleton, short narratives evolve around chosen themes such as

[64] Doyle, Preface to *Irish Cottagers*.

[65] For example, the narrator in 'Ned M'Keown' states that 'The names here are not fictitious. Andy Morrow, a most respectable and intelligent farmer, is not long dead', *TSIP* i. 9.

[66] See Clara I. Grady, 'The Condition and Character of the Irish Peasantry as seen in the *Annals* and *Cottage Dialogues* of Mary Leadbeater', *Women and Literature*, 3/1 (1975), 28–38. Grady takes literally this conventional claim, arguing that Leadbeater's representations are based directly on her neighbours in Ballitore and that her dialogues contain 'a literal transcript of peasant language', ibid. 32.

[67] More, *The Shepherd of Salisbury Plain*, 15 n.

[68] Rolf and Magda Loeber, 'Fiction Written to and for Cottagers', 149.

'calculation', 'economy', 'early training', and 'perseverance'. Specific characters personify these particular values, such as Polly, a virtuous servant girl who learns to read from her improving mistress, Mrs Brampton, who also provided her with 'profitable books', ensuring that 'she did not make a bad use of her learning.'[69] In fact, Polly exemplifies lower-class literacy that is put to useful rather than immoral, radical, or simply useless ends, demonstrating how literacy can be harnessed for the good once enlightened individuals such as Mrs Brampton intervene. Polly spends her time reading the Bible, religious texts, and, interestingly, 'Miss Edgeworth's *Popular Tales* and *Castle Rackrent*' rather than those 'foolish or immoral ballads' to be found everywhere.[70] Such virtuous reading material will not only improve Polly's mind, but should enhance her earning power, instilling the kind of instruction that is necessary to advance steadily in a modernizing society. The narrator states that these texts 'afforded as much pleasure and instruction' in the kitchen as in the parlour of Mrs Brampton's house, indicating that they could be read by all classes and successfully create a common discourse across class and religious divides, between upstairs and downstairs, and from the big house to the cottage. Like More, Leadbeater and Skackleton were explicitly attempting to encourage a shared frame of reference between rich and poor rather than reaffirming a strict division between high and low culture (without, of course, threatening to dismantle specific class divisions). This rhetoric would itself appear to be novelistically inspired, invoking the democratized idiom of the novel to unify disparate communities and interests. Leadbeater and Shackleton present this image of the benevolent woman of the house, who enacts—by textual means—a tranquil middle-ground between servants and masters, connecting the diverse groups that constitute her household through a persuasive improving rhetoric. The possibilities of realizing a liberal public sphere are enacted within this representation of a tightly integrated household, instructing through a series of domestic metaphors—rooted in novelistic discourse—the means by which moderation in language, sensibility, and even physical bearing could be achieved in the broader terms of society as a whole.[71]

69 Mary Leadbeater and Elizabeth Shackleton, *Tales for Cottagers, Accommodated to the Present Condition of the Irish Peasantry* (Dublin, 1814), 29.
70 Ibid. 29.
71 For an analysis of the relationship between particular representations of domesticity in English conduct books and the emergence of a middle-class liberal tradition in the English novel, see Armstrong, *Desire and Domestic Fiction*.

In the model household depicted in *Tales for Cottagers*, a generic preference was expressed for prose over poetry, the former deemed a more measured and appropriate medium for instructive themes while intrinsically embodying the restraint of improvement. Poetry was clearly equated with the very literary excess that troubled improvement writers and novelists such as Edgeworth. In Leadbeater's *The Landlord's Friend*, a landowner, Lady Seraphina, maintains a library for tenants on her estate: 'I do not introduce much poetry,' she explains. 'The poor have not time to seek instruction in the winding walks of fancy, *the direct road of plain prose* is better suited to their attainment of that end.'[72] Leadbeater nonetheless proves herself incapable of writing in plain prose—her call for literalism expressed in figurative language. Indeed, the problems attributed to imaginative writing are also described figuratively: 'winding walks of fancy'. 'Fancy' is, of course, supposed to connote poetic discourse (which is also equated with women) and that which leads one astray from the material world. Improving rhetoric seeks to characterize itself as being unambiguous and linear in the manner of prose (as though prose was by definition transparent), dispelling in particular the fictionality of republican discourses. The factual qualities of improvement prose were to counter the allegedly deluded pretensions and fictions of the lower classes. Lady Seraphina then claims that her 'labourer only reads plain English, which is now nothing rare; the point is to direct his reading and that reading which inculcates humility and simplicity is what I propose for him'.[73] The apparent linearity and transparency offered by prose, embodied particularly in 'plain English', is, it seems, capable of instilling instruction more readily than the equivocal and circular nature of poetry or, indeed, as will be evident in Chapter 3, the Irish language. The terms of discourse are rewritten so that plainness of language will necessarily encourage 'simplicity' in bearing and expectation. This has the inevitable effect, however, of calling attention to the conventionality of notions such as 'plainness' and 'simplicity'. It would appear that Leadbeater as well as More and Edgeworth assert prose and, increasingly, despite themselves, the novel, against poetry, associated by them with an excess (linked to gender as well as to politics and language) from which they wanted to distance their particular literary endeavour.

The construction of this fictional library betrays a desire to define a literary 'canon'. The library thus excludes many novels and 'much poetry', seeking to keep the shelves free of impractical, immoral, and

---

[72] Leadbeater, *The Landlord's Friend*, 107, emphasis added.   [73] Ibid. 111.

politicized books.[74] As with Mrs Brampton's model household in *Tales for Cottagers*, this library is not just intended for the tenants on Lady Seraphina's estate: the books are clearly selected in the hope that they may become the preferred reading material for the entire community. Her library is naturally stocked with the Bible, the New Testament, and Willan's *Life of Christ*. Other books such as *Pilgrim's Progress* are included for their ability to maintain a 'steady place' within the tradition 'while many a high wrought novel and many a tuneful lay has appeared, been gazed upon, and then glided down the stream to oblivion' (yet another figurative phrase).[75] Certain works of non-novelistic prose were guaranteed a place on the shelves, such as *The Life of Benjamin Franklin*, whose essentially improving quality 'encourages to temperance and frugality' while displaying 'a pure and plain style'.[76] These prosaic texts are presumed to be properly realistic, grounding and orienting the reader in the world rather than away from it in some form of poetic reverie, escapist romance, political idealism, or philosophical transcendence.

The issue of genre troubles the construction of this particular tradition, reflecting the generic anxieties integral to improvement discourse. When Lady Charlotte comments: 'What a constellation of female writers has this age produced!'—most of whom concentrated on the writing of novels—Lady Seraphina explains that she has become 'too sensible of the dangers of novel-reading to admit even ... well imagined and well intended recitals' into her selective library.[77] Interestingly, Leadbeater described her utter disdain for Samuel Richardson's *Pamela* in a letter to George Crabbe, citing the 'dangers' of the novel and recounting how she 'met with one volume' when she 'was young', as did her mother who promptly 'committed it to the flames'.[78] Most novels were, it seems, generically inappropriate for the improvement library, embodying the very rhetoric improvers were determined to displace. It seems that fiction—particularly in the form of the novel—exemplified an essentially unstable political and linguistic situation that had to be suppressed for improvement to be achieved. However, didactic fiction was, nonetheless, a product of the novel and was inescapably mired in literary, novelistic discourse.

In order to counteract the pervasiveness of the novel in popular culture, this fictional library is stocked with the improvement tracts of

---

[74] Leadbeater, *The Landlord's Friend*, 107.   [75] Ibid. 102.   [76] Ibid.
[77] Ibid. 103.
[78] Letter from Mary Leadbeater to George Crabbe, 12 Apr. 1821. Reprinted in Leadbeater, *Papers*, ii. 374.

Hannah More, Sarah Trimmer, Thomas Day, Maria Edgeworth, and Elizabeth Hamilton, many of whom—such as Edgeworth, Hamilton, and More—also wrote novels. For Leadbeater (though also for Edgeworth and More) it is 'highly-wrought' novels that particularly disconcert, those that overstep the mark by veering away from supposedly truthful representations of the material world (as conceived, of course, by liberal improvement). Edgeworth addressed this situation directly by writing novels while Leadbeater and More hoped to resolve the problem of representation by means of the didactic tract.

The didactic tract was an expression of dissatisfaction with the novel, which it then sought to redefine and restructure as resolutely realist and linear. For improvement writers, the appropriate novel was somehow free of both fictionality and literariness. The novel was nonetheless perceived to be more manageable generic terrain than poetry. The frame of reference contained within Leadbeater's fictional library extends, however, to a particular class of poetry. The work of Robert Bloomfield is cited as appropriate poetic writing because the 'natural descriptions in his Farmer's Boy and other poems touch the heart, and are well adapted for the perusal of those in his line of life.'[79] Bloomfield's natural images remained free of ambiguity and excess, exemplifying—albeit within poetry—the literary values of improvement discourse. In a manner, Bloomfield personified the acceptably literate peasant: education did not deter him from his pre-ordained role in life, remaining—as he did—within his station while simultaneously writing poetry that celebrated his lowly existence. According to Alan Richardson, poets such as Bloomfield were acceptable to improvers as his life 'in outline closely resembles the autobiography of self-improvement'.[80] In a discussion between Squires Hartley and Wilfort in *The Landlord's Friend*, Hartley mentions approvingly that Bloomfield composed his 'Farmer's Boy' as he made shoes and that Burns—also permitted into the library—'framed many a sweet lay while he followed the plough'.[81] These poets signify for Hartley the precise integration of labour and

---

[79] Leadbeater, *The Landlord's Friend*, 107.

[80] Alan Richardson, *Literature, Education and Romanticism: Reading as Social Practice 1780–1832* (Cambridge: Cambridge University Press, 1994), 247. On the fashion for 'uneducated poets' in the early nineteenth century, see pp. 247–59.

[81] Leadbeater, *The Landlord's Friend*, 34. On Burns, see David Buchan, 'The Expressive Poetry of Nineteenth-Century Scottish Farm Servants', in T. M. Devine (ed.), *Farm Servants and Labour in Lowland Scotland, 1770–1914* (Edinburgh: John Donald, 1984), 226–42, and Richardson, *Literature, Education and Romanticism*, 250–1.

literacy that lay at the heart of the improvement imagination. This presumes that there is, or should be, a direct continuity between representation and ordinary experience. It is the task of improvement realism to recover this essential relationship between experience and representation and, thereby, restore a natural order of things. According to this rhetoric, satisfaction can really only inhere within such an order of utility and restraint, all other possibilities resulting in inevitable disappointment. Education did not compel Bloomfield and Burns to forsake their humble roles in life; rather, it made them appreciate that humility all the more. It is as though the potential excessiveness (or transcendental impulses) of the literary can be reined in when conducted alongside the ploughing of fields, the making of shoes, administration, and commerce.

For Leadbeater, poets such as Bloomfield and Burns, both drawn from lower social ranks, personify a raw, natural eloquence, untainted by any conventionality. Squire Hartley tries to convince Wilfort that such eloquence is already—and naturally—abundant amongst the Irish peasantry and is not just to be found in the novels of Maria Edgeworth:

> Be assured, the Irish character in the lower classes, is a continual source of entertainment, if that only were in question. You delight in Miss Edgeworth's pictures of their language and manners. She has selected and generalized with the pencil of genius—but she is the most faithful of painters—and believe me, you would find much amusement in comparing her exquisite sketches with that real life from which she has so successfully copied.[82]

The fiction of Edgeworth supposedly corresponds perfectly with the reality it purports to represent. Even more rewarding is the fact that one can take pleasure in her depiction of the lower classes on the pages of her novels and then experience it within the realm of real life itself. There is a professed correspondence between representation and reality in Edgeworth's writing (and implicitly in Leadbeater's own writing) as in improvement fiction in general, much like that which is claimed by Hartley to exist in the writings of Bloomfield and Burns. Any mode of representation which calls attention to textuality and convention is accordingly shunned. Hartley claims that the linguistic pleasures provided by Edgeworth's fiction can be experienced regularly as a resident landlord, citing an example of a recent encounter with 'a

---

[82] Leadbeater, *The Landlord's Friend*, 14–15.

female orator' who was, appropriately, digging potatoes. She interrupted her work to pronounce 'a lamentation for a deceased neighbour, an elderly man, of whom she claimed: "He died on a naked board, and left no children to say, Why did you die?"' Hartley proceeds to interpret the woman's language, supposing that 'the metaphor of the naked board was meant to express the solitary state of a single life, which we see our peasantry so careful to avoid.'[83] Such exegesis of the speech of peasants is akin to the process of editing in Edgeworth's *Castle Rackrent* and her edition of *Cottage Dialogues* which provide an editor to perform this exact interpretive function. Edgeworth's novels demonstrated for Leadbeater how Hiberno-English could be represented and rendered acceptable as literary language and how, by extension, Irish character could be absorbed within a broader British identity. The implication is that Irish peasant character, once educated and improved, would be more than capable of literary accomplishment, like that of a Burns or Bloomfield, without representing any threat to the social order; in fact, according to the overly optimistic and simplistic interpretations of Leadbeater's fictional landowners, they would enforce that very order. However, a cautionary note is made by Richardson who describes how Bloomfield died in 1823 'impoverished despite his huge success with *The Farmer's Boy*, falling victim both to changing fashion and to suspicions regarding his political loyalties'.[84] Leadbeater's optimistic faith in the ability of improvement education to produce apolitical, rustic poets rather than political extremists reflects a related desire to subsume the supposedly 'difficult' Irish peasantry within a standardized Britishness.

Leadbeater justifies the creation of her library on the terms that: 'Not one of these books tends to foster that false refinement which introduces discontent, and many are written expressly to reconcile the mind to a lowly lot in life.'[85] Leadbeater connects 'false refinement' with political disturbance, unfulfilled desire often expressing itself in the form of linguistic, literary, or political excess. It was presumed that this excess then returns to haunt the public sphere, unleashing a frightening array of barbarous impulses. Improvement fiction is supposed to offset any such desire or ambition by demonstrating the value of an ordinary, plain life, one stabilized by the intrinsic order and regularity of modernization.

---

[83] Ibid. 15–16.   [84] Richardson, *Literature, Education and Romanticism*, 249.
[85] Leadbeater, *The Landlord's Friend*, 109.

Leadbeater's 'false refinement' echoes Wordsworth's Preface to the *Lyrical Ballads* in which the exact same phrase is used to describe some of the more unfortunate characteristics of late eighteenth-century poetry.[86] Leadbeater denounces any literature that embodies 'false refinement' in any form as, she presumed, it was contrary to her own rigorous realism. Perhaps surprisingly, Wordsworth's poetry is included in her model library on the grounds that 'notwithstanding their overstrained simplicity' his poems 'have merit enough with me to find a place here, because I believe their author intended to adapt them to the comprehension of those who were not accustomed to refinement.'[87] Leadbeater installs Wordsworth in her library but still reproaches him for not achieving a more convincing 'simplicity' or literalism. Leadbeater thus concedes that 'simplicity' is a convention which can be 'overstrained', rendered artificial, when not—as in the case of Wordsworth—deployed carefully. In fact, Leadbeater confesses in a letter to Crabbe that she does not find Wordsworth's poetry 'understandable' and, in a later letter, she claims that 'The Excursion' is 'obscure at times'.[88] It appears that Wordsworth's poetry should not be both plain and obscure at once, written in 'real' language but yet truly difficult to understand. This poetry probably suggested to Leadbeater the impossibility of her own project, the extent to which her plain realism could not be achieved in either literary or linguistic terms. Though Wordsworth explicitly invoked 'the very language of men' for his poetry, Leadbeater is critical of his work for not being sufficiently prosaic. [89] It could be argued that Wordsworth's (prosaic) lyrics suggested the impossibility of transparency within prose, 'the very language of men' by no means ensuring literalism but alluding instead to the figurative nature of all language.

The disdain for 'refinement'—which simultaneously connotes the artificial and mediated—links the discourses of both Romanticism and improvement. Mary Jacobus and, more recently, Angela Keane have commented on the connections between More's Cheap Repository Tracts and Wordsworth's *Lyrical Ballads*. Jacobus claims that 'Hannah More's aim, to combine popular appeal with 'religious and useful knowledge', is matched by Wordsworth's claim for his poems, 'that

---

[86] William Wordsworth, Preface, *Lyrical Ballads*, 1800, ed. W. J. B. Owen (Oxford: Oxford University Press, 1969), 157.

[87] Leadbeater, *The Landlord's Friend*, 107.

[88] See Mary Leadbeater's letters to George Crabbe, 9 Nov. 1824, p. 394 and 3 Apr. 1825. Reprinted in Leadbeater, *Papers*, 396–7.

[89] Wordsworth, Preface, 161.

each of them has a worthy purpose'.[90] For Jacobus, Wordsworth was subverting 'a genre which his contemporaries were accustomed to think of as educating the poor not only in virtue, but in acceptance of the status quo'. Jacobus suggests that More's 'moral ballads', such as 'The Carpenter, or The Danger of Evil Company', which were inserted into the Cheap Repository Tracts, were the inspiration for some of Wordsworth's poems, such as 'Goody Blake and Harry Gill'. In Jacobus's thinking, the difference between each project is that 'More wished to edify the semi-literate' whereas 'Wordsworth was asking his literate readers to think about their own code.'[91] However, as noted in the discussion of *The Shepherd of Salisbury Plain*, More's tracts were also addressed to fully—even excessively—'literate readers' as well as to the semi-literate, explicitly encouraging the educated upper classes to modify and restrain their own use of language for counter-revolutionary purposes. In this sense, More too could be said to be asking her upper-class readers 'to think about their own code', though she was by no means encouraging subversion of the social values of the 'status quo'. As shown earlier in this chapter, More's ballads and tracts were written to protect against that very kind of subversion.

Wordsworth's ambition in the *Lyrical Ballads* was, in part, to 'counteract' the excesses of an expanded print culture in an industrializing age. As such, his project was similar to More's sustained effort to dominate the literary marketplace with her Cheap Repository Tracts. Angela Keane notes how 'like Wordsworth in the Preface to the *Lyrical Ballads*, More sought not to woo a new class of readers, but to instruct a known constituency in a new aesthetic.'[92] For More, however, the scourge of popular literature had to be displaced to curtail revolutionary discourse and preserve an existing social hierarchy which was itself represented, indeed upheld, by a specific aesthetic code. In her mind, that social hierarchy was directly threatened by the work of Romantic writers. Indeed, More's project articulated all too clearly the very cultural tradition which is, in many respects, destabilized and undermined in the *Lyrical Ballads*.

Wordsworth's 'low' subject matter cannot be equated with, say, the plain poor of More's tracts or Leadbeater's Irish peasants. The project of both More and Leadbeater was to assimilate difference—in part

---

[90] Mary Jacobus, *Tradition and Experiment in Wordsworth's Lyrical Ballads* (Oxford: Oxford University Press, 1976), 237–8.
[91] Ibid. 237.   [92] Keane, *Women Writers and the English Nation in the 1790s*, 150.

epitomized by the poor and marginal figures of Wordsworth's *Lyrical Ballads*, such as 'The Mad Mother' or 'The Idiot Boy'—into the mainstream. Wordsworth was attempting to uncover the very 'passions' and feelings that improvement writers sought to work and narrativize beyond. For improvement writers, those passions lay at the root of a dissatisfaction that was often expressed in politics, violence, and despondent idleness. Improvement writers declare that this unhappiness could be resolved by work (but would, they warn, be deepened by aesthetic or speculative inwardness). Improvement progress would dissolve all difficulty by providing satisfaction in a life of order and discipline. Indeed, that satisfaction was presented as the proper and true order of things. Wordsworth's interest in 'low and rustic life' was entirely at odds with the plainness of improvement discourse, which sought to suppress the troubling truths excavated in many of the *Lyrical Ballads*.[93] Wordsworth's related desire to restore the 'sympathies of men' to poetic discourse is a democratization (or republicanization) of literary language. [94] In his Preface, Wordsworth comments on the relationship between 'the revolutions not of literature alone but likewise of society itself' that were then talking place, his *Lyrical Ballads* a contribution to both.[95]

In improvement discourse, plainness was asserted on the level of rhetoric as a means of allaying the proliferation of signs produced by the technologies of print and factory production. Improvement discourse embodies a fear that 'theory'—or speculation—could actually be put into practice again (having already occurred with the Revolution in France). For Wordsworth, plainness does not endorse a given social hierarchy, but is invoked to transcend imaginatively the very order expressed by More's evangelical tradition. One of More's biographers notes that in the 1790s, she was especially sceptical of the work of Romantic poets, whose 'republicanism and "semi-atheism" put their work in these years automatically outside her sphere of interest or approval.'[96] It seems to me that in reacting to the French Revolution, More was implicitly responding to a particular literary and intellectual tradition exemplified in England by the early work of Wordsworth and

[93] Wordsworth, Preface, 156.

[94] Joshua Wilner notes 'the breakdown, clearly heralded by Wordsworth's "Preface to Lyrical Ballads", of the foundational generic distinction between the language of poetry and the language of prose.' *Feeding on Infinity: Readings in the Romantic Rhetoric of Internalization* (Baltimore: Johns Hopkins University Press, 2000), 6.

[95] Wordsworth, Preface, 154–5.   [96] Jones, *Hannah More*, 224–5.

in France by Rousseau.[97] More's tracts generally present themselves as resolutely prosaic, immersed in the immediacy of the present rather than embodying the 'eternal' values of an explicitly aesthetic enterprise. For More, the aesthetic is always immersed in the material world, empirically given in life itself, as though such value inhered within a plain prose, which itself could only be found in specific worldly situations. This also typifies Leadbeater's improvement fiction, as well as the novels of Edgeworth. In *Cottage Dialogues*, for example, emphasis is strictly placed on practical matters while speculation on metaphysical questions, or any urge to transcendence, is strongly, indeed vehemently, discouraged. Writers such as More, Leadbeater, and Edgeworth all articulate an early anxious response to Romanticism. In Edgeworth's *The Absentee*, the exemplary agent Mr Burke—a figure of the model statesman—is described as being 'a plain man' who 'made it a rule not to meddle with speculative points, and to avoid all irritating discussions. He was not to rule the country but to live in it and make others live as happily as he could.'[98] This figure of the modern statesman and, indeed, author—grounded in the world rather than situated above it—signifies both secular liberalism and realism, defined against both an oppressive, feudal past and the feared republicanization of literary and political representation.

Two particular strands of improvement discourse have been discussed here: economic and social modernization and, in line with this, a (perceived) necessary privileging of the literal over the figurative. Improvement fiction sought to assert and emphasize the value of an ordinary and practical life, by representing an existence and aesthetic which functioned in the absence of any metaphysical and linguistic complexity. In an apparently naive manner, improvement fiction sought transparency in order to provide a literal and entirely unambiguous representation of morality, economics, and the general practicalities of life. For Hannah More, this literalism was necessary for the protection of a threatened social order. In Irish improvement fiction, however, this pursuit of a plain language—which runs through the writings of Leadbeater, Bardin, Doyle, and Carleton—reflects a broader desire for a liberal, secular society. There was no allowance for theoretical reflection on meaning and language; what was written had to be understood and

---

[97] I would suggest that More is reacting to 'theory' as defined by Paul De Man in *The Resistance to Theory* (Minneapolis: University of Minnesota Press, 1986).

[98] Maria Edgeworth, *The Absentee* (London, 1812), 134.

then put into practice exactly as intended. Otherwise—or so it was perceived—there could be no reform or improvement and conditions would be ripe for revolution (and, indeed, an overly alienated and aestheticized literature). The desire to transcend ambiguity and confusion results in the utter literalism to be found in improvement writing, despite its obvious rootedness in literary discourses. In a discussion of Rousseau's *Second Discourse*, Paul De Man notes that 'without this literalization' of metaphoric language 'there could be no society.'[99] The emphatic literalism of language and representation of improvement tracts was a means of creating an improved society in post-Union Ireland. As an aesthetic, plain writing was credited with an ability to clarify, to transcend the disorderliness of the pre-modern past and, in the process, create a liberal society through the act of representation. Plainness was also linked to the attainment of the kind of satisfaction in the present which did not appear to be otherwise achievable. However, the more these writers insist on the realism and factuality of their fiction, the more they emphasize the literary nature of their project. In so doing, improvement writers reveal themselves to be implicated in the very social and political situation they sought to transform. I will demonstrate in the chapters that follow how the imagining of an improved society in Ireland depended, paradoxically, on an assertion of plainness within fictional (metaphoric) conventions.

[99] Paul De Man, 'Metaphor (Second Discourse)', *Allegories of Reading: Figural Language in Rousseau, Nietzsche, Rilke and Proust* (New Haven: Yale University Press, 1979), 155.

2

Improvement and Nostalgia: Society Schools and Hedge Schools

IMPROVEMENT writers asserted the lasting pleasures of hard work and the most banal of tasks from weeding to cleaning the kitchen floor. The educational programme of liberal improvement reflects this faith in the value of physical work, stressing that life was best lived at the most material, indeed, literal of levels. Improvement schools would teach children a range of practical skills to prepare them for survival in a modernizing economy. The curriculum of these institutions would be notably different from that of the many hedge schools throughout the country where subjects such as Latin and Greek were, it seems, wastefully taught instead of necessary vocational skills. This chapter will show how improvement writers shaped their educational curriculum against that of the hedge school, emphasizing a strongly functional education in place of what they saw as the overly academic and useless instruction on offer in such institutions. Improvement discourse represents the hedge school as perpetuating the values of the pre-modern, prolonging the hand-to-mouth economy of the rural poor by teaching classical languages instead of sewing, ploughing, and horticulture. In the process, improvement writers were able to proclaim their own strongly empirical values. I will demonstrate in what follows how Carleton's writing participates in these educational debates, at once deriding the backward hedge school and condemning the unduly strict improved school.

Hedge schools thrived throughout the Penal era, answering the educational needs of Catholics and even, on occasion, Anglicans and Presbyterians when there were no other institutions to attend.[1] In an era of strident anti-Catholicism, hedge schools were the proud establishments of dispossessed Catholics, providing instruction in reading and writing

---

[1] See e.g. an account of a hedge school from a Presbyterian perspective in J. L. Porter, *Life and Times of Dr. Cooke* (Belfast: William Mullan, 1875), 11.

as well as preparing young men to study for the priesthood at Catholic universities across Europe and in Maynooth after the establishment of a seminary there in 1795.[2] Hedge schools proliferated in the late eighteenth and early nineteenth centuries as many Catholics refused to send their children to the proselytizing institutions administered by the established church, such as the charter schools, parochial schools, and various establishments which functioned under the auspices of evangelical organizations such as the Association of Discountenancing Vice.[3] The unofficial nature of hedge schools was invariably a source of anxiety throughout the post-revolutionary 1790s and early nineteenth century when, as noted in my Introduction, political pamphlets and tracts were widely distributed and—according to contemporary accounts—used as reading materials in hedge schools.[4] Hedge schoolmasters were often accused of sectarianism and extremism, even though the evangelical tracts of Hannah More and Sarah Trimmer were used in some hedge schools and Protestant catechisms were found in others, the latter catering for the occasionally multi-denominational character of the student body.[5]

A proposal for official multi-denominational education was contained in the 1791 educational report, which recommended that schools be administered by a mostly secular body and that Roman Catholics be fairly represented on the board of every school.[6] The report sought to prevent further proselytizing by permitting representatives of all religions to instruct their own congregations. However, the report was suppressed and languished in administrative obscurity until it resurfaced as a frame of reference for the education inquiries of 1799 and 1806–12. This provided the official context for interest in the state of Irish education, which was reawakened by the publication of R. L. and Maria Edgeworth's *Practical Education* in 1798, a pedagogic manual for parents on the effective instruction of children. In 1799, Edgeworth

---

[2] On this hedge-school tradition, see P. J. Dowling, *The Hedge Schools of Ireland* (Cork: Mercier Press, 1968), and Antonia McManus, *The Irish Hedge School and its Books, 1695–1831* (Dublin: Four Courts Press, 2002).

[3] See D. H. Akenson, *The Irish Education Experiment: The National System of Education in the Nineteenth Century* (London: Routledge, 1970), 1–123. See also Kenneth Milne, *The Irish Charter Schools, 1730–1830* (Dublin: Four Courts Press, 1997).

[4] See Dowling, *The Hedge Schools of Ireland* and McManus, *The Irish Hedge School and its Books*. See also Áine Hyland and Kenneth Milne (eds.), *Irish Educational Documents*, i. 61–98.

[5] On the curriculum of hedge schools, see McManus, *The Irish Hedge School and its Books*, 118–35.

[6] See Hyland and Milne, *Irish Educational Documents*, i. 58–9, and Akenson, *The Irish Education Experiment*, 73.

himself initiated a parliamentary inquiry into education in Ireland. The resulting report recommended the establishment of schools in every parish for the education of the lower classes. These schools were to provide equal education for both Catholics and Protestants, which was to be overseen by the respective parochial clergy. It also stipulated that 'for the space of five years no books shall be used in said schools, but such as shall have been previously approved of by persons appointed for that purpose by the Lord Lieutenant.'[7] Clearly, such a measure was intended to safeguard education from the perceived scourge of popular or seditious literature. The report honoured Edgeworth's non-denominational liberalism in its assurance that 'no master or mistress of any catholic school shall be required to use any book in his or her school which shall be disapproved of by the majority of the catholic clergy.'[8]

The particular curriculum recommended for the parochial schools by Edgeworth's report reappears in almost every improvement pamphlet discussed in this chapter:

Whereas, the state of education of the lower orders of the people of this kingdom is materially defective and requires the interposition of parliament. Be it enacted

That one or more schools with a house for the residence of the master, or mistress thereof be erected, in manner hereafter mentioned, in every parish or union of parishes in this kingdom for the education of children in such parish or union in reading, writing, arithmetic mensuration, and such other things as may be suited to their several destinations, and capacities; and for the instruction of the said children in husbandry, gardening, planting; in plain-work, knitting, weaving of lace, and other useful occupations, according to their different sexes, and ages.[9]

This report calls for a vocational education for the lower classes which would educate in useful, practical skills. The emphasis on 'husbandry' and 'gardening' for boys and 'knitting' and 'weaving of lace' for girls was to be reiterated in the numerous model schools depicted in improvement pamphlets in the early nineteenth century. A bill was prepared on the commission's findings and presented to the Irish Parliament in 1799, but was soon abandoned, presumably a victim of impending Union with Britain.[10]

In the post-Union period, controversy continued to surround the educational institutions of the Church of Ireland and the unofficial hedge

[7] 'A Bill for the Improvement of the Education of the Lower Orders of People in this Kingdom', in Hyland and Milne, *Irish Educational Documents*, i. 63.
[8] Ibid. [9] Ibid. 62. [10] Ibid. 75.

schools. The new administration was obliged to concern itself with educational provision and accordingly established the 1806 commission (with Edgeworth again serving as a commissioner). The commission produced fourteen reports in total, in which hedge schools were strongly condemned for poor instruction, the employment of ignorant schoolmasters, and the use of inappropriate chapbooks in the classroom. The general impoverishment of hedge schools ensured that the teachers were unable to purchase 'books as are fit for children to read'. This meant that 'instead of being improved by religious and moral instruction' the children were 'corrupted by books' which deepened superstition, criminality, and dissent.[11] It was therefore seen to be too dangerous for the state not to regulate both education and the books permitted into Irish schools.

The final report produced by the Board in 1812 declared that an education commission should be established which would oversee educational provision and award grants for the establishment of new institutions throughout the country. In short, the Report recommended that education in Ireland be fully nationalized and administered by the state. It was deemed necessary that teachers be professionally educated for employment in these schools. The Report accordingly recommended the creation of an official system of teacher-education, no doubt drawing inspiration from the Edgeworths' own *Practical Education*.

The assertion of a non-denominational ethos was much stronger in the 1812 document than in any previous report. Education was to be 'clear of all interference with the particular religious tenets of any' group. By such means, the Report envisaged an educational culture which could 'induce the whole to receive its benefits as one undivided body, under one and the same system, and in the same establishments'.[12] The dread of both evangelical proselytizing and an overly politicized Catholicism was undoubtedly to the fore in the composition of this Report. It is evident that education was seen to provide the best means of eradicating traditional antagonisms and divisions and should no longer be used as a means of propagating them. Indeed, according to the Report, education was to be charged with the creation of a single community, literate and civilized, which would replace the fractured society of post-Union Ireland.

---

[11] 'Fourteenth Report of the Commissioners of the Board of Education in Ireland', in Hyland and Milne, *Irish Educational Documents*, i 66.

[12] Ibid. 64.

Robert Peel, upon his appointment as Chief Secretary in 1812, attempted unsuccessfully to implement the Report's recommendations and encountered firm opposition from the Church of Ireland. Many of the Report's suggestions remained unheeded; however, the non-denominational rhetoric endured through to the establishment of the National Schools in 1831. Peel's solution to the difficulty of reforming education in Ireland was for the commission to fund voluntary educational organizations, which broadly embodied the recommendations of the educational reports. The most exemplary of these organizations was the Society for Promoting the Education of the Poor in Ireland (also known as the Kildare Place Society, founded in 1811), which accordingly received the largest government grant for its inter-denominational teacher-training college, printing press, and, later, in 1816, its own publishing house.[13] The Kildare Place patronized many schools throughout the country and supplied affordable educational textbooks directly to both schools and pedlars in an attempt to compete directly with the staples of the popular chapbook market.[14]

Many strongly proselytizing agencies also succeeded in procuring grants: the Association for Discountenancing Vice, the London Hibernian Society, and the Sunday School Society all received government funds for their explicit proselytizing ventures. However, the Kildare Place Society did strive to remain non-denominational in practice and, according to Akenson, at least succeeded in being so at the outset.[15] To begin with, Daniel O'Connell served on the board of the Society and the Catholic Church tolerated its existence. In order to placate the evangelical component of the Kildare Place committee, the Bible was read every day (supposedly without any additional doctrinal instruction) in both the teacher-training college and schools overseen by the Society. However, the presence of the Bible in the classroom always implied the possibility of evangelical proselytizing and this commitment to Bible-reading would later prove to be the Society's undoing. O'Connell and

---

[13] On Kildare Place, see Susan Parkes, *Kildare Place: The History of the Church of Ireland Training College, 1811–1969* (Dublin: Church of Ireland College of Education, 1984) and Harold Hislop, 'The Kildare Place Society 1811–1831: An Irish Experiment in Popular Education', PhD thesis, University of Dublin, 1990.

[14] See Akenson, *The Irish Education Experiment*, 86–94; Parkes, *Kildare Place*; Hislop, 'The Kildare Place Society, 1811–1831'; Niall Ó Ciosáin, *Print and Popular Culture in Ireland, 1750–1850* (Basingstoke: Macmillan, 1997), and McManus, *The Irish Hedge School and its Books*, 47–68.

[15] Akenson, *The Irish Education Experiment*, 86.

the Catholic Church eventually broke from the Society in 1825–6 over its insistence on Bible-reading and support for schools administered by the proselytizing agencies. Desmond Bowen recounts that 'the Roman Catholics were unhappy about the Protestant majority on the managing committee ... and they did not really like the policy of reading the Holy Scriptures without note or comment.'[16] Unfortunately for the Society, their educational experiment was under way in the years leading up to and during the Second Reformation of the 1820s, a period of vehement evangelicalism in sections of the Church of Ireland. This evangelicalism was by no means universal in the church but the staunch anti-Romish pronouncements of specific bishops, particularly William Magee, the Archbishop of Dublin in the 1820s, fed into Catholic anxieties.

The Kildare Place Society became a focal point for Catholic suspicion of institutional authority in the years leading up to Catholic Emancipation in 1829. Bowen claims that by 1822 'Roman Catholics were generally united in their opposition to the Kildare Place Society, which was then believed to have become an agency for propagating Protestant religion and British culture.'[17] At this point, the Kildare Place Society was widely perceived by Catholics to have lapsed into being little more than an evangelizing Protestant institution in practice, and Catholic disenchantment increased. Continued Catholic dissatisfaction with the Society forced the establishment of another education commission in 1824 and again in 1828, which was, a few years after Catholic Emancipation, to lead to the establishment of the National School system.[18] From the late eighteenth century through to the immediate post-Union period, a period of relative 'religious peace' had characterized Irish affairs; after all, figures such as O'Connell were sitting on the board of an educational body alongside members of the Protestant establishment. These relatively amicable relations were, however, threatened by the so-called Second Reformation. It was, therefore, unsurprising that the Kildare Place Society should arouse suspicion in the Catholic community despite the fact that its improvement ethos depended upon a highly rationalized social code purged of all fanaticism, prophecy, and extremism. Improvement discourse in Ireland required a suppression of rancour and the achievement of moderation. Clearly, the furious

---

[16] Desmond Bowen, *The Protestant Crusade in Ireland, 1800–70* (Dublin: Gill and Macmillan, 1978), 96.

[17] Ibid. 97.

[18] For an account of the establishment of the national schools from the education debates of the late 1820s, see Akenson, *The Irish Education Experiment*, 96–122.

polemics of Protestant evangelicalism in these years were entirely at odds with the project of liberal improvement in Ireland. Proselytism was probably deployed in certain schools under the jurisdiction of the Kildare Place Society, but the Society itself would not have officially endorsed or encouraged these practices.

A constituency in the Church of Ireland was disinclined to countenance the existence of schools that did not provide religious instruction and, consequently, refused to support the National Schools on the same basis. The same was true of the Catholic Church. It is nonetheless evident that the Society failed to instil non-denominationalism in a convincingly comprehensive manner and was incapable of preventing certain schools from falling prey to the ministrations of an extremist voice in the Church of Ireland. It would probably have been impossible for an institution such as the Kildare Place Society to survive the turbulent religious controversies of the 1820s. Ironically, in light of its own commitment to the eradication of zealousness, the Society fell victim to the extreme constituencies in both Catholic and Protestant communities. Despite strong opposition to the Kildare Place Society in the 1820s, the National Schools were closely modelled on its non-denominational and pedagogical policies. Interestingly, the fact that many Church of Ireland evangelicals refused to support the National School system effectively rendered it a Catholic institution in nineteenth-century Ireland.[19]

Studies of Irish education history tend to simplify the particular controversies of the early nineteenth century into a predictable evangelical versus secular or conservative versus liberal debate. Secular-liberal educationalists such as R. L. Edgeworth and Maria Edgeworth were supposedly influenced by the educational philosophies of both John Locke and Jean-Jacques Rousseau, despite the important differences between these two philosophers.[20] In *Émile* (1762), Rousseau explicitly rejects Lockean education when he states: ' "Reason with children" was Locke's chief maxim; it is the height of fashion at present, and I hardly think it is justified by its results ... If children understood

---

[19] *Bowen, The Protestant Crusade,* 77–8.
[20] See e.g. Hislop, 'The Kildare Place Society, 1811–1831', 22. See Jean-Jacques Rousseau, *Émile,* 1762, trans. by Barbara Foxley (repri. London: Dent, 1974). For an analysis of *Émile,* see Brian O'Hagan, *Rousseau* (London: Routledge, 1999), 59–87, and Geraint Parry, '*Émile*: Learning to Be Men, Women, and Citizens', in Patrick Riley (ed.), *The Cambridge Companion to Rousseau* (Cambridge: Cambridge University Press, 2001), 247–72.

reason, they would not need education.'[21] In her biography of Maria Edgeworth, Marilyn Butler notes that Locke was the 'favourite author' of her grandmother, Jane Edgeworth. Butler claims that 'inspired' by 'the belief that a child's mind and character were formed by his environment rather than by heredity ... she devoted herself to her children's education from their infancy.'[22] Richard Lovell inherited his mother's interest in the rational-empiricism of Locke, which led him to explore the associationism of David Hartley and the work of the utilitarian and scientist Joseph Priestley (a fellow member of the Lunar Society). This interest also shaped the educational projects Richard Lovell engaged in with his daughter which culminated in the publication of the collaborative *Practical Education* (1798).[23] This empirical tradition was of course enforced by Richard Lovell's enthusiasm for science and membership of the Lunar Society which was, in Butler's terms, 'a pioneer industrial research establishment'.[24]

In fact, R. L. Edgeworth's early interest in Rousseau's *Émile* was itself expressed in a classic scientific manner when he set about translating theory into practice. Edgeworth 'experimented' with Rousseau's educational theory by practising on his son, also called Richard, for five years until the 'experiment' was cut short when Edgeworth was distracted from his educational duties by building conveyor belts in Lyons.[25] The experimentation with Rousseau's child-centred theory was thus never completed. Interestingly, Butler records that Edgeworth predictably disliked the cumulative effects of five years of Rousseauist methods on his son, who afterwards defied several teachers and his parents before being packed off to a traditional English boarding school.[26] Rousseau's call for children's education to be conducted in accordance with 'nature'—so that they will be 'children before they are men'—resulted in a wilfulness in the young Richard that disturbed the intensely pragmatic Edgeworth, whose empiricism long outlasted whatever interest he once took in the educational theory of *Émile*.[27]

Although critics consistently refer to Edgeworth as 'Rousseauist' or as 'an advocate of Rousseau's ideas on education', he espoused an

---

[21] Rousseau, *Émile*, 53.

[22] Marilyn Butler, *Maria Edgeworth: A Literary Biography* (Oxford: Clarendon Press, 1972), 19.

[23] Ibid. 169–71 on the collaborative process behind the composition of *Practical Education*, which, aside from Richard Lovell and Maria, included Thomas Beddoes and Lovell Edgeworth.

[24] Ibid. 34.   [25] Ibid. 43–4.   [26] Ibid. 51.   [27] Rousseau, *Émile*, 54.

educational and political philosophy that would most certainly have outraged the French theorist.[28] Rousseau wrote against the Lockean tradition by, in part, emphasizing the pre-eminence of imagination as a faculty over both reason and sense experience:

It is only in this primitive condition [of childhood] that we find the equilibrium between desire and power, and then alone man is not unhappy. As soon as his potential powers of mind begin to function, imagination, more powerful than all the rest, awakes and precedes all the rest. It is imagination which enlarges the bounds of possibility for us, whether for good or ill, and therefore stimulates and feeds desires by the hope of satisfying them.[29]

The education recommended by Edgeworth for the Irish lower classes— or that embedded within the didacticism of his daughter's fiction—was by no means predicated on Rousseau's concept of 'imagination' as the most 'powerful' faculty. In fact, an Edgeworthian education was directly defined against such a concept on the assumption that a rational educational model would invariably produce civility and enlightenment, protecting against the vagaries of 'imagination'. Edgeworthian education was supposed to root out all of that Romantic excess of imagination and desire. It was assumed within improvement education that desire—as described by Rousseau throughout *Émile*—could be rationalized. However, *Émile* suggests that the activity of imagination cannot be eradicated 'whether for good or ill'. In other words, Rousseau's treatise would indicate the impossibility of achieving the education articulated in improvement discourse. Instead of citing Rousseau's *Émile* as the influence behind liberal educational policy in Ireland, that book should more properly be read for its insights into the impossibility of educational enlightenment or, indeed, improvement. Rousseau's writing

---

[28] Ó Ciosáin, *Print and Popular Culture in Ireland, 1750–1850*, 139. See also Hislop, 'The Kildare Place Society, 1811–1831', 22; and Antonia McManus, *The Irish Hedge School and its Books, 1690–1931*, 40–1. An exception is Marilyn Butler, who states that Edgeworth's educational work 'is often misunderstood ... because it is easily confused with his earlier dabbling with the ideas of Rousseau', even though he turned 'to an entirely different educational approach'. See Butler, *Maria Edgeworth*, 58–9. However, Butler's more recent characterization of Maria Edgeworth's politics as republican is at one with those claims that R. L. Edgeworth was 'Rousseauist'. Maria Edgeworth was no more republican than her father was Rousseauist. This study seeks to show the extent to which the work of improvers (such as the Edgeworths) in Ireland should be seen as counter-Romantic and counter-revolutionary (or republican). See Butler, 'Edgeworth, United Irishmen, and "More Intelligent Treason" ', in Heidi Kaufman and Chris Fauske (eds.), *An Uncomfortable Authority: Maria Edgeworth and her Contexts*, (Newark: University of Delaware Press, 2004), 33–62.

[29] Rousseau, *Émile*, 44.

elsewhere—particularly in his *Discourse on the Origin of Inequality*—
suggests that there could never have been a time when society did not
exist (however 'uncivil' it might have been according to the conventions
of liberal improvement). For Rousseau, the 'origin' of society was inextricable from the 'origin' of language. Hence, society has existed as long
as there has been a need to communicate through signs (linguistic or
otherwise).[30]

It is unsurprising that Edgeworth would be instinctively drawn to the
Lockean educational model, given the history of the family's Irish estate
and pressing political and educational issues in Ireland itself. Geraint
Parry claims that Lockean education 'was predicated on producing the
young man who could contribute to the rational administration of his
father's estate'.[31] Edgeworth himself displays the same anti-theoretical
tendencies that are such a characteristic feature of the novels and didactic
tales of his daughter and, indeed, of the Irish improvement project itself.
Practicality was asserted against a perceived theoretical threat, which
had supposedly been politically embodied in the French Revolution
and feared to be a continual danger in Ireland (directly experienced
by the Edgeworths during the Rebellion in 1798). Far from being
Rousseauist, then, the liberal Edgeworths despised the political fiction
they associated with revolutionary politics, Romantic idealism, and the
writer of *Émile*.[32]

The Edgeworths' interest in education was expressed in a range of educational projects, such as their pedagogic manual (*Practical Education*,
1798), educational programmes for their Irish tenants, Maria's didactic
tales for children and young adults, and, of course, her Irish novels.[33]
Her father established himself on his Irish estate as a reforming landowner, educating his tenants in agriculture and supposedly exercising
fair leasing and rental policies. The Edgeworthian educational philosophy was reiterated throughout the course of Irish improvement
writing and education in the early nineteenth century, even if, as
Butler maintains, their 'educational methods, directed at the individual

---

[30] Jean-Jacques Rousseau, *Discourse on the Origin of Inequality*, trans. and ed. Donald
A. Cress, repr. in *Basic Political Writing of Jean-Jacques Rousseau* (Indianapolis: Hackett
Publishing Company, 1988), 25–111.

[31] Parry, '*Émile*: Learning to be Men, Women, and Citizens', 253.

[32] See esp. Maria Edgeworth, 'Forester', *Moral Tales* (London, 1802), i. 1–194. Like
many of these didactic pieces, 'Forester' warns steadily against Romantic idealism.

[33] For a fascinating analysis of writing, pedagogy, and social class, see Aileen Douglas,
'Maria Edgeworth's Writing Classes', *Eighteenth-Century Fiction*, 14 3–4 (Apr.–July
2002), 371–90.

child, were essentially experimental, and could never have been put to large-scale use.'[34] As will be clear later, that need would be met by the efficient monitorial methods of Andrew Bell and Joseph Lancaster, precisely designed to provide efficient mass education in the colonies, countryside, and expanding industrial centres.

The Edgeworths should be seen as educational pragmatists motivated by the same counter-revolutionary ideology as the evangelical faction of the Church of Ireland, a tradition that echoes through the work of Leadbeater, Doyle, and the Kildare Place Society. As noted above, Irish educational history has been repeatedly depicted as a debate between conservatives and liberals. Conservative educational thought in the 1790s and post-Union period was clearly formed in reaction to the French Revolution and the 1798 Rebellion. Opinion may have been divided as to the best means of educating the 'lower classes', but liberals and conservatives generally worked towards the same ends: the avoidance of revolution and, in the process, the creation of 'civil' society in post-Union Ireland. Conservatives held to the belief that the best means of avoiding revolution and achieving 'civilization' was by converting the masses from Catholicism to Protestantism, whereas liberals were opposed to all proselytizing in the schoolroom or beyond. Proselytism was perceived to be dangerous practice by many in the Church of Ireland, antagonizing the Catholic population and leading to intense suspicion of Protestantism. Many Catholic parents rapidly pulled their children out of schools that engaged in evangelical proselytizing. The cause of improvement education in Ireland was destined to fail if evangelical proselytizing was allowed to intrude in the schoolroom. Liberal educationalists such as the Edgeworths emphasized that an enlightened, practical education—free of all harsh proselytizing and Catholic polemic—would, in and of itself, encourage conformity by consensus. Directly invoking this liberal tradition, improvement writers in Ireland stressed that a solid practical education should make the poor less receptive to revolutionary idealism as well as eradicating the superstitions and backwardness of a dominantly oral, backward culture. Attention would be directed to the empirical reality of hard work, subsuming politics within the inherently satisfying and rewarding labour (or mechanics) of improvement. In time, the hand-to-mouth economy that nourished the intense orality of Irish Catholicism would be displaced by the literate rationality of markets. The archaism of

[34] Butler, *Maria Edgeworth*, 172.

superstition and, ultimately, Catholicism would thus recede naturally within a modernizing economy.

Leadbeater's improving pamphlets were of course written to contribute directly to the cause of improvement education on Edgeworthian lines. *Cottage Dialogues* (1811) was intended for Irish schools as well as the rural cabin while *The Landlord's Friend* (1813) was an attempt to encourage landowners throughout Ireland to establish schools and reform the administration of their estates. *The Landlord's Friend* dispensed advice on the creation of an improvement school which, we are told, 'gives to the *liberal* mind such true pleasure'.[35] The values behind improvement education are described through a dialogue between Squire Hartley (surely named after David Hartley) and Squire Wilfort—the latter questioning the sense of teaching the poor at all when they are 'destined to till the ground, and to whom the book and the pen, are equally useless from weariness of body and stupidity of mind'.[36] Hartley retorts that the poor all too frequently display a 'depth' and 'acuteness of intellect' and that education should be provided so that 'these struggling talents' could 'break into day'.[37] Education is thus essential in order to diffuse the weight of orality and liberate the poor from the darkness of ignorance and superstition that overwhelms them. Predictably, Wilfort worries that this education would encourage the poor to abandon their station in pursuit of greater wealth and status, thereby leaving 'the potatoes unplanted, and the corn unsown'.[38] Hartley assures Wilfort that, unlike in the hedge schools, an improvement education would result in the integration of literacy and labour, the act of ploughing as valued by properly literate peasants as reading and writing. As discussed in Chapter 1, the possibility of unifying labour and education was exemplified by (pastoral) poet-labourers such as Burns and Bloomfield, who remained attached to their rural occupations while supposedly composing inoffensive, yet pleasing, verse.

Leadbeater advises Irish landowners that the establishment of schools on their estates would prevent agrarian unrest and thereby protect their own landed interests. In the process, they could ensure that their tenants received an appropriately 'practical education' which would prove to them that their own interests were best served by hard, disciplined work rather than, say, membership of secret societies. Leadbeater comments that the task of organizing these educational programmes on Irish estates

---

[35] Mary Leadbeater, *The Landlord's Friend* (Dublin, 1813), 33 [my italics].
[36] Ibid.   [37] Ibid. 34.   [38] Ibid.

was a particularly suitable occupation for women: 'Did a few young ladies unite in establishing a school, even on a small scale, any trouble of thought which it cost, any self-denial which it might demand, would be so amply repaid, that they would reluctantly resign such a never-failing resource against ennui'.[39] The boredom of aristocratic culture would be eradicated by this kind of administrative work, which would invariably improve the 'young ladies' themselves as well as the pupils enrolled in the schools. Leadbeater's improving landowners are invigorated by residence on their estates, engagement with their tenants and a return to a simpler, plainer existence. Leadbeater's very use of the word 'ennui' in the passage quoted above is, of course, an explicit reference to Edgeworth's novel *Ennui* (1809). Edgeworth had demonstrated the importance of improvement to the psychology of landlords as well as tenants in her novel. Leadbeater had originally included material on improving landlords in the early draft of *Cottage Dialogues* she sent to Edgeworth. In the correspondence between Leadbeater and Edgeworth throughout 1810, the latter recommends that the material relating to landowners be extracted from *Cottage Dialogues* as it was 'intended for another rank of reader and would spoil the effect and the sale for schools and for the poor.'[40] Leadbeater accordingly developed *Cottage Dialogues* and *The Landlord's Friend* as distinct texts with specific implied audiences. *Cottage Dialogues* was primarily addressed to the peasantry, although it was always assumed that landowners would nonetheless constitute a significant portion of the readership. *The Landlord's Friend*, meanwhile, was principally directed at landowners, seeking thorough reform of ascendancy practice in Ireland.

In *The Landlord's Friend*, landowners are provided with detailed advice on the improvement of estates through fictional representations of tidy cottages and a literate, satisfied tenantry. On viewing the civilized estate of Lady Seraphina, Lady Charlotte exclaims:

Is it possible that these are the dwellings of the idle, savage race which I have heard your tenants represented [*sic*]. I was told that there was not a tree upon your estate, that the hovels were like the styes of dogs, that they were filled with smoke, and that the squalid figures who peeped out of them were scarcely like human beings.[41]

[39] Ibid. 97.

[40] Letter from Maria Edgeworth to Mary Leadbeater, 5 July 1810, Ballitore Papers: Letters of Maria Edgeworth on Literary Matters (National Library of Ireland), Bundle E, 1–40, n. 1008 p. 1090. Hereafter cited as Ballitore Papers.

[41] Leadbeater, *The Landlord's Friend*, 61.

Lady Seraphina replies that 'your picture is too faithful a representation of the situation in which I found my poor cottagers. Was it not worth a little pains to amend it?'[42] The possibility of creating civility out of savagery and wildness is thus confirmed by Lady Seraphina's improved estate. By means of her intervention, the estate was transformed from a gothic fiction to an improvement fiction, the darker forces of Irish life successfully displaced by enlightenment. Lady Seraphina creates civil society on her estate, the barbarity of orality subsumed by the civilizing tropes of domesticity and modern work patterns.

The children in Lady Seraphina's school are only permitted to wear the plainest of clothes and no one leaves 'till fit to be an apprentice or servant'.[43] The plainness of clothing thus reflects the plainness of the occupations for which the pupils are being prepared. Social class is unambiguously displayed in the clothes worn by the pupils in the school, successfully reversing the erosion of 'the hierarchy of appearances'. The previous chapter explored the manner in which that hierarchy was perceived to be under threat by the proliferation of factory-produced clothing.[44] The education on offer in the school is appropriately measured for menial roles, confined to meeting the particular demands of specific lower-class occupations. There is no wasteful instruction in academic subjects that will not be of use in efficiently fulfilling the roles of servant or skilled farm labourer. In this education, the poor will not be unnecessarily burdened with academic study that, as in the hedge school, would only instil unrealistic expectations and ideals and contribute further to 'the confusion of ranks' that was increasingly characterizing social life while suggesting the utterly artificial nature of such distinctions in the first place.[45] The education on offer in Lady Seraphina's school would, by contrast, always match skills with expectations and counteract any tendency to idealization. The pupils would only ever be educated to expect whatever could be obtained from a life in service in the big house or on the farm. In the process, Lady Seraphina's school would keep the social order intact, reforming and tidying social practice, but by no means revolutionizing it. As if the reader could possibly be in any doubt as to Leadbeater's reforming rather than revolutionizing tendencies, she feels compelled to have Lady Seraphina state that 'I am

---

[42] Leadbeater, *The Landlord's Friend*, 61.   [43] Ibid. 99.

[44] See Daniel Roche, *The Culture of Clothing: Dress and Fashion in the Ancien Regime* (Cambridge: Cambridge University Press, 1994), 20.

[45] Ibid. 50.

persuaded that it is often a dangerous experiment to change established forms. The natural and gradual progress of learning and civilization, and consequent intelligence, will cause gradual amendment without any hasty overthrow.'[46] Improvement presented as entirely 'natural' a fit between physical appearance and learning in order to maintain critical social distinctions. The reconciliation of expectation with material reality was implicit in the structure of Leadbeater's fictional schools.

The improved schools of Leadbeater's pamphlets were structured on the colonial monitorialism of Joseph Lancaster. Leadbeater was unsurprisingly more inclined to advocate the secular monitorial model of Lancaster—himself a member of the Society of Friends—than the religious monitorialism of Andrew Bell which was closely associated with the established church.[47] The secularism of Lancaster's monitorialism was controversial in England, but, for Leadbeater, it would have provided the only solution to the religious disputes that beset the provision of education in Ireland. The monitorial method, considered the most efficient—indeed industrial—means of educating the 'lower orders', was the dominant educational model of both society and estate schools and the Kildare Place teacher-training college instructed its pupils in Lancastrian monitiorialism. Leadbeater was herself involved in the management of a Lancastrian school in Ballitore, which in 1816—as recounted in a disappointed tone in her *Papers*—was abandoned by most of the Catholic pupils after the school authorities refused to permit the schoolmaster to teach 'the children of that persuasion their catechism in the schoolroom after school hours'.[48] Directed by the local Catholic priest, the Catholic pupils accordingly deserted the school en masse and established their own institution.

In *Tales for Cottagers* (1814), Leadbeater and Shackleton describe the effects of a Lancastrian education on one of their more exemplary characters:

James had fortunately been educated at a Lancastrian school, and was so happy as to be supplied with good and useful books, which enabled him to calculate what actions and what mode of life would tend to make him happy. His own observation, and his reading, had shown him how necessary sweetness

---

[46] Leadbeater, *The Landlord's Friend*, 51.

[47] On the monitorial systems of Lancaster and Bell, see Alan Richardson, *Literature, Education and Romanticism* (Cambridge: Cambridge University Press, 1994), 91–8.

[48] Leadbeater, *Papers: The Annals of Ballitore with a Memoir of the Author; Letters from Edmund Burke Heretofore Unpublished and the Correspondence of Mrs. R. Trench and Rev. George Crabbe* (London: Bell and Daldy, 1862), i. 360–1. Hereafter cited as *Papers*.

of temper, cleanliness, industry and economy are to the happiness of married life.[49]

The rationality and discipline implicit within a Lancastrian education perfectly equipped James for making the calculations and decisions necessary for achieving genuine contentment. James demonstrates how discipline was successfully internalized through the monitorial method, the structure of his education preparing him for the decisions and calculations that constitute successful domestication. The education he received in this school was shown to be endlessly applicable in real life, the books he read foreshadowing the precise situations he would later encounter in everyday experience. While James had been adequately prepared for life by this truthful, practical education, his peers, who were unfortunate to attend hedge schools, were mostly doomed to a life of error and dissatisfaction. In this fictional representation, fiction itself is shown to foreshadow, and indeed determine, the 'real'.

Leadbeater's fictional schools guaranteed that truth and transparency would prevail in all matters from the dress of peasants to communication between landowner and tenant. The reader is informed in a footnote in *The Landlord's Friend* that Lady Seraphina's institution 'is an exact account of a school successfully carried on by Miss T. at Portarlington.'[50] Leadbeater tries to make her fiction more convincing by claiming that her representations are closely modelled on a reality in which improvement is already occurring and being achieved. Lady Seraphina's school is supposedly a mere copy of a real institution and not a fictional construct. Leadbeater attempts to present her improvement fiction as transparent, a representation of a state of affairs that is clearly obtainable as it already exists. The fictionality of the improved society of her pamphlets had to be denied as that could suggest the impossibility of its ever being achieved. It seems that the danger of improvement fiction as a genre is the implication that improvement was itself a fiction. And yet, at the same time, Leadbeater was obliged to present her pamphlets as fictional entertainment in order to secure readers, competing directly with the many 'lively' popular chapbooks available. Thus, improvement writers paradoxically proclaim the truth of their writing while repeatedly trying to pass it off as fictional. In short, the

[49] Leadbeater and Shackleton, *Tales for Cottagers* (Dublin, 1814), 27.
[50] Leadbeater, *The Landlord's Friend*, 99.

rhetoric of improvement was inevitably threatened by the fictionality of the pamphlets themselves.

Despite Leadbeater's insistence that her tracts are all based on her own truthful observations, she recounts in a letter to George Crabbe that she had to rely on a range of sources for the composition of *The Pedlars* (1826):

The Society for the Education of the Poor in Ireland have employed me to write a little book for each of our provinces, descriptive of scenery, ruins, remarkable buildings, celebrated persons, customs, & c, with suggestions for improvement. Perhaps I overrated my abilities, yet I undertook the task. From my own observation and from a variety of books I have collected materials.[51]

Clearly, Leadbeater sought information from travel narratives and surveys—Arthur Young's *Travels in Ireland* and William Shaw Mason's *Statistical Account* of 1814–19 come to mind—to write her pamphlet. By her own admission, Leadbeater's 'own observation' of Ireland was greatly curtailed by the fact that she rarely left Ballitore. In 1810 she claimed in a letter to Edgeworth that she had 'never but once spent six months out of her own village'.[52] Throughout her correspondence with Crabbe, she emphasizes her provinciality and ignorance of metropolitan life. Unable to work from her own empirical observation, Leadbeater would have had to rely on a large quantity of written sources—themselves implicated in a range of discourses—to write *The Pedlars*, which, ironically, is written in the form of a travel narrative.

In this pamphlet, Leadbeater sent her pedlar characters, Darby and Pat, travelling through the east of Ireland and, invariably, to William Hickey's agricultural seminary at Bannow in Co. Wexford, which she had undoubtedly read about in the newspapers. Darby and Pat discuss the curriculum at Bannow, which is notably practical: reading, writing, and mathematics are taught alongside improved agricultural techniques.[53] The educational ethos in practice at Bannow was reiterated in the agricultural manuals and fiction Hickey wrote (under the pseudonym

---

[51] Letter from Mary Leadbeater to George Crabbe, 1 Oct. 1824. Repr. in Leadbeater, *Papers*, ii. 391.

[52] Letter from Mary Leadbeater to Maria Edgeworth [n.d.]. Ballitore Papers. It is clear from the correspondence that the letter was written in 1810.

[53] The Scrapbook of Mrs. William Hickey, National Library of Ireland: MS 407. This contains information on improvement on William Boyce's estate at Bannow where William Hickey established his agricultural school with the assistance of Boyce. According to the scrapbook, Hickey was friends with both Daniel O'Connell and Thomas Moore.

Martin Doyle), which strongly urged a technical education for the poor and even for the middle and upper classes (who were themselves in need of thorough practical instruction in modern agriculture).

By contrast, the standard Irish hedge school is characterized in strongly disapproving terms in Doyle's tracts. Doyle explicitly declares that 'education is of two kinds—the bad and the good', hedge schools the former and improvement or vocational schools the latter. Doyle describes a wealthy farmer of his acquaintance who was determined that his sons should be educated as he himself had not been to school. This farmer was himself hard-working and invested the profits gleaned from agricultural improvement into the education of his sons. Much to Doyle's dismay, this man decided that his sons should be educated in Greek and Latin rather than agriculture. These 'stout lads' were consequently 'far advanced ... in Sallust and Lucian' and fully removed from the material world of ploughs, seeds, and physical labour.[54] The utter impracticality of classical, bookish education in rural Ireland greatly irritated Doyle, who cautions that 'a school of this description is a nuisance among you: the master is wrapped up in the pride of classical knowledge, and despises lower branches of instruction, which would be ten-fold more valuable to your children than all his Greek and Latin.'[55] Doyle enquired as to why this farmer chose to send his sons to 'a Latin school', only to be told that he was informed how 'it was a fine thing to know the *dead languages* and *to be put through the authors.*'[56]

Doyle emphasized the extreme impracticality of traditional classical education, claiming that he would 'rather see' young men 'knock down a partridge or a hare, than hear them read a sentence in the books they are taught'.[57] A hedge-school education was thought to pay no attention to the pressing material needs of rural life, refusing to acknowledge the dreadful economic reality of rural Ireland. Doyle claims that he once visited a hedge school in Kerry where the schoolmaster taught both Latin and Greek. The schoolmaster encouraged him to observe a student 'be put through his author', in this case, Virgil, despite Doyle's insistence that he 'was a bad judge of these matters', professing not to know any language other than English.[58] Of course, this is untrue as Doyle had studied classics at Trinity College, Dublin, but he labours to cultivate

---

[54] Doyle, *Hints Addressed to the Smallholders and Peasantry of Ireland on Subjects Connected with Health, Temperance, and Morals* (Dublin, 1833), 75.

[55] Ibid.   [56] Ibid. 76. Original emphasis.   [57] Ibid. 77.

[58] Ibid. For information on Doyle's education, see the Scrapbook of Mrs. William Hickey.

the 'voice' of the 'ordinary' practical farmer in all his pamphlets. This hedge schoolmaster declares his immense pride in the education he provides: 'Oh, Sir, it does one's heart good to hear a little jockey of this sort doing the thing as grand as Dryden. That's the way I tache my boys; I would not give a sod of turf for any thing else: I'd rather they missed the sinse altogether, than not consthrue it freely'.[59] The schoolmaster's pride in classical education is shown to be entirely out of place within the context of a struggling primitive economy. Typically, the teacher professes not to care if his pupils actually 'miss the sinse' of the passages once they are able to deliver a fluent translation. Doyle claims that such education 'is not only useless but injurious for the lower classes', stating that 'a smattering of that sort of knowledge is dangerous, and always sure to end in disappointment.'[60] One wonders if such 'disappointment' was to be felt politically, metaphysically, or both. Clearly, for Doyle, classical education is not only without practical value, but it fosters unrealistic expectations by bearing no relation to the reality of life in post-Union Ireland; by contrast, an improved education could never disappoint as it would not engender unrealistic expectations in the first place. Doyle's fiction strives to represent situations in which practical education—be it as simple as reading a farming manual and then applying it in practice—always leads to greater prosperity and even happiness. Classical education, however, necessarily deludes the poor, making 'a man think that he is born to be a learned man, and that the handles of a plough or the business of the counter would disgrace him.'[61] It seems that agriculture had to be equated with commerce, signifying the nascent capitalism of improvement. An education in Latin and Greek produces unwarranted pride, making one averse to the materiality of both physical labour and commerce. According to Doyle, classical education, for the poor at least, is both 'uncertain and deceitful', perpetuating, it seems, the lies and delusions of oral, pre-modern economies. This kind of classical education fails to demonstrate the necessary connections between work and material gain and, by extension, civility and progress. For an improver such as Doyle, classical education prevents the peasantry from comprehending that genuine, temporal contentment can be derived from immersion in the raw physicality of 'modern' work and administration. Doyle clearly aligns the classics with an educational and cultural tradition which he perceives to be dangerously at odds with his programme of modernization. That

---

[59] Doyle, *Hints*, 77–8.   [60] Ibid. 78.   [61] Ibid.

tradition was most particularly expressed in a 'high' literary mode—here exemplified by 'classical' writers such as Virgil—and those political ideologies that promise a form of liberation or freedom that cannot possibly be fulfilled in the given material conditions of post-Union Ireland (or, indeed, anywhere else).

According to the discourse of improvement, education should be simple and practical (indeed, realistic), conveying unequivocal instruction and bearing a direct relationship to the ordinary circumstances of life as well as applicability to the reality of a rural peasant existence:

let the useful knowledge acquired be applied usefully and humbly, and not in the way of boasting over those who have not learned as quickly or as much as yourselves, and keep clear of Latin and Greek, and parties and politics, and cut up each of you a leaf of red deal, and make a little book-shelf and it shall soon be occupied with nice little books, full of the good advice and practical instructions of your sincere friend and hearty well-wisher, Martin Doyle.[62]

In Doyle's thinking, hedge schools, classical education, and secret societies are all curiously entwined in the same primitive economy of excess. The relationship between agrarian violence, classical instruction, and hedge schools is simply assumed, as though reading Virgil automatically fed into the political extremism of Ribbonmen. In the hands of the hedge schoolmasters of Doyle's pamphlets, a classical education is reduced to the practices and rituals of oral culture, inevitably subsumed within the compulsive orality of a pre-modern economy. Irrespective of the literacy of the curriculum, the hedge school could only ever be depicted as intensely oral and thus disruptive of the rationalizing project of modernization. As Doyle's representation of the Kerry hedge school is supposed to demonstrate, this orality was exemplified by the oral translation of Latin authors, such as Virgil. It is evident, however, that the construction of Irish peasant culture as irredeemably oral was essential to the definition of improvement discourse itself. Central to the articulation of improvement was the claim that political idealism and literary aestheticism were wildly impractical and worryingly at odds with progress and 'getting on' in life. Doyle argued that the education in most hedge schools was only appropriate for a minority of students—'one in ten thousand' is his approximate prediction in *Irish Cottagers*.[63] He urges that the impractical hedge school be displaced by the establishment of institutions modelled on

62 Doyle, *Hints*, 91–2.   63 Ibid. 73.

the exemplary estate school of Lady Seraphina in *The Landlord's Friend* or that of Mr Bruce in *Irish Cottagers*. The latter institution, administered by an exemplary teacher, was strictly practical, instructing in applicable skills and all the time infusing values such as modesty and simplicity:

He was singularly free from the pomposity and self-importance, so generally indicative of the pedagogue. His language was simple and unaffected, and his habits precisely suited to his office; he was really too well informed not to feel how ignorant man is at best, and too prudent to indulge in the petty dogmatism which so often marks the scholastic tribe.[64]

The teacher in an improvement school is naturally free of the self-importance and pomposity of the 'typical' hedge schoolmaster, embodying instead genuine virtues such as humility and prudence. There is no confusion or disjunction between appearance and reality: the schoolmaster's character appears exactly as it really is and should be. The humility of his physical bearing is reflected in the humility of his language. While the hedge schoolmaster may be infamous for exaggerated, hyperbolic language, this teacher only adopts 'simple and unaffected' speech, ensuring that he is always understood exactly as intended. In this particular social situation, deception and confusion are impossible.

This model schoolteacher was complemented by the exemplary domestic virtues of his wife, who was 'tidy in her own person, and waging uncompromising war with dirt and cobwebs'.[65] This woman divided her time appropriately between reading and 'all kinds of needlework'. In so doing, she thus represented the harmonious combination of literacy and technical skill suitable for the modern woman within an improved economy. The couple were thus exemplary role models for the pupils in the school, impeccably representing the gendered structure of both domestic and political economy.

Mr Bruce's school was strictly non-denominational, educating children from a variety of religious backgrounds. Confronted by a schoolroom which was 'divided, as his scholars were, into Protestant and Roman Catholic', the schoolmaster instinctively understood the necessity of 'abstaining from offending those from whom he differed in religious views'.[66] A core value of liberal improvement is thus shown to function in practice, as this schoolmaster exercised 'the utmost limits

---

[64] Doyle, *Irish Cottagers* (Dublin, 1833), 29. [65] Ibid. 30. [66] Ibid. 29.

of toleration' in the schoolroom which naturally resulted in a truly liberal, pluralist environment.[67] In this pamphlet—as in improvement fiction as a whole—the school is a model for the public sphere, enlightening and instructing in the values of modern civility. The school is presented as a working model of liberal toleration, demonstrating the feasibility of dissolving religious and political tensions by prohibiting discussion of all such matters in the classroom. Mr Bruce's fictional school is supposed to serve as an example of how a liberal society can be achieved and maintained. In practice, of course, the professed toleration of many of these institutions frequently collapsed as underlying tensions made their way to the surface. This is even evident within Doyle's improved, fictional school. The schoolmaster was clearly only forced to exercise toleration ('without any compromise of principle') towards his Catholic pupils, requiring him to resist 'attacking their ignorance, and prejudices, or insulting their superstitions (the surest mode of perpetuating their errors)'.[68] Catholicism was the only religion demanding restraint on the part of the schoolmaster. The subtext of Doyle's pamphlet is that the more objectionable elements of Catholicism would soon disappear through education, toleration, and the intrinsically rationalizing nature of improvement and modernization.

The fiction of Leadbeater and Doyle constructs a culture in which language, education, and work are all infused with the same values of plainness and transparency. Needless to say, these elements all function harmoniously in a strengthened and entirely legible social order. The capability of a reforming, improving society to offset revolution and insurrection is represented through images of a stable, contented rural community. In this economy of the moderate and plain, the mediated language of orality has been displaced from both speech and the written page by the unmediated vocabulary of improved English. Ironically, these explicitly practical and assertively realistic writings all construct a fiction of language functioning in such a transparent manner. How after all could improvement writers possibly hope, in Paul De Man's terms, 'to escape ... from the duplicity, the confusion, the untruth that we take for granted in the everyday use of language'.[69] However, the realistic prose of improvement writers was supposed to provide a recourse from

---

[67] Doyle, *Irish Cottagers*, 29.   [68] Ibid.

[69] Paul De Man, 'Criticism and Crisis', *Blindness and Insight: Essays in the Rhetoric of Contemporary Criticism* (1971; repr., London: Routledge, 1996), 9.

that condition and, in the process, both embody and perpetuate a transparency that was otherwise absent.

The plain language of Doyle's model teacher is notably different from that of Carleton's hedge schoolmasters. Indeed, Carleton's fictional schoolmasters are supposed to provide a rationale for both improvement education and the comprehensive reform of Irish society. Apparently drawing on his own experiences, Carleton's work documents in detail the numerous alleged abuses and dangers of the hedge school. Carleton's schoolmasters are drunken, sectarian, and, more than often, politically extreme. Their professed learning is an elaborate pretence that conceals an immense ignorance. Many stories suggest that hedge schoolmasters were entirely uneducated, merely duping their poor neighbors into believing that they possessed great learning. Their knowledge of classical languages is shown to be utterly false, as they recite reams of meaningless 'bog' Latin and textbook 'King's English'. Their deception of the rural poor is the same as that of the prophecy-man, cosherer, seanachai, and the other stock characters of Carleton's represented 'oral' culture.[70] In Carleton's representation, these schoolmasters are shown to intensify the backwardness of rural Ireland, prolonging that already painful transitional state from Irish to English, barbarity to civility, and an oral to written culture.

Carleton's fiction at once documents the persistence of this culture of hedge schools and its rapid demise and displacement by both improved and National Schools. The oral culture of rural Ireland is always about to be subsumed into the commercial world of literacy and the English language. Likewise, the senseless speech and writing of schoolmasters is forever disappearing and being replaced by common sense. Carleton's writing explicitly professes a desire to overwhelm the incoherence of his schoolmasters—who epitomize the condition of Hiberno-English—with a solidly literate and truthful language. In *The Emigrants of Ahadarra* (1848), Hyey Burke's obscure, hedge-school language is supposed to signify the downfall that ultimately awaits him. Needless to say, he has to be banished before an improved society can be properly achieved. The novel partly represents the potential ascendancy of the plainness of improvement in a fictional rural community and, for Carleton, the possibility of a realist prose accompanying resident, improving landlords.

---

[70] 'Cosherer': a gossip, one who spreads tales; 'seanachie': storyteller.

The linguistic archaism of the hedge school is reflected in the primitive political culture it embodies. Carleton's hedge schoolmasters nurture political extremism and sectarianism, endlessly repeating a story of dispossession and ultimate millennial redemption. In the fiction, hedge schools are shown to be responsible for the illiterate political culture of rural Ireland. The excessively polemical content of the hedge school curriculum is described in detail in 'The Hedge School', which depicts hedge schoolmasters as political fanatics:

Their weapons of controversy were drawn from the Fifty Reasons, the Doleful Fall of Andrew Sall, the Catholic Christian, the grounds of the Catholic Doctrine, a Net for the Fishers of Men, and several other publications of the same class. The books of amusement read in these schools, including the first-mentioned in this list, were, the Seven Champions of Christendom, the Seven Wise Masters and Mistresses of Rome, Don Belianus of Greece, the Royal Fairy Tales, the Arabian Nights Entertainments, Valentine and Orson, Gesta Romanorum, Dorastes and Faunia, the History of Reynard the Fox, the Chevalier Fabulax; to these I may add, the Battle of Aughrim, Siege of Londonderry, History of the Young Ascanius, a name by which the Pretender was designated, and the Renowned History of the Siege of Troy, the Forty Thieves, Robin Hood's Garland, the Garden of Love and Royal Flower of Fidelity, Parismus and Parismenos; along with others, the names of which shall not appear on these pages.) With this specimen of education before our eyes, is it not extraordinary that the people of Ireland should be, in general, so moral and civilized a people as they are? (*TSIP*, i. 313)

In this description, a hedge-school education is shown to be steeped in cheap, extremist Catholic propaganda and inappropriate chapbooks such as the *Arabian Nights Entertainment*. The reading-list catalogues the very titles and genres that provoked intense anxiety regarding popular literacy and education in the early nineteenth century. Carleton knows exactly which titles will most outrage his improving, reforming readers and he accordingly lists them. The atmosphere of this hedge school was thus both politicized and tense, the very act of learning to read and write deeply embedded in never-ending political and religious disputes as well as crime and immorality. In Carleton's account, the hedge school enhanced the prejudices and backwardness of orality by teaching reading and writing through the medium of these chapbooks and pamphlets. For Carleton, as for improvement writers, instruction in reading and writing by means of 'seditious', crude, and immoral chapbooks cancelled whatever benefits were otherwise gained by literacy.

The overly frantic and restless environment of the hedge school was far removed from the orderly, disciplined atmosphere of the improved school, which insisted on individualism and silence rather than community and speech. Carleton's hedge school is the antithesis of the improved school, freely espousing sectarianism and polemic in a manner repugnant to liberal improvement. The hedge schools of Carleton's fiction are supposed to be the Catholic equivalent of evangelical institutions such as the Association for Discountenancing Vice (ADV), icons of a heavily sectarian and polemical culture that has to be displaced by the disciplined restraint of liberal toleration.

Carleton tries to demonstrate in his fiction how the values represented within these overly imaginative chapbooks and pamphlets were reiterated daily in the setting of the hedge schoolroom as pupils were encouraged to engage in and thus perpetuate local factional disputes, as recounted in 'The Battle of the Factions', or larger sectarian clashes such as those between Catholics and Protestants which are described in detail in 'The Party Fight and Funeral'. In his *Autobiography*, Carleton recounts how plays such as *The Battle of Aughrim* (1756) by Robert Ashton,[71] which were read in hedge schools, were dramatized in a heightened realist mode as Protestants and Catholics divided according to denomination into the parts of opposing sides in theatrical re-enactments of the battle, culminating eventually in actual bloodshed and serious injury (*Autobiography*, 34–6). These dramatizations indicate a literalization of fiction, however rooted the original text may have been in actual historical events.

In the tradition of Leadbeater and Doyle, Carleton's hedge school is dangerously alienated from the economic realities of pre-Famine Ireland. His hedge schoolmasters are, of course, dependent upon the isolation of peasant Ireland from the modernizing mainstream. These schoolmasters could only survive in a context of chronic backwardness, their 'orality' unsustainable in an improved social order. Appended to a footnote in 'The Hedge School' is a public proclamation in which a schoolmaster painstakingly defends his scholarly reputation after being denounced as a fraud by a competing teacher. The footnote informs the reader that the proclamation gives 'an excellent notion of the mortal feuds and jealousies that subsist between persons of this class':

[71] The full title is *The Battle of Aughrim, or the Fall of Monsieur St. Ruth* by Robert Ashton. The original text explicitly declares itself to be a tragedy.

To the public.—Having read a printed document, emanating, as it were from a vile, mean, and ignorant miscreant of the name of —— calumniating and vituperating me; it is evidently the production of a vain, supercilious, disappointed, frantic, purblind maniac of the name of ——, a bedlamite to all intents and purposes, a demon in the disguise of virtue, and a herald of hell in the paradise of innocence, possessing neither principle, honour, nor honesty; a vain and vapid creature whom nature plumed out for the annoyance of —— and its vicinity.

It is well known and appreciated by an enlightened and discerning public, that I am as competently qualified to conduct the duties of a Schoolmaster as any Teacher in Munster, (Here I pause, stimulated by dove-eyed humility, and by the fine and exalted feelings of nature, to make a few honourable exceptions …

The notorious impostor and biped animal already alluded to, actuated by an overweening desire of notoriety, and in order to catch the applause of someone, groveling in the morasses of insignificance and vice, like himself leaves his native obscurity, and indulges in falsehood, calumny, and defamation. I am convinced that none of the highly respected teachers of —— has had any participation in this scurrilous transaction, as I consider them to be sober, moral, exemplary, well-conducted men, possessed of excellent literary abilities, but this expatriated ruffian and abandoned profligate, being aware of the marked and unremitting attention which I have heretofore invariably paid to the scholars committed to my care, and the astonishing proficiency which, generally speaking, will be an accompaniment of competency, instruction, assiduity, and perseverance, devised this detestable and fiendish course in order to tarnish and injure my unsullied character. (*TSIP*, i. 296–7 n.)

Carleton claims that this public proclamation is 'an authentic produc- tion' of a schoolmaster named John O'Kelly. However, this notice—like most of the footnotes in the *Traits and Stories*—is, of course, part of Carleton's elaborate comic fiction of schoolmasters, the supposed fac- tuality of the footnotes working to deepen the fictionality of the story as well as to textualize its orality. Carleton repeatedly strives to validate his stories as truth, asserting the authenticity of his writing at every opportunity, fearing that it would otherwise be tainted by the perceived deception of orality and, indeed, fiction (or the 'literary'). Carleton's main concern here is to draw attention to the ludicrousness of hedge schoolmaster English, emphasizing the duplicity and dishonesty of such language within a struggling backward economy. Carleton's schoolmas- ters signify the very literary indulgence that was seen to be detrimental to the work of progress.

The indulgent language of schoolmasters is notably at odds with the hunger and scarcity of means that surrounded the typical hedge school. Indeed, the rhetorical excess of these schoolmasters is highlighted by the utter emptiness of so many cabins and, indeed, stomachs. The language of schoolmasters is supposed to represent an economic imbalance caused in part—it seems—by this abundance of rhetoric. This hedge-school language is supposed to represent a linguistic excess which makes poor peasants unfit to participate in economic development. The convoluted fictions of schoolmasters are shown to disguise the miserable material reality of post-Union Ireland. Improvement writers were explicitly committed to reinstating clarity and common sense to this linguistic and narrative economy, restoring a solid plainness of diction to language while conveying an ethos of hard work and discipline. By such means, language would be fully reconciled with the reality of lived physical experience.

Carleton's schoolmasters were often appointed to 'the clerkship of the parish', which would have entailed the writing of notices, surveying, and other scribal tasks on behalf of the local community (*TSIP*, i. 322). This role placed them at the centre of village life as described in 'The Hedge School':

It was highly amusing to observe the peculiarity which the consciousness of superior knowledge impressed upon the conversation and personal appearance of this decaying race. Whatever might have been the original conformation of their original structure, it was sure, by the force of acquired habit, to transform itself into a stiff, erect, consequential, and unbending manner, ludicrously characteristic of an inflated sense of their extraordinary knowledge, and a proud and commiserating contempt of the dark ignorance by which, in despite of their own light, they were surrounded. Their conversation, like their own *crambos*, was dark and difficult to be understood; their words, truly sesquipedalian; their voice, loud and commanding in its tones, their deportment, grave and dictatorial, but completely indescribable, and certainly original to the last degree, in those instances where the ready, genuine humour of their country maintained an unyielding rivalry in their disposition, against the natural solemnity which was considered necessary to keep up the due dignity of their character. (*TSIP*, i. 276)

In Carleton's characterization, schoolmasters were consistently per-forming a role in the community, assuming immense superiority and self-importance while speaking and teaching nonsense in real-ity. This overreaching in linguistic and narrative terms was, it is implied, unacceptable within a modernizing economy which required modesty and restraint.

In Carleton's fictional schools, literacy was always subsumed within the overwhelming orality of the hedge-school environment. All educational activities were reduced to the most fundamentally oral of levels. As with all 'oral' discourses represented in Carleton's fiction, the language of hedge schoolmasters tended towards a heterogeneity of sound and meaning rather than homogenization. The loudness of the hedge schoolroom is described in detail in 'The Hedge School', which attempts to reproduce the particular atmosphere of the schoolroom on the printed page: ('Come, boys, rehearse—(buz, buz, buz)—I'll soon be after calling up the first spelling lesson—(buz, buz, buz)' *TSIP*, i. 302). Carleton's description emphasizes the intense orality of the classroom, showing how all disciplines were ultimately brought within this strongly oral world. As language endlessly proliferated in this setting, there could be no agreement regarding either definition or broader meaning. In such a linguistic environment, language did not possess any pragmatic function, existing only in a fictional, hyperbolic state. The language of schoolmasters could at once mean everything and nothing at all, making the development of an official, written standard of English both all the more urgent and difficult.

The redundancy of the primitive, pre-modern economy of the rural poor was encapsulated by the language of schoolmasters, which was shown by Carleton to be outmoded in a world of print. This redundancy is particularly exemplified by the speech of Denis O'Shaughnessy, the young scholar of Carleton's story 'Going to Maynooth'. Denis is considered a fit candidate for Maynooth on account of his grasp of the 'King's English' and Latin. A hedge-school education leads him into ever greater darkness and obscurity rather than clarity and knowledge. Denis's knowledge of grammatical terms provides him with a stock of 'difficult' words and phrases which serve to confirm his learning in the minds of his audience. Denis literally speaks within the idiom of dictionaries and grammar texts and can supposedly 'rattle off the high English, and the larned Latin, jist as if he was born wid an English dictionary in one cheek, and the larned Latin Neksuggawn in the other' (*TSIP*, ii. 99). Though such dictionaries and grammars were clearly written and published in order to standardize a set of definitions, they are reduced to the heterogeneity of orality in the environment of the hedge school. Fixed definitions and grammatical standards are dissolved by the habitual orality of a hedge-school education.

The disregard of language as communication is embodied in the meaningless iteration of Latinate words and phrases. Schoolmaster Latin encapsulates the manner in which sound is valued over sense and the fictional over the real. The language of hedge schoolmasters is endlessly repetitive from story to story—words from grammar texts and dictionaries are spat out monotonously and repetitively by Carleton's schoolmasters. Carleton implies that it would be impossible for a culture to modernize and develop on such excessively metaphoric terms (which of course presumes that it was not modern already). Carleton strives to differentiate his writing from the compulsive orality of hedge schoolmasters, distinguishing his written fiction from the meaningless wordiness of a Denis O'Shaughnessy or Mat Kavanagh.

Carleton notes in his *Autobiography* that his language had once been 'as fine a specimen of the preposterous and the pedantic as ever was spoken' by any of his schoolmasters (*Autobiography*, 96). He thus presents schoolmaster pedantry as factual, his representations of fictional schoolmasters supposedly grounded in his own personal experiences as a young scholar:

I took a fancy for strolling through the country in search of adventures, and on these occasions I uniformly assumed a studious aspect—always had some classical or other book in my hand, and walked with a mock-heroic gait, which, had the people been gifted with common sense, would have made me ridiculous. I was, however, excessively fond of histrionics, and strutted about uttering such sesquipedalian and stilted nonsense as was never heard. (*Autobiography*, 96)

This description is reminiscent of numerous characters from Carleton's stories and novels, his fiction reflecting the reality of peasant life. However, it is tempting to speculate that, writing soon before his death in 1869, Carleton was basing his autobiographical self on his fiction and forcing biographical details to correspond with the fictional world created in his writing. Carleton claims in his *Autobiography* that, like his schoolmasters, he once copied Latin prose when he had no school to attend:

Writing Latin was a great amusement of mine. I imitated the flowing and redundant style of lines as well, at all events, as I could; but that which baffled me most, and tried my powers of imitation severely, was my attempt to imitate the curt condensed style of Sallust. After several efforts at imitating the Latin historian, I ultimately gave up. (*Autobiography*, 92)

The redundancy of Latin appealed to Carleton and, presumably, to his fictional schoolmasters, the language providing yet another convention or mode of representation (like the King's English). Many aspects of Carleton's fiction can be traced to the autobiographical claims recounted in the 'General Introduction' to the 1842–4 edition and the *Autobiography* itself, convincing the reader of the authenticity of the detail contained in the fiction. However, the so-called fact of the *Autobiography* is probably rooted in the fiction, Carleton's younger scholarly self modelled on characters from stories such as 'The Hedge School'. Like his schoolmasters, Carleton cannot resist the impulse to fictionalize, irrespective of his commitment to exposing the duplicitous practices of the stock characters of Irish oral culture.

The modernization of the rural economy was by no means in the interest of Carleton's schoolmasters, who thrived within a context of ignorance and impoverishment. These characters are shown to benefit from speaking in a dense, convoluted manner, their deception concealed by a thick mass of wordiness. By contrast, improvement writers demanded that language function in a literal manner, so that a civil society could be created out of the clouded fictional environment that was early nineteenth-century Ireland and to which—it must be noted—improvement writers were themselves actively contributing. Writers such as Doyle, Leadbeater, and Carleton presented their writing as, in part, a revelation of the density of self-deception and illusion in rural Ireland which was typified by the hedge school. It was only once matters had been 'restored' to a literal state that improvement could be communicated and then, possibly, occur. Despite the strongly fictional nature of improvement, these writers insist on the truthfulness and utter integrity of their representations, a trope that Carleton carries over into his writing. Writers such as Doyle and Leadbeater paradoxically assert that they are writing—to use Carleton's phrase—'truthful fiction' so that they can all the more effectively fictionalize (Preface, *Art Maguire*, p. viii). Hedge schoolmasters were derided for perpetuating a culture of profound fictionality, speaking an utterly false hybrid of languages, sprouting ludicrous prophecies from *Pastorini*, and passing themselves off as serious classical scholars. Improvement writers characterize that body of fiction as orality, the deluded expression of a people oppressed by governmental neglect, absenteeism, Catholicism, and poverty, while, by contrast, their fictional output is resolutely realistic and thus truthful and transparent. However, the 'truthfulness' of improvement discourse is immediately called into question by the fictional dialogues and narratives of pamphlets such as *The Landlord's*

Friend and *Irish Cottagers*, a truthfulness irredeemably enmeshed in the convoluted world of fiction.

Despite Carleton's portrayal of the hedge school as anachronistic and illiterate, it is notable that he appears to be unwilling to relinquish the 'orality' of the schoolroom entirely. The harsh depictions of the hedge school simultaneously express a longing for the social world supposedly embodied in these institutions. There is a confusion in his ideology which borders on nostalgia for the hedge school when he writes:

I think it a mistake to suppose that silence, among a number of children in school, is conducive to the improvement of health or intellect. That the chest and lungs are benefited by giving full play to the voice, I think will not be disputed; and that a child is capable of more intense study and abstraction in the din of a schoolroom, than in partial silence, (if I may be permitted that word,) is a fact, which I think any rational observation would establish. There is something cheering and cheerful in the noise of friendly voices about us—it is a restraint taken off the mind, and it will run the lighter for it—it produces more excitement and puts the intellect in a better frame for study. The obligation to silence, though it may give the master more ease, imposes a new moral duty upon the child, the sense of which must necessarily weaken his application. Let the boy speak aloud, if he pleases, that is, to a certain pitch; let his blood circulate; let the natural secretions take place, and the physical effluvia be thrown off by a free exercise of voice and limbs: but do not keep him dumb and motionless as a statue—his blood and his intellect both in a state of stagnation and his spirit below zero. Do not send him in quest of knowledge alone, but let him have cheerful companionship on his way. (*TSIP*, i. 306–7)

Carleton's hedge schools are typically loud, noisy, and chaotic while his society and National Schools are silent, disciplined, and ordered. It is striking that, in this instance, Carleton professes a preference for the disordered world of the hedge schoolroom, claiming that the stiff atmosphere of the society school was too dreary for learning when compared with the lively, stimulating environment of the typical hedge schoolroom of his fiction. In the same story, Carleton exclaims 'what noble materials for composing a national character, of which humanity might be justly proud, do the lower orders of the Irish possess, if raised and cultivated by an enlightened education' (*TSIP*, i. 295). However, he then proceeds to criticize the very 'enlightened education' on offer in Ireland in the early nineteenth century. Carleton's hedge school is filled with the presence of community rather than the empty individualism demanded in society schools. Learning in the hedge school is an intensely vocal, physical activity, mental and physical resources united in the vigorous acquisition of knowledge. Carleton claims that education is best conducted within a noisy, oral environment and not in the deadening atmosphere of silence and solitude insisted upon by modern pedagogy. This could be understood as an ambivalence towards the general discourse of improvement, which encouraged solitary reading and writing over communal fireside storytelling and the values of individualism over those of community. Improvement writers generally feared the particular form of community built upon oral storytelling, alcohol, tea-drinking, and 'talk' which was believed to enforce the illiterate politics of secret societies and a hand-to-mouth economy rather than the enlightenment of 'progress', pluralism, and markets. Despite Carleton's insistence on the importance of creating a literate, industrialized society, his writing nonetheless articulates a discomfort with the apparent dissolution of community wrought by modernization. Carleton expresses a sense of longing for the loss of an 'oral' community. In this respect, he differs from Doyle and Leadbeater, for whom nostalgia is a necessary Christian value, which is both rooted in the biblical traditions they inhabit and intrinsic to their concept of modernization. It seems to me that for improvement writers such as Doyle and Leadbeater the 'modern' was already located in a lost past. For Carleton, loss and nostalgia were the negative yet necessary consequences of modernization and by no means offered affirmation of religious faith or theological principle. This could be Carleton's Catholic past once more expressing itself.

It is notable that an English convert to Catholicism, John Henry Newman, should have been invited to assist in the establishment of a Catholic University in Ireland in 1851. Newman's university, as outlined in *The Idea of a University*, sought to overturn the very utilitarianism (or improvement) which he associated with English Protestantism. Indeed, in *The Idea of a University*, he denounced the term 'improvement' as 'Protestant language'.[72] For Newman, non-denominationalism was synonymous with both Protestantism and liberalism and, therefore, a wretched utilitarianism as well.[73]

---

[72] John Henry Newman, *The Idea of A University*, ed. I. T. Kerr (Oxford: Clarendon Press, 1976), 247.

[73] On Newman and liberalism, see Seamus Deane, 'Newman: Converting the Empire', *Foreign Affections: Essays on Edmund Burke* (Cork: Cork University Press/Field Day, 2005), 147–68.

However, Newman arrived in Ireland at a time when—as this chapter has demonstrated—improvement utilitarianism was controlling Irish education and seeking to displace the last remaining vestiges of a classical (and Catholic) educational tradition. Newman's university experiment was an attempt to protect that very educational tradition from those utilitarian forces. Ironically, in light of the material examined here, Ireland appeared to offer that possibility to Newman in the mid-nineteenth century despite the fact that the country's educational culture was being comprehensively reshaped by an improvement liberalism which he believed to be detrimental to 'culture' and, indeed, to the course of civilization itself.

Though Carleton frequently condemns hedge schools in his fiction, he claims in 'The Hedge School' that they were pedagogically superior to society schools. According to Carleton, the hedge school developed 'the monitorial system of instruction' long before it was formulated by Lancaster and Bell (*TSIP*, i. 306). In the hands of the hedge schoolmaster, this innovative educational method was supposedly 'applied ... more judiciously' than in society schools, allowing for a fuller mental and physical development than was possible in an oppressively silent, regulated classroom (ibid.).

It might be suggested that Carleton's denunciation of the society school derives from his own miserable experiences as a teacher in institutions administered by the ADV in Mullingar and Carlow in the early 1820s. Contrary to the recommendations in R. L. Edgeworth's Report of 1812, there was no fixed school building in Mullingar when Carleton arrived there as schoolmaster, suggesting that the institution had just been established and that he was the first schoolmaster to be appointed to the post.[74] Carleton describes the dispiriting scene which awaited him on entering the temporary classroom: 'our school opened to about sixteen or eighteen of the most wretched-looking creatures—boys and girls—I ever laid my eyes upon. "And this", thought I bitterly, "is after all my struggles and hopes, what I have come to." It was a melancholy position' (*Autobiography*, 219). He states later that he mostly 'detested the duties of the school altogether' (p. 232). Carleton provides no additional information on his melancholic experiences as a teacher in Mullingar and his *Autobiography* abruptly finishes at the point when he has just been appointed to the school in Carlow, which is described as 'similar to that which I had left in Mullingar' (p. 237). The society school

---

[74] Unfortunately, the Church of Ireland records for Mullingar no longer exist.

was probably associated by Carleton with his own personal hardship as an employee. Conditions became increasingly difficult in Mullingar, culminating in his arrest and imprisonment for debt (pp. 233–7).

The records for the school in Carlow do not provide any information on Carleton's tenure in the school aside from noting that he 'was a fit and proper person to undertake the management' of the schoolroom,[75] and recording the dates of his appointment and subsequent resignation.[76] The school had been desperate to find a schoolmaster throughout 1823 and they wrote to 'the secretary of the Society for Promoting the Education of the Poor of Ireland in Kildare Place to recommend a young man of … character … properly qualified to conduct this school in the Lancastrian plan.'[77] However, Kildare Place refused to recommend a teacher and the school authorities were clearly forced to turn to the ADV for assistance. Strangely, it transpired that Carleton, soon after his release from debtors' prison and most certainly unqualified 'in the Lancastrian plan', was appointed to the post, having been recommended by the ADV.[78] Carleton's experiences as a schoolmaster in these institutions made him sceptical of the monitorial model of the society school and, by the time he was writing, the newly established National Schools as well.

The hedge schools represented in Carleton's fiction tend to manifest the strength of community rather than the isolation of individualism. This sense of community provided a sharp contrast to Carleton's own particular isolation as a writer in an urban environment. The community represented by the hedge school may be poor, impoverished, and undeveloped, but it probably seemed preferable to the isolation of reading and writing. The schoolmasters reside at the centre of this community, their utterances unmediated by publishers and an absent readership, where they are always respected in an immediate and palpable manner by the local people. Mat Kavanagh in 'The Hedge School' is described as 'the contented lord of his little realm' (*TSIP*, i. 310), basking 'in the enjoyment of unlimited authority' (*TSIP*, i. 300). Raymond Williams has characteristically described how the 'nostalgic portraits of parson and schoolmaster' in Goldsmith's 'The Deserted Village' 'are of men independent and honoured in their own place, supported by a whole way of living in which independence and

[75] Minute Book: Carlow Parish School, Oct. 1819–Mar. 1839 (RCB Library, P. 317–13), 29 Feb. 1824.

[76] Ibid. 27 Feb. 1825, School Minutes: Carlow, Oct. 1819–Mar. 1839.

[77] Ibid. [n.d.]   [78] Ibid. 25 May 1823.

community are actual'.[79] Carleton's schoolmasters inhabit a similar actuality of community and independence, financially and morally supported by integrated communities, however poor and backward.

Williams claims that the nostalgia of Goldsmith was an expression of his own immediate situation as a poet and was not by any means a reliable document of a particular moment of social and historical change. In Carleton's fiction, historical circumstances are similarly absorbed within his own struggle to support himself as a writer. Carleton was unable to achieve either independence or community throughout his literary career (the letters collected together by David O'Donoghue into the second volume of the *Autobiography* provide abundant detail of Carleton's struggles with publishers, government pensions, and finances).[80] Independence is consistently denied to him during a career which begins by writing anti-Catholic polemic for the evangelical *Christian Examiner* and culminates in the production of excessively sentimental Victorian parlour novels in a desperate attempt to make ends meet. As Williams notes in relation to Goldsmith, 'the exposure and suffering of the writer, in his own social situation, are identified with the facts of a social history that is beyond him.'[81] Carleton's famine novel *The Black Prophet* (1847), his ascendancy polemic *Valentine M'Clutchy* (1845), and the ludicrous pro-tithe novel *The Tithe Proctor* (1849)—all assertively political—are projections of his own particular difficulties as a writer in the 1830s, 1840s, and 1850s. As well as offering representations of famine, corrupt agents, or agrarian violence, Carleton's work, then, can be read as a record of the isolation of writing and the instability of the literary profession, qualities which he presumed did not characterize the 'oral' world constructed in his fiction. Oral peasant Ireland is thus consistently *constructed* in Carleton's fiction as an opposition to writing, as what writing is not. Orality is, in this sense, the negative identity of text. For Carleton, representations of orality were necessary in order to understand and define the processes of writing itself. The schoolmaster is paraded through the stories and novels to

[79] Raymond Williams, *The Country and the City* (London: Chatto and Windus, 1973), 78. For a different perspective on nostalgia in Goldsmith, see Declan Kiberd, 'Nostalgia as Protest: Goldsmith's "Deserted Village" ', in *Irish Classics* (London: Granta, 2000), 107–24. Kiberd argues that nostalgia in Irish literature should be understood as radical rather than reactionary.

[80] See *The Life of William Carleton*, ed. David O'Donoghue, 2 vols. (London: Downey and Co., 1896), esp. ii. 104–23 and 140–57.

[81] Williams, *The Country and the City*, 78.

signify both the despised values of oral culture and the positive values of orality—presence, immediacy, community—which, it seemed, had been displaced by an alienated world of writing.

As we have seen, this fiction of orality is also depicted in the improvement writing of Leadbeater and Doyle, as it provides a necessary, presumed point of origin for improvement discourse, an origin that in turn relies upon a deeply fictional, textual world of hungry peasants endlessly repeating the same oral stories around the fireplace. The peasantry represent a sort of 'primitive originality' upon which improvement writers construct their concept of civil society. In the pamphlets, tracts, and stories under discussion here, this civility is always necessarily represented in the generic, fictional terms of tolerant schoolmasters, tidy pupils, and an integrated social order. However, these representations tend to suggest the fictional nature of improvement itself rather than the feasibility and ease of progress. In this respect, the practicality of improvement education is undermined by the rhetoric of its writing.

3

The Silence of Irish

In *Sketches in Ireland*, Caesar Otway describes a young girl on Cape Clear island who

appeared to be of the peculiar and indigenous, and fixed breed of the island, as did the sheep and lambs ... and this girl, I never did see such a specimen of an untaught and untutored savage—her hair was of a deep madder red, her eyes, ferret-like, sparkled from under hair unacquainted with comb or cleanliness. When she neared us, apparently to avoid the stranger and the enemy, as she considered us, she ran off, barefooted, on the stony rock, whining and jabbering Irish.[1]

This description exemplifies the manner in which the Irish language came to be equated with orality in the nineteenth century. The girl's utterances in Irish are in keeping with her dirtiness and 'untaught and untutored' state, her savagery further epitomized by the 'madder' redness of her hair. According to Otway, education and tutoring of a particular kind would entail cleanliness, civility, and the adoption of the English language. Otway equates the sound of Irish with the unimproved recesses of the country and—being 'peculiar and indigenous'—as emblematic of an absence of writing and civilization. The girl's use of language fails to distinguish her from the utter naturalness of the environment—instead, the Irish language places her at one with the sheep, lambs, and 'stony rock' of the island.

Otway's description of this 'untutored savage' on Cape Clear encapsulates the very perceived incivility, rooted in the Irish language, which improvement writers were attempting to displace throughout the early nineteenth century. The Irish language is itself rarely discussed in the improvement fiction and pamphlets of writers such as Leadbeater and Doyle. The language almost never appears as a topic of debate in dialogues dispensing instruction on growing vegetables and managing the

---

[1] Caesar Otway, *Sketches in Ireland: Descriptive of Interesting Portions of the Counties of Donegal, Cork, and Kerry*, 1827 (Dublin, 1838), 214–15.

household economy. Leadbeater's improved peasants remain untroubled by the national language as they find themselves busily improving their cottage, small farm, and overall domestic economy. English was simply assumed to be the language of improvement, the pamphlets themselves conveying the virtues of an improved idiom which was at once plain and truthful as compared with the abundant obfuscation and fiction to be found elsewhere.

An improved English would provide the necessary set of terms for commercial transactions, the creation of a viable public sphere, and the writing of a realistic literature, which, it was assumed, the Irish language would have been unable to achieve. Improved English would amend narrative and even the subject matter of stories, displacing the diffuse and erratic oral storytelling culture of the past. Carleton invoked an improved English for the act of writing stories because, for him, Irish was firmly equated with orality and considered an inappropriate medium for written storytelling. In Carleton's representation, the Irish language exemplifies the heritage of legends, tales, and folklore that made up the oral tradition, a body of material metaphysically and culturally at odds with the social order envisaged in his writing. That order was itself most clearly outlined within improvement fiction and discourse, which urged a break with the specific economic, social, narrative, and linguistic patterns of the past.

Those regions of Ireland that had the greatest concentration of Irish speakers were destined to be, by definition, the least developed. Improvement, it seems, could only arrive in the form of 'modern' languages such as English. In his 1845 pamphlet, *The Labouring Classes in Ireland: An Inquiry*, Doyle compares the Irish and Breton peasant and attributes their similarities to common 'Celtic' origins:

> It is a remarkable coincidence that Brittany is the poorest and most backward province in France, and that its inhabitants are sprung from the same Celtic origin as those of the west and south of Ireland. The vernacular language is so nearly identical that the natives to the two countries can understand each other. The Breton in many localities of his province does not speak, or comprehend a word of French, just as many of the inhabitants of Munster or Connaught are at fault with regard to the English language; the peasantry in both lands cling to their original tongue, though from the progress of education, the modern languages are in each case so rapidly superseding it, that in twenty years at farthest the Celtic tongue will have ceased to be the medium of intercourse.[2]

[2] Martin Doyle, *The Labouring Classes in Ireland: An Inquiry* (Dublin, 1845), 2.

Doyle would have known that Irish and Breton speakers were unable to understand each other; however, as a highly educated Church of Ireland clergyman, who had studied classical languages, he felt the need to emulate the perceived insularity of the ordinary, practical farmer. It was necessary for Doyle to cultivate the 'voice' of a pragmatic man of commerce who was immersed entirely in the very physical work of agricultural improvement and impatient with any 'impediment' to modernization (be it language, religion, or classical education). For Doyle, all languages classified as 'Celtic' merely lapse into the one barbaric 'tongue'. These vernacular languages were, in his mind, forever confined within orality and unable to evolve into modern written forms. Such intensely oral languages had impeded development in regions such as the west of Ireland and Brittany.[3] The existence of Irish in a locality was an indication for Doyle that education—as defined in his various pamphlets—had not yet progressed there. Doyle claims that, in Ireland, linguistic homogenization had still not been achieved in 1845; the poor progress of so many peasants in achieving fluency in English was intertwined in an overall lack of economic development.

The particular linguistic backwardness of Munster was described by Doyle *Hints Addressed to the smallholders and Peasantry of Ireland* (1833), where he recounts an encounter he once had with a goat-herd in Kerry:

I recollect, some years back, riding through a valley in that country, and seeing a ragged fellow on a high rock, herding goats; I beckoned to him to come down, and asked him some questions about the romantic spot in which I stood. He did not understand a word I said, but addressed me very fluently in Latin. I was as badly off there—it being a little out of Martin's line—and we parted as wise as we met; for the native language which he also tried on me, was thrown away upon a Wexford man. It struck me that he must have been taught the Latin in Irish, for not one word of English could he speak, or I believe, understand.[4]

In this impossible situation, Irish and Latin are both considered to be 'dead' languages, each somehow exemplifying the orality of the region, itself locked within a primitive agricultural economy (typified by goat-herding on high rocks). The 'ragged fellow'—unimproved and

---

[3] However, Niall Ó Ciosáin records the presence of a strong literate culture in Brittany in the nineteenth century. See Ó Ciosáin, 'Printed Popular Literature in Irish 1750–1850: Presence and Absence', in Mary Daly and David Dickson (eds.), *The Origins of Popular Literacy in Ireland: Language Change and Educational Development 1700–1920* (Dublin: Trinity College and University College, 1990), 50–2.

[4] Martin Doyle, *Hints Addressed to the Smallholders and Peasantry of Ireland on Subjects Connected with Health, Temperance, Morals* (Dublin, 1833), 76.

unable to speak English—was incapable of communicating within the linguistic and commercial conditions of the modern world. This goat-herd had probably learnt Latin through Irish in a Kerry hedge school, an institution which, for Doyle, compounded backwardness and linguistic confusion, instructing students in Latin and Greek whilst confining them in rags. The existence of these particular languages confirmed the absence of any means to undertake modernization. Hedge schools were responsible for a profusion of languages and the prevalence of rags.[5]

This linguistic profusion is replicated on the pages of Carleton's writing, in an attempt, paradoxically, to clear the way for a monoglot writing culture. Carleton writes on the assumption that representation necessarily organizes and unifies, that the depiction of the heterogeneity of languages on the written page will result in inevitable standard-ization. For Carleton, this process of representation was necessary in order to create an Irish national literature in English. In Carleton's writing, Irish is deemed pre-modern and oral, fated to the endless reiteration of prophecies, superstitions, and legends of dubious his-torical authenticity. It seems that the Irish language was contrary to the concept of a national literature and the particular frame of refer-ence it embodied. In his 'General Introduction' to the 1842 edition of the *Traits and Stories*, Carleton comments that the absence of an Irish national literature had been an embarrassment, exemplifying the chaotic conditions of a backward orality (*TSIP*, i. p.v). For Carleton, a national literature signified the coherence and order of modernization. The Irish language suggested variety and difference whereas a national literature (as existed in Scotland) signified uniformity and stability. In one respect, Carleton brought the various characters of Irish-language popular culture—from the seanachie to the prophecy-man and fid-dler—to the fore on the written page in order to demonstrate their incongruity with writing, English, and print. Carleton represented this culture to demonstrate how it could not be accommodated with-in a modernizing society. His representation of Irish orality speaks for his sense of the language as an obstacle to modernization and improvement.[6]

---

[5] On the issue of the survival of languages, see Seán De Fréine, *The Great Silence* (Dublin: Foilseacháin Naisiúnta Teoranta, 1965), 132. On the particular case of Irish, see Garret Fitzgerald, 'The Decline of the Irish Language 1771–1871', in Daly and Dickson, *The Origins of Popular Literacy in Ireland*, 59–72.

[6] On this theme, see David Lloyd, 'Writing in the Shit: Beckett, Nationalism and the Colonial Subject', 44–6 and, in relation to Young Ireland and the Irish language,

Carleton's writing represents an effort to nationalize language and form, moving from a strongly oral Irish to a resolutely literate English. The linguistic transition between Irish and English preoccupied Carleton, invariably and, for him, regrettably, becoming characteristic of his own writing style:

The language of our people has been for centuries, and is up to the present day, in a transition state. The English tongue is gradually superseding the Irish. In my own native place, for instance, there is not by any means so much Irish spoken now, as there was about twenty or five and twenty years ago. This fact then, will easily account for the ridicule which is, and I fear ever will be, unjustly heaped upon those who are found to use a language which they do not properly understand. In the early periods of communication between the countries, when they stood in a hostile relation to each other, and even long afterwards, it was not surprising that 'the wild Irishman' who expressed himself with difficulty, and often impressed the idiom of his own language upon one with which he was not familiar, should incur, in the opinion of those who were strongly prejudiced against him, the character of making the bulls and blunders attributed to him. ('General Introduction', *TSIP*, i. p. ii)

Carleton seeks to present his writing as marking the climax of this transition, while conceding that language in Ireland has always been transitional. While Irish speech was disappearing, Carleton's fiction implies that Irish writing did not exist at all. In describing the character of Irish-language literacy in the early eighteenth century, Louis Cullen claims that even 'people of little means ... were literate in Irish' at the time. According to Cullen, literacy seems to have decreased as the century progressed, 'becoming less commonplace as a command of English increased'.[7] Mary Daly and David Dickson cite the evidence of the 1806 educational survey to suggest the possibility that 20,000 people were literate in Irish in the late eighteenth century.[8] 'The amount published in Irish in the early years of the nineteenth century was', according to Sean De Fréine, 'of necessity, slight but it is significant.' De Fréine notes the 'wide popularity' and extensive distribution of texts such as Tadhg Gaelach Ó Súilleabháin's *Pious Miscellany* and other religious material such as O'Gallagher's Sermons and Ó Duinnshléibhe's

---

see 'Adulteration and the Nation', 90–4, in *Anomalous States: Irish Writing and the Post-Colonial Moment* (Dublin: Lilliput Press, 1993).

   [7] Louis M. Cullen, 'Patrons, Teachers and Literacy in Irish: 1700–1850' in Daly and Dickson, *The Origins of Popular Literacy in Ireland*, 32.

   [8] Daly and Dickson, Preface, *The Origins of Popular Literacy in Ireland*, p. ix.

Catechism, which confirm the existence of literacy in Irish in the early nineteenth century.[9] The printed Irish-language material available on the chapbook market was mostly devotional literature and catechisms. The most famous text in this genre was the *Pious Miscellany*, which, as Niall Ó Ciosáin notes, 'had 18 or more editions between 1800 and 1850 in south and south-eastern Ireland'.[10] Yet, as Ó Ciosáin claims elsewhere, 'printing in Irish, and the literacy implied by it, was heavily influenced by print literacy in English, and could even be described as a transitional phenomenon in the trend towards a wider print culture and popular literacy in English.'[11] Additionally, few hedge schools taught Irish and the language was excluded, indeed prohibited, from the National Schools when they were established in 1831. Moreover, Daniel O'Connell conducted most of his campaign for Catholic Emancipation through English, a point bitterly noted by Douglas Hyde at the outset of his project to 'revive' the Irish language in the late nineteenth century.[12] O'Connell clearly perceived the Irish language to be at odds with his political objectives, which depended in part on Catholic Ireland being accepted into the British mainstream. It was central to O'Connell's programme—as indeed it was to Carleton's—that Ireland no longer be thought of as different and strange, its peculiarity obliterated by the homogenizing and secularizing process of modernization.

In Carleton's fiction, the Irish language is concentrated within the world of speech and dialogue and always differentiated from written prose by quotation marks. In these stories and novels, Irish-language literacy is entirely absent even though it most certainly existed. The unrepresentability of Irish in writing became an established convention in the early nineteenth century and the language was often only depicted in the writing of the period to confirm its distance from English-language print culture. Irish was nonetheless made to serve a textual function in the early nineteenth century by evoking a culture—pre-modern, oral,

---

[9] De Fréine, *The Great Silence*, 129. De Fréine also mentions an English army recruitment poster of 1806 which was published in Irish, 129. Louis Cullen has noted the regional basis of Irish-language publishing: 'the early attempts at printing in Irish came exclusively from Munster' where Irish-language literacy was strongest. See Cullen, 'Patrons, Teachers and Literacy in Irish, 1700–1850', in Daly and Dickson, *The Origins of Popular Literacy in Ireland*, 34.

[10] Niall Ó Ciosáin, *Print and Popular Culture in Ireland, 1750–1850* (Basingstoke: Macmillan, 1997), 118.

[11] Ó Ciosáin, 'Printed Popular Literature in Irish 1750–1850', 47.

[12] Douglas Hyde, Preface, *Beside the Fire: A Collection of Irish Gaelic Folk Stories* (London: D. Nutt, 1890), p. xxiii.

and overly emotional—which was being superseded by the rationality of writing and print. The silence of Irish was therefore a textual convention upon which improved English relied.

In 1820, the Kildare Place Society published an *Irish-English Primer*, to facilitate the learning of English in Irish-language regions.[13] In its Preface to the volume, the Society claims that

having observed, that the population of several districts are prevented from receiving the advantages of education, by their ignorance of the English language, have caused the following spelling book to be compiled. It is sufficiently obvious that many disadvantages arise to the peasantry, in places where two different tongues are spoken, if they be not both of them spoken by the inhabitants. Such a circumstance must very much prevent the intercourse between the peasant and the landlord, the magistrate, the clergyman, the lawyer, the physician and the trader, to whom he may have occasion to resort for assistance or for advice.

The present work is, therefore, for the poor of Ireland, with a view to aid them in their future communications with those, from whom many of their comforts must naturally flow.[14]

The Irish-speaking poor were disconnected from the institutions of the state and unable to receive an enlightened education on account of their ignorance of English. This linguistic reality made it impossible for the Kildare Place to instil improvement education in, perhaps, the very places that were presumed to need it most. The *Primer* depicts the Irish and English alphabets side by side and provides a dictionary of terms. When necessary, it seems that print could readily accommodate Irish characters and vocabulary. The Kildare Place *Primer* was an explicit attempt to institute English as the 'national' language, clearly viewing the continued existence of Irish as an obstacle to the creation of the transparent communication necessary to achieve a viable public sphere. In addition, economic improvement was frustrated by the existence of Irish, the necessary ease of commercial transaction impeded by linguistic difference. By its very existence, the *Primer* sought to mark the disappearance of Irish from the linguistic landscape, while also, ironically, providing a means for greater communication between languages and so allowing for the (partial) continuance of Irish in both printed and spoken forms.

[13] Harold Hislop, 'The Kildare Place Society: An Irish Experiment in Popular Education', unpublished PhD thesis, University of Dublin, 1990, 153–4.

[14] Preface, *Irish-English Primer* (Dublin, 1820).

It seems that Irish was constructed in terms of orality and illiteracy in order to assert the rationality of English-language literary discourse. Carleton's fiction portrays the disappearance of Irish from written discourse in the very process of its occurrence. In Carleton's writing, the Irish language was equated with an oral and fragmented world against which the stability of English-language prose was supposed to be definable. English-language publications are the only texts ever mentioned in Carleton's fiction in his accounts of hedge schools and the books to be found in Irish cabins. The books stored in Irish homes were considered precious objects which were 'most carefully laid up'—often unread—in the home 'under the hope that some young relation might be able to read them' (*Autobiography*, 7). Books were no doubt intended for children who would be educated to be readers and writers. The distinction between Irish as oral and English as written is encapsulated by the very existence of such English-language book collections in the cabins of Carleton's fiction. English-language chapbooks were probably purchased from pedlars with a similar enthusiasm as factory-produced clothing was bought at markets and fairs. As noted in earlier chapters, popular print and dress combined to instil anxiety amongst improvement writers regarding the development of a culture of consumption amongst the rural poor. Such consumption suggested the indeterminacy of the very social, moral, and intellectual order improvement writers insisted upon.

The continued presence of the Irish language suggested the indeterminacy of the linguistic code of improvement discourse itself. The need to achieve a common language in Ireland had the effect of calling attention to the difficulty of creating a shared discourse within the English language. However, these difficulties were always projected onto the Irish language and a perceived entrenched 'orality'. Carleton's representations of Irish were complicated by the combination of his deeply bilingual background and commitment to an English-language print culture. In his 'General Introduction' to the 1842–4 edition of the *Traits and Stories*, he describes this background, recounting how his father

spoke the Irish and English languages with nearly equal fluency. With all kinds of charms, old ranns, or poems, old prophecies, religious superstitions, tales of pilgrims, miracles and pilgrimages, anecdotes of blessed priests and friars, revelations from ghosts and fairies, was he thoroughly acquainted and so strongly were all these impressed upon my mind, by frequent repetition on his part, and the indescribable delight they gave me on mine, that I have hardly ever since heard, during a tolerably enlarged intercourse with Irish society, both educated and uneducated—with the antiquary, the scholar, or the humble seanachie—any single tradition, usage or legend, that, as far as I can at present recollect, was perfectly new to me or unheard before, in some similar or cognate dress. ('General Introduction', *TSIP*, i. pp. viii–ix)

This oral material was suffused by superstition, prophecy, and revelation, all of which was allegedly narrated within the allegorical and repetitive storytelling patterns of oral culture. Writing, in the mode of a 'national literature', was presumed to offer the possibility of creating symbolic narratives, at once engendering and expressing a broader linguistic and social unity, defined in the 'General Introduction' as 'a national spirit that rose above the narrow distinctions of creed and party' (*TSIP*, i. p. vii). Carleton claims to possess a comprehensive knowledge of the Irish oral tradition, asserting that he is an authority on folklore and oral culture in the Irish-language original as well as translation:

What rendered this besides of such peculiar advantage to me in after life, as a literary man, was that I heard them as often in the Irish language as in the English, if not oftener; a circumstance which enabled me in my writing to transfer the genius, the idiomatic peculiarity and conversational spirit of the one language into the other, precisely as the people themselves do in their dialogue, whenever the heart or imagination happens to be moved by the darker or better passions. ('General Introduction', *TSIP*, i. pp. viii–ix)

In this account, translation is depicted as an essential part of narrative, becoming a mode of representation in and of itself. Some of Carleton's stories are even presented within the form of transcriptions (or copies) and translations (i.e. the entire fireside setting of the first series of *Traits and Stories*), which become, in effect, narrative constructs and part of the fictional setting. Carleton attempts to present the linguistic and cultural heritage of his parents as advantageous to his literary career even though his writing often implicitly represents it as a hindrance to the creation of a national literature.

Carleton professes to admire the Irish-language heritage of his parents while writing that subject matter and language out of existence in his own fiction. Both Irish and Hiberno-English were supposed to be neutralized—or refined—by representation in Carleton's texts, where they were to be absorbed within the unifying capability of English-language writing. In the process, these dialects would acquire the benign qualities of literary convention. For Carleton, the Irish language suggested superstition, prophecy, and oral storytelling—and was supposed to evoke as much in his writing—whereas a national literature in English implied reason, writing, and a unified national culture. In Carleton's fiction, there is a desire for the former to be incorporated within the terms of the latter. At the same time, the failure of an English-language print culture to perform this unifying role is apparent in the representations of both Irish and orality in Carleton's writing. Irish is made to embody the difficulty—and perhaps impossibility—of achieving the linguistic and cultural standardization deemed essential for both improvement and a national literature. This tension is also evident in the various explications of Hiberno-English and Irish produced by the Edgeworths. In all of their annotations—for the *Essay on Irish Bulls, Castle Rackrent*, and the English edition of Leadbeater's *Cottage Dialogues*—the problems supposedly represented by both Irish and Hiberno-English seem to signify the tensions within the Edgeworths' own discourses of nationality and modernization.

In *Sketches in Ireland*, Otway describes how Irish had become an interior language, confined to personal and domestic concerns, while English was the language of the public sphere, social institutions, and commerce. In a cottage in West Cork, Otway questioned a man about religion and, receiving very unsatisfactory answers, turned to his travelling companion to bemoan the man's theological ignorance. However, his companion cautioned, 'Not so fast with your judgment ... what if you prove very much mistaken in this instance concerning the knowledge of this man: Recollect you are now speaking to him in a foreign tongue.' Otway's companion then posed the same questions to the man in Irish:

it was quite surprising to see how the man, as soon as the Irish was spoken, brightened up in countenance, and I could see from the smile that played on the face of my friend, how he rejoiced in the realization of his prognostic, and he began to translate for me ... The man gave in Irish clear and feeling answers to questions, concerning which, when addressed in English, he appeared quite ignorant; and yet of common English words and phrases he had the use; but like most of his countrymen in the south, his mind was groping in foreign parts when conversing in English, and he only seemed to think in Irish; the one was the language of his commerce, the other of his heart.[15]

In the travel writing and literature of the period, Irish is readily perceived and constructed in these terms. The language is made to serve this representative role—oral, hidden, and emotional—and is

[15] Otway, *Sketches in Ireland*, 312–13.

thus called upon to signify the opposite of English-language writing. In the process, the language is divested of any public or institutional value or possibility

Carleton's 'oral characters'—those who signify orality within his texts—inhabit a bilingual world: English and Irish are often uttered within single sentences, the former frequently providing a translation of the latter. They thus speak tautologically. In 'Wildgoose Lodge', for example, the Captain states: 'Bee dhu husth; ha bihil anam inh:—hold your tongue, it is not yet time' or 'Gutsho nish, avohelhee—come hither now, boys' (*TSIP*, ii. 353–5). In 'Tubber Derg', a woman tells her sons to give up their places at the fire to Owen M'Carthy's cold and hungry children in the following manner: 'Eiree suas, a wadhee bradagh, agus go mah a shin!—be off wid yez, ye lazy divils' (*TSIP*, ii. 390). When Jemmy returns home an ordained priest at the conclusion of 'The Poor Scholar', he speaks to his mother in Irish, declaring that 'it will go directly to her heart—*Mhair, avourneen, tha ma, laht, anish!*—Mother, my darling I am with you at last' (*TSIP*, ii. 348). The conversation is then conducted between them in both Irish and English, the former supposed to signify an unmediated orality not available in the latter. In the same story, the priest's sermon is delivered in English and then translated into Irish by members of the congregation (*TSIP*, ii. 264–8). On one level, Carleton presents translation as a feature of everyday, common exchanges, organizing and structuring speech patterns, and even, it seems, thought processes. However, these passages make Irish appear entirely redundant, a language which has effectively become a tautology and which is, by itself, incapable of communication, let alone literary representation. The apparent linguistic inclusiveness of Carleton's fiction is far from democratic: Irish is, paradoxically, brought in only to be excluded in the end. The language is never used as a medium of representation in and of itself; the presence of the language in Carleton's writing is entirely conventional within the terms of nineteenth-century Irish writing.

Irish is depicted as being comfortably embedded in the Hiberno-English of Carleton's fiction in such idiomatic phrases as 'millia failte ghud', as though it had been seamlessly absorbed into the English language. However, the existence of Irish is often only registered in the form of isolated and increasingly banal idioms, such as 'asthore' or 'machree'. Irish could only, it seems, make the transition to the written text through these idioms and phrases rather than as a medium for written storytelling. Far from invoking Irish as a living language, these phrases comprise a literary convention in the nineteenth-century Irish novel, which is supposed to convey sentimentality and melodrama—then novelistic conventions—and intended to appeal to such expectations in a non-Irish readership, providing at once sentimental figures of speech and a 'Hibernian' prose. It thus appears that Irish, which is supposedly oral and illiterate, comes to signify the sentimentality and melodrama of the novel.

In certain works, Carleton refuses to represent the language even when allegedly spoken by characters within the fiction. In these instances, the Irish language is represented by means of its absence from the printed page, though the reader is assured that Irish is being spoken. One such example is the speech of Mary O'Regan in *Valentine M'Clutchy*, praying that her husband will die before the officers can arrive to arrest him:

'They are gallopin'! they are gallopin'!' she said, 'and they will find life in him!' she then wrung her hands, but shed not a tear—'speed, Hugh,' she said, 'speed, speed, husband of my heart—the arms of God are they not open for you, and why do you stay?' These sentiments, we should have informed our readers, were uttered or rather chaunted in a recitative of sorrow, in Irish; Irish being the language in which the peasantry, who happen to speak both it and English, always express themselves when more than usually excited. (*Valentine M'Clutchy*, 115)

This character does not so much speak Irish as 'chaunt' the language. As this passage demonstrates, the excessive orality of Irish is even occasionally beyond speech itself, belonging to a pre-linguistic order entirely.[16] It seems that in this instance it is almost impossible to embody Irish in speech, let alone within writing. For many of Carleton's characters, Irish is the only medium for emotional, mournful expression, but this form of articulation cannot, it seems, be depicted on the printed page in its original form. The narrator writes the words in English while stating that they were actually uttered in Irish. The Irish language is depicted throughout the novel as the voice of an excessively emotional state which can only be phrased in oral terms, or else translated into the intrinsic restraint of English and print. The mere mention of Irish is supposed to suggest an intense emotion beyond the scope of both the English language and written prose.

[16] On the issue of speech and representation, see Seamus Deane, *Strange Country: Modernity and Nationhood in Irish Writing since 1790* (Oxford: Clarendon Press, 1997), 63–6.

Writing and Irish are supposed to be irreconcilable, each representative of distinct social conditions and even historical periods. When Mary O'Regan's husband and son die, she sings 'an old and melancholy Irish air, in a voice whose wild sweetness was in singular keeping with its mournful spirit' (*Valentine M'Clutchy*, 127). Irish has become 'wild', 'old', 'melancholy', and utterly feminized, associated with death, mourning, and the past in comparison with the contemporaneity of the printed page. The Irish 'air' serves as a connection back into the past, though the song itself is not transcribed on the page. Irish is particularly and uniquely embodied in song, exemplifying its distance from language as a practical, usable, and literal tool of communication. Irish is, therefore, always supplying pathos and melodrama in the background of the novel. In *Valentine M'Clutchy*, the language has disappeared from the reach of written representation, while also being designated a specific representational role.[17]

In his 'General Introduction', Carleton praises Irish for possessing 'the finest and most copious vocabulary in the world for the expression of either sorrow or love' (*TSIP*, i. p. xxiii). The Irish language has come to be equated with an irrationality, which—Carleton seems to be claiming—could not exist within English. Irish has thus become a convenient way to represent irrationality. The fact that Irish is not typographically represented in *Valentine M'Clutchy* demonstrates how the language was perceived to have become archaic for the needs of modern narrative as well as commerce and education. Declaring the absence of Irish from the novel is also a trope in Gerald Griffin's *The Collegians*, which notes that the language is being spoken by certain characters even though it is not represented on the page: 'In a little time the boatman rested on his oars, and a voice from the interior of the cave was heard exclaiming in Irish, "Is it himself?" "It is", said the boatman in the same language.'[18] Irish is invoked and suggested but never actually made to appear on the printed page. It could be argued that Carleton's representation of Irish suggests the incapacity of many of his readers to understand written Irish, yet they are being urged to conceive of the language in a very specific set of terms: absent, irrational, feminine, and figurative. In this respect, the Irish language serves very

[17] For an example of an illicit distiller who has literally gone underground, see William Carleton, 'Bob Pentland, or The Gauger Outwitted', *Irish Penny Journal*, 1/16 (17 Oct. 1840), 125–7 and for the fairies and their underground, see 'Irish Superstitions: Ghosts and Fairies; The Rival Kempers', *Irish Penny Journal*, 1/24 (12 Dec. 1840), 188–91.

[18] Gerald Griffin, *The Collegians*, 1829 (repr. Belfast: Appletree Press, 1992), 100.

specific textual, literary purposes, becoming, in effect, a melodramatic trope.

The implication in Carleton's fiction is that the Irish language is too figurative to be contained within prose; in *Valentine M'Clutchy*, the narrator comments that 'the conversation which followed was in Irish, a circumstance which accounts for its figurative style and tendencies of expression' (*Valentine M'Clutchy*, 93). This figurativeness, of form as well as content, is supposed to distinguish Irish from the literalism of English. In this writing—Otway, Doyle, and Carleton—it seems that Irish was actually becoming a foreign language, signifying foreigness and, therefore, a threat in some form. For Carleton, Irish orality could only become literal when translated into written English. Irish is thus characterized as a poetic language, which is too figurative for the expression of improved narratives. In a similar manner, Irish cannot exist within the supposedly practical world of literary prose and commerce, not possessing the necessary resources of vocabulary or structure for either realm. In 'Tubber Derg', Carleton describes the Irish speech of Owen M'Carthy as conveying 'much of that vivid feeling, and strong figurative language, inseparable from the habits of thought and language of the old Irish families' (*TSIP*, ii. 409). Owen M'Carthy not only spoke in Irish, but thought in accordance with the structures of the language. When speaking Irish, M'Carthy falls back into these patterns of speech (figurative) and thought (archaic).

English-language prose, at once practical and literal, could not, for Carleton, unambiguously accommodate a storytelling culture of legends, prophecies, and ballads. Carleton demonstrates how this subject matter was, like the Irish language, already disappearing, having been replaced by a 'reading and, consequently, a thinking culture' (*TSIP*, i. pp. vi–vii). However, his writing professed to be representing this oral culture in the literate terms of English-language prose, as though the transcription of this culture was necessary for the development of a national literature and was, therefore, integral to the process of improvement. On one level, Carleton presented himself as recording or copying the practices and traditions of oral culture, expediting its demise and eventual replacement with a solidly literate culture. However, such transcription always entailed fictionalization, an absorption of this 'remembered' orality within a range of textual conventions. His fiction also demonstrates the extent to which the act of copying was definitive of the process of writing, as exemplified by the replication of previous improvement narratives and novelistic conventions on the pages of his stories and novels. Clearly, there could not be an unmediated oral culture represented on the written page, orality necessarily displaced once brought within the forms of writing.

If Carleton's fiction marks—as he claims—a transitional state between languages, the literary culture of the 1830s and 1840s must also manifest this particular instability. The various journals of the period would likewise be transitional in character, explicitly mediating between an oral culture of rural Ireland and a metropolitan print culture. It should also be noted that literary history traces an Irish revival of the early nineteenth century to the development of a periodical, print culture in Dublin in the late 1820s.[19] Many of Carleton's stories were first published in journals, such as the *Christian Examiner* and the *Monthly Magazine*, and were surely shaped by the nature of this medium as well as by the ideological stance of the publications themselves. Penny Fielding notes that journals in the early nineteenth century 'can be seen to combine characteristics associated with orality with those of a newly forged literary establishment'. It is tempting to see Irish journals of the early nineteenth century as transitional entities, inhabiting, like Carleton's stories 'a border territory linking oral transmission to controlled literary circulation'.[20] As well as signifying a transitional stage from orality to print, journals in Ireland could also be seen as signalling a shift from Irish to English and from the provisionality of the manuscript to the 'finality' of print.[21] It would be difficult, however, to classify a journal such as the *Christian Examiner* in this manner. It seems to me that the *Examiner*, a strongly, evangelical, Protestant publication, was clearly rooted in a textual culture and, indeed, existed to engage directly with texts, such as the Bible, theological scholarship, and the literature of the period (there are, for example, numerous references to Coleridge in the *Examiner*). Indeed, it is not really possible to classify any journal of the period as 'transitional': established organs such as *Dublin University Magazine* and less successful journals, such as the *Irish Penny Journal*, all emerge from within a written, textual culture rather

---

[19] See Barbara Hayley, 'Irish Periodicals from the Union to the Nation', *Anglo Irish Studies*, 1/2 (1976), and Seamus Deane, *A Short History of Irish Literature* (London: Hutchinson, 1986), 60–89.

[20] Penny Fielding, *Writing and Orality: Nationality, Culture, and Nineteenth-Century Scottish Fiction* (Oxford: Clarendon Press, 1996), 125–6.

[21] I am here invoking the simplistic and overly optimistic terms of Walter Ong in *Orality and Literacy: The Technologizing of the Word* (London and New York: Methuen, 1982), 132.

than an oral one. These journals do not appear to be mediating between
a form of raw orality and print. Even the *Irish Penny Journal*, which was
explicitly addressed to the poor and priced accordingly, was itself the
product of improvement discourse. These journals mediate from one
form of textual activity to another and do not spring from oral culture.
Additionally, the representations of peasant orality contained in these
publications are themselves heavily mediated by the literary culture of
the early nineteenth century, as manifest, in particular, in the novels of
Maria Edgeworth and Walter Scott as well as the improvement tracts
of Leadbeater, the Kildare Place Society, Doyle, and Carleton. The idea
that Carleton (or anyone) was a 'transitional' writer seems, then, to be
somewhat redundant; these 'transitions' have always been with us.

The *Irish Penny Journal* expressed its editorial objectives in the
characteristic terms of Irish improvement discourse, thereby placing
itself within a specific literary tradition of the early nineteenth century :

The want of a cheap literary publication for the great body of the people of this
country, suited to their tastes and habits, combining instruction with amusement, avoiding the exciting and pointless discussion of politics or polemical
questions, and placed within the reach of their humble means, has long been
a matter of regret to those reflecting and benevolent minds who are anxious
for the advancement and civilization of Ireland—and the reflection has been
rather a humiliating one, that while England and Scotland abound with such
cheap publications ... Ireland, with a population so extensive, and so strongly
characterized by a thirst for knowledge, has not even one work of this class. It
is impossible to believe that such an anomaly can have originated in any other
cause than the want of spirit and enterprise on the part of those who ought to
endeavour to enlighten their countrymen, and thereby elevate their condition,
even though the effort should be attended with risk and trouble to themselves.[22]

In accordance with this objective, the articles published in the *Irish Penny
Journal* counselled on economic matters, child-rearing, horticulture,
and, in the case of Carleton's contributions, educated on the absurdity
of superstition and archaism of many traditional practices. In so doing,
the journal was attempting to institute consensus on both a practical
and an abstract level, seeking uniformity on matters from gardening to
ideology. The explicitly improving tone was provided by Martin Doyle's
contributions, which predictably encouraged kindness to animals and
the (profitable) rearing of geese, and recommended 'occupations for the
young' (such as gardening and botany).

---

[22] 'To Our Readers', *Irish Penny Journal*, 1/1 (4 July 1840), 8.

Carleton's articles for the *Irish Penny Journal* were centred on various representative characters of Irish oral culture, such as the cosherer, the prophecy-man, and the matchmaker. These characters were supposed to personify a pre-literate culture, pre-modern economy, and even particular modes of narrative, such as 'word of mouth', fireside storytelling, and prophecy. In 'The Irish Matchmaker', Carleton describes this culture in strongly disapproving terms:

Characters like Rose [the cosherer] are fast disappearing in Ireland; and indeed in a country where the means of life were generally inadequate to the wants of the population, they were calculated, however warmly the heart may look back upon the memory of their services, to do more harm than good, by inducing young folks to enter into early and improvident marriages. They certainly sprang up from a state of society not thoroughly formed by proper education and knowledge—where the language of a people, too, was in many extensive districts in such a state of transition as in the interchange of affection to render an interpreter absolutely necessary. We have ourselves witnessed marriages where the husband and wife spoke the one English and the other Irish, each being able with difficulty to understand the other.[23]

The hand-to-mouth economy of oral culture is perpetuated by characters such as the cosherer, who lures young people into careless and reckless marriages by gossiping from house to house. Carleton presumes that the culture exemplified by matchmaking, prophecy, and superstition would be reformed by his writing. In a series entitled 'Irish Superstitions', he describes and recounts various folk and fairy beliefs, but attempts to account scientifically and rationally for, what he terms 'spectral phenomena'. In one sketch, he describes the experiences of a young girl who claimed to have seen a ghost. However, we are assured that the ghost 'was a pure case of spectral illusion, and precisely similar to that detailed so philosophically by Nicolai, the German bookseller, and to others mentioned by Hibbert'.[24] In 'Frank Martin and the Fairies', another story in the same series, Carleton mentions that 'we cannot avoid regretting that we have not by us copies of two most valuable works upon [the fairies] from the pen of our learned and admirable countryman, Thomas Keightley—we allude to his Fairy Mythology and his history

---

[23] William Carleton, 'The Irish Matchmaker', *Irish Penny Journal*, 1/14 (2 Oct. 1840), 119.
[24] William Carleton, 'Irish Superstitions: Ghosts and Fairies', *Irish Penny Journal*, 1/21 (21 Nov. 1840), 165. I have been unable to trace the allusion to Nicolai and Hibbert.

of the transmission of popular fictions.'[25] A copy of Thomas Keightley's *Fairy Mythology* was sent to Carleton by Henry Cooke Taylor, with whom he corresponded in the 1830s. Keightley's book is here invoked as an authority on the subject of fairy and folklore.[26] Irish superstition is supposed to be discredited when brought within the 'learned' researches of a Hibbert or Keightley. Interestingly, Keightley fabricated, indeed fictionalized, his contribution to Crofton Croker's *Fairy Legends of the South of Ireland* entitled 'The Soul Gages'. According to Brian Earls, this story 'was entirely the invention of Keightley who had rewritten a legend of the Brothers Grimm, adding Hiberno-English dialogue and providing it with an Irish setting'.[27] It is notable that Carleton should refer to Keightley as an authoritative folklorist, who was, like himself, committed to analysis of 'popular fictions' in order to expose them as duplicitous nonsense. In the process of revealing the fictionality of oral culture, writers such as Keightley and Carleton created elaborate fictions of their own. Though Carleton presents his *Penny Journal* sketches as articles and ethnographic reports, they should be read as fictional narratives. In this instance, Carleton was forced to construct his own fiction of Irish culture because he did not have Keightley's book at hand to help him. It is necessary to emphasize the textual sources of Carleton's fiction and supposedly authentic representations of peasant orality. The oral culture represented in Carleton's fiction is based on a range of conventions and discourses, most of which were themselves explicitly fictional.

The oppressiveness of peasant superstition is supposed to be eliminated when represented in writing: 'As the old monsters of the mythologies disappeared before reason and religion, so also will ghosts, fairies, and all such nonsense, vanish when men shall be taught to reason upon them as they ought.'[28] Reasoning upon superstition is only made possible by means of written representation—presented here as an evolutionary stage in the history of civilization—which immediately rationalizes superstitious folk belief, eliminating the eccentricity of orality. The act

---

[25] Carleton, 'The Rival Kempers', *Irish Penny Journal* 1/24 (12 Dec. 1840), 188.

[26] See *The Life of William Carleton*, ed. D. J. O'Donoghue (London: Downey and Co., 1896), 26. Letter from William Cooke Taylor to Carleton: 'I now enclose a copy of Keightley's "Fairy Mythology"', in which I have speculated as proprietor.' This suggests that Cooke Taylor had a material stake in the production of Keightley's book.

[27] Brian Earls, 'Supernatural Legends in Nineteenth-Century Irish Writing', *Béaloideas*, 60–1 (1992–3), 101–2.

[28] William Carleton, 'Irish Superstitions—no. III, Ghosts and Fairies', *Irish Penny Journal*, 1/34 (20 Feb. 1841), 269.

of reading is also simultaneously an act of reasoning: the reader intrinsically analyses and rationalizes the material being read. Writing dispels
the terror of fiction, which was supposedly inhabited by the Catholic
poor, and replaces it with truth and rationality. The monstrousness
of superstition was to be displaced by reason and, paradoxically, the
'factuality' disseminated by the very existence of Carleton's fiction. A
fiction of orality was therefore to be replaced by a fiction of writing.
These *Irish Penny Journal* stories were supposedly directed at the exposure of superstition in writing in a manner that would not, it seems,
have been possible within an oral exposition. Carleton presented his
writing as marking an end to superstition, making way for the freedom
implied by 'reason'. There is a precedent for Carleton's exposure of
superstitious beliefs in a story entitled 'Ghosts' in Leadbeater's *Short
Stories for Cottagers* (1813). In this 'tale', the alleged sighting of a ghost
is shown to be entirely delusional: it transpires that the 'ghost' is really a
piece of white fabric strewn in a ditch.[29] Leabeater's first improvement
tract, *Anecdotes Taken from Real Life, for the Improvement of Children*,
counsels children against being drawn in by 'the pernicious nonsense
of ghosts and fairies' and urges them instead to develop a taste for the
realistic stories contained in her pamphlet.[30] In the process, Leadbeater
was trying to shift the attention of her readers (and herself?) from gothic
to realist fiction.

For Carleton, writing rationalizes superstition while simultaneously
providing authoritative and truthful narratives in a manner supposedly
not feasible within oral culture.[31] In 'The Castle of Aughentain', the
narrator declares that most oral legends of the peasant Irish are 'woefully
deficient in authenticity, as indeed those of most countries are'. He then
proceeds to explain how the particular legend of the castle at Aughentain
is '*ex post facto* or *postliminious*' by claiming that the story has no basis
whatsoever in any historical record and was probably 'of Scotch origin,
as indeed the names would seem to suggest'.[32] The fictionality of the
oral tradition is exemplified by the absence of authority and truthfulness

[29] Mary Leadbeater, *Short Stories for Cottagers Intended to Accompany Cottage Dialogues* (Dublin, 1813), 69.
[30] Mary Leadbeater, *Anecdotes Taken from Real Life, for the Improvement of Children* (Dublin, 1809), p. ii.
[31] On the issue of truth and orality, see the discussion of James Hogg in Fielding,
Writing and Orality, 122–31.
[32] William Carleton, 'The Castle of Aughentain, or a Legend of the Brown Coat: A
Tale of Tom Greissy the Shanahus', *Irish Penny Journal*, 1/40 (5 June 1841), 389.

that, for Carleton, characterized oral discourse. The suggestion is that oral narratives are intrinsically spurious and fictional, amassing bits and pieces from numerous different sources without reference to authorship or source. By comparison, written narratives are supposedly made to conform to a specific standard of truth, compelled to become part of an established record, which is both factual and transparent. Carleton is claiming that his written accounts of Irish 'orality' are an infinitely more reliable and authentic version than those uttered by most of his countrymen. He is attempting to assert the superiority of his writing over the oral tradition, thereby presenting his fiction as, paradoxically, a truer representation of orality than could ever be possible within the conventions of oral culture itself. In Carleton's fiction, the assumption is that the 'truth' of oral culture can only be discovered in writing despite the fact that this orality was clearly a fictional construct in his writing.

Indeed, Carleton's fiction was praised for bringing oral culture to account by improving and enlightening social practice through fictional representation. According to Caesar Otway, Carleton's story 'The Station' actually led to a welcome decline in this backward practice in rural Ireland:

'The Station' shows how the writer can deal with the follies that are associated with the religion of the people, without bitterness or ill will. And yet the description has told—since the publication of this abuse, the old fashion of the station dinners has been rapidly passing away—and this quiet and not ill-natured exposure of the practices on these occasions has told more on its objects than could the publication of the severest strictures or the most fearful invective.[33]

Irish popular culture is reformed and improved by means of written representation within fiction, as though the mere act of writing necessarily rationalized and reformed it. In addition, reading awakened people to particular realities, such as abuses within the church or the irrationality of superstition, in a manner that would not be possible in the reception of oral narratives. Otway originally published Carleton's writing as it took the familiar materials and landmarks associated with Irish oral, Catholic culture—corrupt priests, pilgrimages, superstition—and presented them as an authentic, first-hand record of the excesses of oral Catholicism. According to Otway, Carleton's work should be effective

---

[33] [Caesar Otway], 'Our Portrait Gallery: William Carleton—no. XV', *Dublin University Magazine*, 67/97 (Jan. 1841), 71.

in reforming peasant culture because of its 'quiet and not ill-natured exposure' of Irish Catholic practices. The claim of Leadbeater's Lady Seraphina in *The Landlord's Friend* had clearly become widely accepted: 'I believe that examples in narrative are generally more likely to impress young and uncultivated minds than what is merely didactic.'[34] Hence fiction was seen as the most effective means of impressing social change, fictional representation providing a convincing portrayal of a life lived in accordance with enlightenment and reason. However, the representation of an unenlightened and superstitious culture in dire need of enlightenment was a construct of this fiction, a necessary contrast to a professed rationality and order. Carleton's writing demonstrated for Otway how didactic fiction was a more persuasive discourse than, as Otway phrased it, 'the publication of the severest strictures or the most fearful invective'. Carleton's stories would not have reached a mass peasant readership—particularly when published in journals—but it seemed, somehow, to be sufficient that they had simply come into being and existed within the culture, as though that in itself signified the impossibility of the existing oral culture enduring.

In Carleton's writing, certain aspects of Irish orality were supposedly 'preserved' on the printed page while passing out of existence in social life itself, forever serving as a reminder of the abuses which existed in an uncultivated age. Importantly, for Otway, Carleton's writing showed how this material could, only when written and improved, provide the materials for a national culture, having been transformed from living cultural practice into a 'lesson to respect ourselves':

How many legends of our people are to be rescued from the insecurity of the tradition in which they are each generation receiving new tarnish or suffering cruel injury from decay? How many of the events of her past history supply materials for narratives in which we might be taught the great national as well as individual lesson to respect ourselves? Shall these themes be ever unimproved?—And all these rich sources of the romance of Ireland lie like so many of her valleys desolate and waste.[35]

The materials of the Irish oral tradition would ultimately perish entirely unless collected into a written form, in a manner achieved in Carleton's stories, where they could serve a useful, educational, and 'national' purpose. Carleton's writing had demonstrated for Otway how Irish oral

---

34 Mary Leadbeater, *The Landlord's Friend* (Dublin, 1813), 102.
35 [Otway], 'Our Portrait Gallery: William Carleton', 71.

culture could—though, of course, paradoxically—be absorbed within an instructive and nationalizing rhetoric. The fragmentary and broken nature of Irish oral culture was apparently subsumed into the unity of the written story in Carleton's fiction, where it had been transformed into a civilizing and rationalizing force. The structural disunity and digressiveness of Carleton's writing in a story such as 'The Station' does not seem to trouble Otway. Additionally, Carleton's use of explanatory footnotes throughout his fiction surely indicates the impossibility of achieving formal unity at the level of the written page within a society divided by language, religion, and politics. In other words, the absence of unity is confirmed by the impossibility of telling stories without the need to annotate or translate them.

Otway's anxiety that 'many legends' were in need of rescuing 'from the insecurity' of oral culture may have motivated Carleton in the writing of two his later novels: *Willy Reilly: A Tale Founded upon Fact* (1855) and *The Red-Haired Man's Wife* (1889). Both novels present themselves as translations of old Irish ballads into the novel form. In the Preface to *Willy Reilly*, Carleton states that the source of the novel is a 'rude' ballad of the same name from the 'Penal Era' which he has supposedly retrieved from the obscurity of the oral tradition:

The ballad I found in a state of wretched disorder. It passed from one individual to another by ear alone, and the inconsecutive position of the verses, occasioned by inaccuracy of memory and ignorance, has sadly detracted from its genuine force, as it existed in the oral versions of the populace, the narrative was grossly at variance with the regular progress of circumstances which characterize a trial of any kind, but especially a trial as that which it undertakes to describe. The individuals in it for example are made to speak out of place, and it would appear from all the versions I have heard, as if every stanza was assigned its position by lot. This fact, however, I have just accounted for and remedied, by having restored them to their original places, so that the vigourous but rustic bard is not answerable for the confusion to which unprinted poetry, sung by an uneducated people is liable. As the ballad now stands, the character of the poet is satisfactorily vindicated; and the disorder which crept in during the course of time, though strongly calculated to weaken its influence, has never been able to injure its fame. (Preface, *Willy Reilly*, 6)

Carleton claims to correct all previous oral versions of the ballad as he renders it into a literate mode. The confused and distorted state of the ballad, as Carleton discovered it, was apparently owing to the printless nature of oral culture and the utter unreliability of transmission 'by ear alone' amongst the uneducated, illiterate poor. Carleton thus claims to take the ballad from the oral tradition and to rewrite it in two ways: first by altering its order and sequence (or by restoring and correcting it, as he claims) and secondly by reworking it as a novel. Translation supposedly occurs at two levels in Carleton's novel—from the chaotic nature of oral culture into the orderliness of print and from the structural mode of the ballad into that of the novel.[36] Carleton had to set about correcting and amending the narrative order and sequence of events recounted in the ballad, which, he claims, had become utterly askew in the process of oral transmission. The alleged frustrations Carleton experiences with this ballad inadvertently speak for his own difficulties in making his writing conform to the conventions of realism. In effect, Carleton writes the entire ballad himself, claiming that he had to make the text comply with a specific standard of representation. Contrary to the claim of the subtitle—'a tale founded upon fact'—Carleton's novel is based on a fiction of his own creation.

'Willy Reilly' had to be translated from the formlessness of orality into the formal nature of print in order to be restored to its original form as intended by the (nameless) bard who composed it sometime in the eighteenth century. In so doing, writing amends the weaknesses of the tradition in which this poet would have composed and even, in the process, restores originality to the ballad. Carleton has clearly written the ballad himself from a range of literary and historical sources—such as the genealogy of the O'Reilly family appended to the Preface—despite claiming to have restored it. Carleton's work repeatedly presents itself as truthfully representing the condition of oral culture, but this material is clearly fictionalized. His printed version of 'Willy Reilly' is nonetheless presented as the authoritative and original edition of the ballad, its authority further underlined by the medium of print.[37]

In the Preface to *Willy Reilly*, oral culture is depicted as diffuse and formally unsuitable for either a national literature or the processes of modernization. As noted, however, this material was itself largely fabricated by Carleton to provide sentimental melodrama for his novel. The 'national tale' recounted in the novel is an overly sentimental love-story between a Protestant and a Catholic. The Catholic, Willy Reilly, belongs to 'an old and noble Irish family' and 'his ancestors

---

[36] On the theme of ballads and print, see Hugh Shields, 'Printed Aids to Folk Singing, 1700–1900', in Daly and Dickson *The Origins of Popular Literacy in Ireland*, 139–52.

[37] On print and the Irish language, see Cullen, 'Patrons, Teachers and Literacy in Irish' (n. 7 above), 38–40.

had gone through all the vicissitudes and trials, and been engaged with most of the civil broils and wars, which in Ireland, had characterized the reign of Elizabeth' (*Willy Reilly*, 33). The 'colleen bawn', Helen Folliard, belongs to the ascendancy and the narrative is set at the height of the Penal Laws. In order to offset criticism, Carleton notes in his Preface that 'the demerits of his work may be censured on purely literary grounds' (pp. 6–7). The novel demonstrates the extent to which the national tale had become entirely conventional by the late nineteenth century, providing a predictable formula for the writing of an 'Irish' novel. The national tales and ballads produced in the nineteenth century were supposed to create a coherent and unified national culture, brought within the stable and knowable realm of a written discourse, as exemplified, for example, by Charles Gavan Duffy's concept of the Library of Ireland. A novel such as *Willy Reilly* was clearly one of the more unfortunate products of this discourse, but it nonetheless demonstrates the conventionality of the discourse of nationality by the 1850s. When *Willy Reilly* was written, the national tale had clearly become drained of whatever political significance it once possessed, signifying only the banality and political paralysis of Victorian melodrama.

Carleton's last novel, *The Red Haired Man's Wife* (1889), was likewise based on an Irish ballad and presents itself as a form of translation from the Irish-language song to the English-language novel.[38] In his Preface, Carleton claims that 'the air' of Stagan Varagy 'as well as the song itself, seems balanced between a kind of solemn humour and the deepest pathos' (*The Red-Haired Man's Wife*, 2). The song is translated from the Irish words 'staghan varagy' to the English 'the red-haired man's wife' and, in the process, into the flat melodrama of a Victorian novel. In Carleton's translation of the song in the opening section of the novel, he represents the Irish-language original as well:

The first verse of the Irish runs (I do not spell the Irish grammatically, only as it is pronounced in the north of Ireland):

> Vee misha'n la guil feeid a wulssasha,
> Ca hay cas orrum agh staghan varagy,
> Stagan Varagy, grah na colleene
> Horo! ghud dhee thus slan.

---

[38] *The Red-Haired Man's Wife* was published posthumously in 1889. According to Barbara Hayley, the manuscript had been missing and was discovered after Carleton's death. See Barbara Hayley, *A Bibliography of the Writings of William Carleton* (Gerrards Cross, Bucks.: Colin Smythe, 1985), 136–7.

The translation is as follows:

> As I was one day going through this town,
> Who did I meet but staghan varagy (the market lounger)
> Stagan varagy—the beloved of the girls—
> Horo! fare you well!
>
> (*The Red-Haired Man's Wife*, 2)

Here the Irish is translated phonetically, which deepens its estrangement from print and, indeed, the novel. However, Carleton concedes that there is a grammatical form of writing for the Irish language, but he chooses to transcribe it nonetheless within a phonetic idiom. In writing the Irish words in phonetic form, Carleton emphasizes the complicity of the Irish language with orality. Phonetic representations of Irish were a feature of transcription in manuscripts in the eighteenth century. Louis Cullen explains:

Phonetic scripts were unknown in the mid-eighteenth century, emphasizing that the acquaintance with literacy first derived from Irish and from the literary molds of that language. A generation later, circa 1790, the phonetic scripts begin to appear. They were not numerous in the south, but where they appear they emphasized that individuals were drawing their reading knowledge from English, and that they proceeded to literacy in Irish by models already picked up from English. They thus mark a significant deterioration in the quality of Irish.[39]

Cullen claims that 'phonetic scripts' were particularly 'common in the west' of Ireland, the poetry of the region by figures such as Raftery and the Callanan brothers was transcribed in phonetic script. However, Cullen emphasizes that Irish literacy was particularly strong in Munster where 'familiarity with the written language in Irish reached down the scale quite widely'; hence Doyle's goat-herd in Kerry who had clearly learnt Latin through the medium of Irish. Niall Ó Ciosáin cites instances of ballads which were 'printed in a phonetic spelling and based on English-language orthography', a practice directly echoed by Carleton's transcription of 'The Red-Haired Man's Wife'.[40] For Carleton, however, Irish is exemplified through this cumbersome phonetic representation, the language made to appear awkward within the terms of modern print and orthography. In this respect, Irish is supposed to signify what is

---

[39] Cullen, 'Patrons, Teachers and Literacy in Irish', 32.
[40] Ó Ciosáin, 'Printed Popular Literature in Irish 1750–1850' (n. 3 above), 47.

lost and unrepresentable, a convention which is more often than not represented by its absence.

It so happens that 'The Red-Haired Man's Wife' was a song which Carleton's mother sang but which she refused to perform in English, insisting that it could only be truthfully expressed in the Irish language. In his 'General Introduction' to the *Traits and Stories*, Carleton noted that many of the Irish-language songs performed by his mother 'had never been translated' and that 'some valuable ones, both as to words and airs, have perished with her.' He mentions that his mother's family

> were all imbued with a poetical spirit, and some of her immediate ancestors composed in the Irish tongue, several fine old songs, in the same manner as Carolan did; that is, some in praise of a patron or friend, and others to celebrate rustic beauties, that have long since been sleeping in the dust. For this reason she had many old compositions that were almost peculiar to our family, which I am afraid could not now be procured at all, and are consequently lost, I think her uncle, and I believe her grandfather, were the authors of several Irish poems and songs, because I know that some of them she sang, and others she recited ... At this day I am in possession of Irish airs, which none of our best antiquaries in Irish music have heard, except through me, and of which neither they nor I myself know the names. (*TSIP*, i. pp. ix–x.)

The implication is that oral compositions will inevitably perish unless translated into English and preserved in writing. Carleton suggests that oral culture lacks the conventions necessary to preserve and catalogue this material, resulting in the inevitable loss of many poems and songs. Against the wishes of his mother, Carleton translates 'The Red-Haired Man's Wife' into English and even extends the process of translation and, indeed, preservation by rewriting the song as a novel. There is, then, an absence of a writerly form or order for Irish, as though the language can only exist in the realm of speech and be transported as such onto the written page. The perceived orality of the language is simply assumed, though that characteristic is itself made to serve a particular textual, literary function. In Carleton's writing, Irish is isolated and alienated from the English and print which surrounds it. Ó Ciosáin claims that 'the adaptation of the forms of the language to the needs of an audience literate in English and to the exigencies of a printing trade which functioned primarily in English, could be viewed as a distinct cause of the decline of Irish.'[41] With obvious exceptions—such as Charlotte

---

[41] Ibid. 49. For a discussion of the relationship between typeface and national character, see Seamus Deane, *Strange Country*, 100–9.

Brooke's *Reliques of Irish Poetry*, Hardiman's *Irish Minstrelsy*, and the more suspect case of the Kildare Place *Primer* described above—the Irish language is shown to be unrepresentable within the efficient modes of modern print. Carleton's particular transcription of 'The Red-Haired Man's Wife' calls attention to the absence of a written standard as well as typeface for Irish within the novel. It was impossible to represent Irish within an English-language novel without corrupting and distorting it. Seamus Deane notes how 'what was really authentic could not be retrieved and still retain its original condition. It would bear within it—either in footnotes, headnotes, introductions, translations, glossaries—the marks of its historical transmission.'[42] It seems to me that Carleton felt so burdened by the 'historical transmission' that accompanied any act of representation in Ireland that he had long abandoned the effort to achieve authenticity (if such an objective ever really existed). All acts of description or representation were immediately enmeshed in a web of contemporary and historical cultural discourses. Carleton's translation of the ballad hardly redeemed it for his national literature, instead demonstrating the gaps and inconsistencies within his rhetoric of nationality. The novel's mix of genres and styles from the ballad to Victorian melodrama and romance merely highlights the conventionality of Carleton's rhetoric, confirming the arbitrary manner in which nationality was constructed in nineteenth-century writing. Carleton's 'national literature' was, like improvement tracts, a textual convention which implied coherence and unity. The paradox of Carleton's improving discourse was that nationality could only exist in a stable linguistic culture while such unity was, at the same time, essential for creating stability.

In the writing discussed throughout this chapter, the historical condition of Irish is constructed as oral, illiterate, and archaic in order to define both improvement and nationality. In the process, Irish is made to exemplify a range of literary tropes within English-language writing such as loss, sentimentality, and melodrama and shown to be unfit for print, economics, and incorporation within a larger British polity. Carleton's characterization of Irish-language oral culture as fictional and irrational should be seen as a projection of his own difficulties with English-language genres such as the realist novel and tract. The manner in which Irish orality is represented in Carleton's fiction demonstrates the extent to which that culture is a fictionalized construct in so much

[42] Deane, *Strange Country*, 107.

of the writing of the period. Carleton does not celebrate or preserve Irish-language oral culture in his stories and novels. Instead, his writing shows the extent to which that culture was already mediated by a range of discourses and conventions which effectively prevented any kind of authentic representation in writing.

The organization and orderliness implicit in the organic national community envisaged in the writings of Leadbeater, Doyle, and Carleton could not accommodate either Irish or oral storytelling, both considered diffuse and inherently disorderly. The discourses of both improvement and nationality depended on the displacement of the Irish language, which was seen to hinder both the writing of fiction and the attainment of an improved community unified by a shared language and discourse. Both Irish and 'orality' repeatedly present themselves as obstacles to the achievement of modernization and a national literature, while being conventions invoked by the discourse of improvement.

4

Political Discipline and the Rhetoric
of Moderation

IRISH improvement writers emphasized the importance of moderation
in language, bearing, and ideology as a response to religious and political
extremism. Leadbeater and Doyle insisted that progress could not be
articulated, let alone achieved, within the sectarian and party-political
language that shaped public debate in Ireland. The need for toleration
was asserted in order to create a national community without recourse to
religious extremism, traditional party-political antagonisms, and secret
societies. Improvement discourse in part defined itself against secret
societies, asserting its orderliness by comparison with the supposed
anarchy of Ribbonmen and other agrarian groups. This chapter will
demonstrate how the orderly cottage of improvement fiction became
a symbol of a stable nation state and, in turn, of a coherent national,
or even nationalist, community, as envisaged in the 1840s by Thomas
Davis. It was assumed that an organized cottage would instil personal
and, by extension, political discipline, thereby preventing both domestic
violence and secret-society activity while providing the basis for the
development of civil society.

Carleton's writing expresses a determination to displace agrarian unrest with the stability of an improved society, to subsume violence in
Ireland completely into the rationality, indeed, domesticity, of the printed page. In his *Autobiography*, Carleton recounts how he was inducted
into Ribbonism by chance at an *infare* ('the haling home of a newly-
married bride to the house of her husband') where he was 'forced ... to
take two glasses of poteen' (*Autobiography*, 76). After being led behind a
ditch, Carleton was confronted 'by a red-haired fellow named Hugh Roe
McCahy' who had in his possession 'a *manual*, a book of Roman Catholic
devotion' which 'greatly puzzled' Carleton as he knew McCahy to be illiterate (p. 77). This illiterate man inducted Carleton into Ribbonism by
having him swear an oath on the *manual* he could not himself read. The

oath itself was not of course written, but was 'got by heart' by McCahy. Carleton then describes the Ribbon oath in the following manner:

there was a vagueness and a want of object in this ridiculous oath which gave conclusive evidence that it must have proceeded from a very ignorant source. I subsequently made inquiries into its origin, but could never ascertain the name of any man possessed of the slightest claim to respectability in connection with it. It originated with, and was confined to, the very lowest dregs of the people. (*Autobiography*, 76–80)

The origin of this oath amongst 'the very lowest dregs' of the rural poor is typically obscure and disreputable. Carleton's Ribbonmen are rarely represented as literate even though the local schoolmaster features prominently in their ranks.[1] However, as shown in Chapter 2, even hedge schools were depicted as illiterate institutions, the presence of certain printed materials strengthening orality rather than displacing it. In Carleton's *Autobiography*, Ribbonism—'a senseless but most mischievous system'—is steeped in ignorance, orality, and Catholicism (*Autobiography*, 77). Carleton even claims that 'the whole Catholic population, with the exception of the aged heads of families, was affiliated to Ribbonism' (p. 78). The orality, superstition, and backwardness of secret societies is insisted upon, evoking a gothic threat that in time should be swept away by modernization.

Improvement writers proclaim that domestic and agricultural improvement would eradicate the tension that found expression in extreme rhetoric. Improved characters and settings were represented in order to convey the possibility of a harmonious and domesticated rural order, free of the political difficulties that characterized both past and present rural life. A placid, moderate tone is shown to resolve disputes with ease and effectiveness. In Bardin's *Cottage Fireside*, Jenny comments to her grandmother how 'if the house was—throwing out of the windows, a word from you would settle it again—you speak so mild and gentle, that if one did not hear what you said, your very looks would persuade one you were in the right.'[2] Improvement fiction was partly an attempt to create a textual rhetoric of moderation that served as an antidote to both rural disorder and despotism. Bardin was trying to demonstrate

---

[1] Tom Garvin claims that the semi-literacy of secret-society notices suggests that 'hedge schoolmasters were less universally involved than was sometimes suggested.' See 'Defenders, Ribbonmen and Others', in C. H. E. Philpin (ed.), *Nationalism and Popular Protest in Ireland* (Cambridge: Cambridge University Press, 1987), 240.

[2] Charles Bardin, *The Cottage Fireside* (Dublin, 1826), 10.

how social stability could be achieved through education and example, rather than coercion and extremism. Leadbeater's *Anecdotes Taken from Real Life for the Improvement of Children* attempts to demonstrate how improvement rhetoric could achieve social order:

Afflicted as she has long been by the despotism of iron ignorance, and the exasperations of civil and religious discord, what could have appeased these convulsions, or assimilated the jarring elements of intestine commotion, but the spirit of appropriated instruction, calmly infusing religious and moral principles and pacifying the angry waves by the efficacy of that spirit which said to the sea, 'Be still', and it was hushed into tranquility.[3]

In the world of improvement fiction, a placid and cultivated language pacifies temper and discord. In a similar vein, Leadbeater warns her readers elsewhere against 'flogging' children, harsh discipline creating a rupture between parent and child that is often impossible to resolve in later years.[4] In all her pamphlets, Leadbeater repeatedly invokes domestic metaphors to articulate her concept of a progressive liberal state which would be free of both (colonial?) despotism and insurrection. As indicated throughout this study, that call for moderation was nonetheless often expressed in the most extreme of terms.

In *Cottage Dialogues*, Leadbeater reminds her readers of the United Irishmen and 1798, warning against the temptation to become involved in secret societies. As Tim warns his less improved neighbour:

No good ever comes of such people as us having secrets … Let us remember the Rebellion, and how many people were deceived with fine talking, and lost their lives, and all that they had in the world; they thought they were doing great feats, when they were just made a cat's paw of by those that did not care a straw what became of them later.[5]

Leadbeater cautions that 'fine talking' as opposed to plain instruction invariably leads to hardship and loss, not the possibility of the comfortable home and savings in the bank guaranteed by improvement. The deceptive 'fine talking' (or extravagant orality) of secret societies is compared with the utter practicality and openness of the improvement advice dispensed throughout the *Dialogues*. In effect, the pamphlet presents the reader with a choice between an oral and literate life, the

---

[3] Mary Leadbeater, Preface, *Anecdotes Taken from Real Life for the Improvement of Children, with Appropriate Engravings* (Dublin, 1809), p. iii.

[4] Mary Leadbeater, *Short Stories for Cottagers Intended to Accompany Cottage Dialogues* (Dublin, 1813), 48–9.

[5] Mary Leadbeater, *Cottage Dialogues* (Dublin, 1811), 146–7.

former frequently idle, political, and impoverished and the latter busy, contented, and prosperous; the one unstable and threatening and the other secure and safe. Improvement defines itself against secret societies by eschewing overtly political rhetoric and focusing instead on domestic and agricultural economy. The stability of the modernized cottage and farm of improvement fiction was always represented against the chaos and confusion of the pre-modern. Instead of offering political redemption or promises of 'liberty', improvement fiction instructed in the means of achieving domestic comfort within the particular, and limited, material constraints of pre-Famine Ireland. As such, it opposed the materiality of work and profit to politics and history, suggesting that the impoverishment of the rural poor could not be resolved by political means. These pamphlets insist that economic development would naturally eradicate the tensions of rural society. In keeping with this, progress was itself to be brought into existence by means of a convincing rhetoric of improvement.

In Leadbeater's fictional cottage, women are charged with the domestic organization of the home, ensuring that proper order prevails in all matters from household hygiene to fixed mealtimes. The impeccable domestic skills of Rose in *Cottage Dialogues* successfully placated and civilized her husband's once rash and violent temper. Amicable relations between Rose and Tim eventually yielded to broader domestic and economic stability on their cottage and farm. Similarly, Leadbeater advises, improvement throughout the countryside, diffused by enterprising landlords and middling farmers, would discourage violent, political, and sectarian tendencies amongst the peasantry. Poor management in the home—the responsibility of the woman of the house—was, it seems, at the root of domestic violence and, the *Dialogues* warn, agrarian unrest in rural Ireland generally was the result of the neglectful administration of many estates by landowners and agents.

Leadbeater set herself the task of imagining a responsible and committed landowning class, attuned to the discourses of political and domestic economy. A resident landowner should exemplify the domestic values of hard work, prudence, and frugality that would be simultaneously disseminated throughout the estate by means of personal example and education. In *The Landlord's Friend* (1813), Leadbeater attempted to persuade landowners of the urgency of reform if civil order were to be achieved and maintained in the countryside. In the process, Leadbeater's pamphlet implicitly condemns traditional landlord culture in Ireland, establishing Squire Hartley and Lady Seraphina as the improving, progressive voices in the text. These characters are supposed to convince Squire Wilfort and Lady Charlotte of the necessity and even particular pleasures of improvement. Hartley provides the liberal argument for the reform of estates, while Lady Seraphina's property becomes an example and working model of reformed landlordism. By means of their loyalty, cleanliness, and productivity, the improved tenantry on this exemplary estate signify the immense value of residence, work, and benevolence.

Liberal reform was embedded within a textual culture and could only be achieved through mass literacy. The creation of shared values across the traditional divides of religion and class required the existence of a literate public bound by a fixed frame of reference. A liberal community could only be formed by textual means, the creation of consensus made possible by the stabilizing nature of the printed tracts and pamphlets of improvement discourse. The provision of education on estates throughout the country was thus essential, but the traditional prejudices of the ascendancy had to be overcome first:

Squire W: In my opinion, more harm than good is done by instructing the poor; they get hold of newspapers, become political, grow idle, dissatisfied, and disloyal. Better let them drudge on, happy in ignorance.

Squire H: Sir, we do not want to keep a great body of the community in ignorance to secure their loyalty, nor to prevent them from knowing the state of their own country. The idle, dissatisfied and disloyal will often be found amongst the most ignorant.[6]

For Wilfort, popular literacy is invariably equated with the idleness and politics of the lower classes. Wilfort associates lower-class literacy with popular print and disaffection, invoking ascendancy memory of the distribution of radical newspapers and tracts in the 1790s. Improvement reform was distrusted by many landowners as, in the terms of Wilfort, it could be 'turned to seditious purposes' and become generalized 'disaffection with the government'.[7] However, Leadbeater has Hartley assert that improvement, which would bring together varying constituencies and religions in the shared pursuit of economic prosperity, would actually compel the poor 'to feel increasing attachment to the government, when they can look up to the ranks above them as friends and protectors'.[8] Leadbeater insisted that improvement education would protect against dissatisfaction and disloyalty, dissolving traditional anxieties by

---

[6] Mary Leadbeater, *The Landlord's Friend* (Dublin, 1813), 35.
[7] Ibid. 25–6   [8] Ibid. 26.

means of the rewards of domestic order and material gain. After all, Lady Seraphina successfully created an industrious, satisfied, and loyal tenantry on her estate, contentment embodied in the tasteful cottages and gardens that are scattered throughout the property.

In the voice of unreformed landlordism, Wilfort claims that the Irish peasantry are the 'reverse' of their English counterparts, who are consistently 'steady, regular and punctual'.[9] Hartley retorts, however, that the absence of such characteristics amongst the Irish peasantry is the fault of those 'of a higher rank' who 'partake too much of that unfixed character of which you complain in the lower. We enter warmly into plans of benevolence but these plans as often fail from our own want of stability, as from any other cause'.[10] The dissipation of the lower orders was thus traced back to the upper classes, peasants helplessly emulating the excesses and weaknesses of aristocratic behaviour. Leadbeater recommends that Irish landlords follow the example of their exemplary English peers and, in time, their tenants would also reform and become just like 'the English peasantry'. The decadence of the ascendancy had to be redressed, the indulgent 'convivial parties' of the big house replaced by frugality and responsible administration.[11] By adopting the demeanour of a Squire Hartley or Lady Seraphina, landlords could once again assert control over the economic and political state of the countryside.

The pamphlet is designed to instil enthusiasm for improvement amongst the landed gentry by demonstrating the visible benefits of reform on the fictional estate of Lady Seraphina. Leadbeater insists that only a rhetoric of improvement could possibly endure within the fraught ideological climate of early nineteenth-century Ireland. Traditional landlordism—the pamphlet repeatedly warns—is dangerously unviable in a modernizing economy, such unviablility expressing itself repeatedly in outbursts of agrarian unrest. Like *Cottage Dialogues*, liberalism is embedded in the very structure of *The Landlord's Friend*: liberal and conservative views are each embodied in the opposing voices within the dialogues, but the more enlightened (and liberal) argument always gains ascendancy, convincing—as in this instance—by rationality on the one hand and 'empirical' example on the other.

Leadbeater warns landowners against their characteristic indolence or 'ennui', evident in the rampant neglectfulness of so many estates. The improving Lady Seraphina comments to Lady Charlotte that 'young

⁹ Mary Leadbeater, *The Landlord's Friend* (Dublin, 1813), 24.   ¹⁰ Ibid. 25.
¹¹ Ibid. 25.

ladies' could 'unite in establishing' schools for the poor, which would be altogether so fulfilling that it would prove to be 'a never failing resource against *ennui*'.[12] In this instance, Edgeworth's novel *Ennui* (1809) has clearly yet again worked its way into Leadbeater's representation of ascendancy life. In *Ennui*, improvement is presented as the most effective antidote to aristocratic *ennui*, diffusing the oppressive, accumulated boredom that afflicts the protagonist, Lord Glenthorn. Typically, Edgeworth sends her upper-class characters to work, forcing them to break with traditional propensities to idleness, leisure and, invariably, depressiveness (or Romantic melancholia?). Edgeworth shows how the frightening isolation of the Irish landlord on his country estate is offset by work and absorption in the economic management of property. Improvement not only transforms the economy of estates but provides lasting fulfilment for individual landowners themselves. In *The Landlord's Friend*, Lady Seraphina personifies how the activity of improvement is suffused with meaning and fulfilment when compared with the emptiness and monotony of traditional aristocratic culture.

The satisfactions of improvement extend beyond the fulfilment achieved from the responsible administration of estates. Lady Charlotte is particularly struck by the manner in which Lady Seraphina is admired by her tenants: 'Why this is something. I doubt there are more sparkling eyes at this morning's party, than are here turned upon you, Lady Seraphina. I had rather awaken such feelings, as are displayed here, than all the gallantry of all the beaux there, and you know I don't detest admiration'.[13] The pleasures of the plainness of improvement even outweigh those of courtly admiration and 'gallantry', providing genuine contentment as compared with the essentially shallow satisfaction to be obtained from the artificial displays of courtly society: 'Happy Lady Seraphina! Here she comes, more lovely, adorned with the radiance of benevolence, than when she graces her jewels at court'.[14] As shown in Chapter 1, meaning and truth supposedly reside in plainness, unfussy exteriors, and felt experience as 'benevolence' and improvement radiate from within the reformed body. The need for bodily restraint and control within an improved economy is emphasized, all adornment shown to be entirely meaningless by contrast with the plain truths of improvement. Lady Seraphina's conversations with her tenants seem to eliminate traditional suspicions and hostilities while enforcing her power and authority across the estate. It seems that the authority of the landed

---

[12] Ibid. 97.   [13] Ibid. 62–3.   [14] Ibid. 68.

class would be more secure within this form of benevolent landlordism. The power of the resident, improving landowner is invariably more stable than that of the neglectful absentee. In this respect, the improving landowner restores the traditional power structure of the countryside through liberal reform of social and economic practice and, in so doing, creates the very kind of stability that would discourage the formation of secret societies amongst the lower classes.

Leadbeater confidently asserts that discontent can be resolved once the peasantry are brought within an improved economy. Lady Seraphina recounts Lord Hardwicke's claim that 'the rebellion in Ireland could not have occurred had every county possessed' improving landowners.[15] Rebellion, in other words, could have been averted by the existence of an improvement ethos in every community. Leadbeater has Lady Seraphina declare that she doubts that 'those who feel themselves happy'—fulfilled by the fiction of improvement—'will ever be unwilling to resign that feeling for an uncertainty'.[16] That 'uncertainty' was exemplified by the rhetoric of secret societies (and republicanism) which was seen to propagate entirely unrealistic expectations through 'fine talking'. The task of the improving landowner was to instil certainty, eliminating the very instability that gave rise to lower-class politics by diffusing a rhetoric of moderation. As Lady Charlotte comments of Lady Seraphina's estate, 'It is certain that if your attention to your tenants was universally followed, we need never dread civil discord.'[17] It was presumed that the mere existence of improvement discourse protected against political upheaval by providing a viable rhetorical and ideological alternative to both popular culture and politics.

In *The Landlord's Friend*, Leadbeater called for the comprehensive reform of the ascendancy. Her pleas were reiterated in Martin Doyle's *Irish Cottagers* (1830), which accused landlords of a 'reprehensible negligence with respect to their own and their tenant's interests'. Doyle chastised Irish landlords, the majority of whom were absentee and officiating over estates encumbered by debt and backward agricultural methods. In such a context, the prevalence of agrarian unrest was to be expected:

I wish that the really influential, and well educated part of our landed proprietors were more generally resident, in such case, the great blessing of domestic peace might be expected—the employment of our poor would be more steady and

---

[15] Leadbeater, *The Landlord's Friend*, 112.   [16] Ibid.
[17] Ibid.

extended, and we all know that active occupation is ever accompanied by good order, and tranquility; but as matters now unfortunately stand in many parts of Ireland, it is not a subject of surprise that a neglected, unemployed, and half-starved peasantry, should be ready for every novelty and every mischief.[18]

According to Doyle, 'active occupation' necessarily instils 'domestic peace' in the countryside, the prevalence of secret societies attributed to the idleness and hunger of a 'neglected' peasantry. Landlords possessed the ability to eradicate idleness and therefore politicization by becoming resident and modernizing their estates. In so doing, they would provide ample employment for themselves as well as their tenantry. Doyle assures the reader that improvement reform would, in time, entail homogenization of social practice, which should eradicate all 'turbulence and party dissension'. Homogenization prepared the way for the development of capitalism, the point at which 'peace, plenty and prosperity, become the characteristics of the land' rather than discord, hunger, and scarcity.[19] In Doyle's mind, improvement would gradually depoliticize the landscape, contributing to the creation of a cohesive and unified rural culture bound by economic interests rather than religious and political obsessiveness. In this sense, improvement should be seen as a form of rhetorical and practical preparation for a liberal market economy in which differences of class and religion would, it seems, no longer be relevant.

Both Leadbeater and Doyle insisted, then, that resident, improving landowners, busily advising their tenantry and investing capital, were unlikely to encounter any political trouble on their estates. However, M. R. Beames has shown how agricultural improvement in Tipperary was the cause of the widespread agrarian unrest there in the 1830s. Secret societies were most active in prosperous agricultural regions such as Tipperary where farmers 'had begun to introduce improved stock, the use of clover, the modern ploughs and harrows'.[20] Beames describes how the victims of Whiteboy assassinations in Tipperary tended to be landlords who possessed 'an improving commercial attitude' and those who benefited in some measure from agricultural development, be it occupying the holdings 'from which the allegedly less industrious have

---

[18] Martin Doyle, *Irish Cottagers* (Dublin, 1833), 53–4.
[19] Martin Doyle, *An Address to the Landlords of Ireland on Subjects Connected with the Melioration of the Lower Classes* (Dublin, 1831), 18–19.
[20] M. R. Beames, 'Rural Conflict in Pre-Famine Ireland: Peasant Assassinations in Tipperary, 1837–1847', in Philpin, *Nationalism and Popular Protest*, 265.

been ejected' or working within the improved economy in such positions as ploughman or steward.[21] According to this analysis, secret societies were a product of the 'strong commercial pressures' of an improving economy and not an atavistic force lingering at the margins of rural life.[22] Beames's research suggests that agrarian unrest was not dissolved by agricultural improvement, but was, in some cases at least, caused by it. In this sense, secret societies were implicit in economic development and not a force that could be overcome by the processes of modernization and reform. However, improvement discourse consistently depicts political violence as pre-modern rather than intrinsic to the capitalization of agriculture. In improvement discourse, a rhetoric of domestication and economic progress is shown to eradicate both domestic and political violence, softening tempers and discord.

In her glossary to *Cottage Dialogues*, Edgeworth expresses irritation to 'the English reader' that this rhetoric of domesticity—deemed essential to the creation of a liberal public sphere and, indeed, to the proper development of the novel as a genre—did not yet prevail in Ireland:

All the friends to the British Empire will wish to raise in Ireland that English spirit of independence, which maintains, that 'every man's house is his castle', which scorns to open a gate even for his majesty, unless his majesty (God bless him!) *axes civil*. The more every man is made to think and feel that his house is his castle, the more zealous he will be in the defence of his castle, the more attached to 'that dear hut', his home. This just spirit of independence is far, very far different from a discontented, disaffected temper; far more safe to trust, as well as more pleasant to see than the sneaking, cringing, 'as your honour plases!'—'Sure whatever your honour decrees me!'—'I'll leave it all to your honour!'—'It's not for the likes of us to be speaking to your honour's honour!'—'I'd let your honour walk over me before I'd say a word, good or bad.'[23]

The more civilized, liberal values such as domestic 'independence' are instilled, the less suspiciously obsequious ('sneaking, cringing') will be the manner of speech and behaviour of the peasant Irish. The feudal form of communication between landlords and peasants had to be replaced by a civil mode of interaction, which would be achieved by the existence of shared domestic values across explicit class divisions.

[21] Beames, 'Rural Conflict in Pre-Famine Ireland', 267.
[22] Ibid. 265.
[23] Maria Edgeworth, Glossary to Mary Leadbeater, *Cottage Dialogues* (London, 1811), 332.

Edgeworth suggests that discontent and disaffection are themselves embedded within the overly convoluted and intensely oral speech of so many Irish peasants. It seems that discontent was not only evident in acts of agrarian unrest, but was deeply ingrained within the very idiom of the Irish peasantry. Outmoded political relations are inscribed within this form of speech, suggesting immense social divisions between landlords and tenants not yet united by the shared language of domesticity and markets. It seems that for Edgeworth the hyperbolic mode of address of the Irish peasantry obscures the existence of dark discontent, the extravagance of obsequious speech at once expressing and masking disloyal, even murderous, tendencies.

Improved communities would be unified by a shared discipline and morality rather than riven by political and religious antagonisms. For improvement writers, the instilling of discipline was essential within a popular culture dominated by the public house and the consumption of alcohol, the latter always linked to the excitement of passion and temper. In *The Cottage Fireside* (1826), Charles Bardin warns the reader that 'when the liqour once gets into your head, all thought is gone, you are no longer master of yourself, but a fit instrument in the hands of the devil, to pull destruction on your own head and that of others.'[24] Once consumed, alcohol instantly works to suppress self-control and reason, leaving one susceptible to all kinds of dangerous temptations which are frequently political in nature. The reader is warned of the possibility—even inevitability—of being drawn into the ranks of secret societies when under the influence of alcohol:

Ill-designing men who wish to make mischief, and fish in troubled waters, take these opportunities, when a number of young fellows are got together, and warm with liquor, to make foolish harangues, about things which they nor their hearers understand; and under pretence of revealing some important secret, get them to take oaths of secrecy—many have I known unfortunately drawn in this way, into plots and combinations, which they would never have entered into, had they been sober; you may easily judge what sort of secrets these are, which require such means to conceal them.[25]

'Plots and combinations' thrive in the presence of alcohol when rational defences are suppressed and people easily seduced into the swearing of oaths. Orality and drinking are intimately linked: idealistic talk and 'foolish harangues' easily entice the drunken into oath-bound

---

[24] Bardin, *The Cottage Fireside*, 96.   [25] Ibid. 96–7.

societies and, before long, the perpetration of political crime. Bardin affirms the necessity of transforming Irish popular culture by linking the consumption of alcohol directly to the consequent development of secret societies.[26] In so doing, Bardin forges the necessary connections between orality and violence, each irrevocably bound up with the other. As in all improvement pamphlets, links between political idealism and orality are firmly established. In fact, all idealism is shown to thrive in those conditions produced by the absence or breakdown of a specific mode of rationality. As such, this so-called idealism is equated with both orality and barbarity. Restraint in the consumption of alcohol would correspond with the bodily discipline and order deemed essential for improvement reform, providing a way out of the chaos or messiness produced by 'idle' political speculation.

Much like Hannah More, Leadbeater and Shackleton warn their readers in *Tales for Cottagers* (1814) that physical beauty was fragile and could be readily destroyed by the presence of a bad temper: 'a fine face', for example, could be distorted by 'passion' which can, in time, leave 'traces behind it'.[27] Leadbeater and Shackleton typically equated physical beauty and material ostentation with passion—often expressed through politics or a violent temper—which they were eager to replace with moderation. In *The Pedlars* (1826), the model domestic woman, Rose, is described as 'not what is called a pretty girl'; however, the reader is assured that 'it was pleasant to look on her benevolent countenance, her sweet smile, her smooth and open forehead, with her clear intelligence, yet rather thoughtful brow.'[28] Improved women are never endowed with physical beauty or passion, such traits threatening the possibility of domestic and broader social stability. Plain women reign over an improved domestic economy, moderation in appearance confirming the necessary physical and moral discipline essential for survival. In improvement fiction, 'pretty', showy women are never allowed to marry sensible men and they are frequently killed off, inevitable victims of the process of modernization.

Restraint had to extend to one's entire social bearing, determining composure in public and ensuring a rigidity in all forms of expression. In *The Pedlars*, for example, the narrator states that Darby, a model improving character

---

[26] Bardin, *The Cottage Fireside*, 98.
[27] Mary Leadbeater and Elizabeth Shackleton, *Tales for Cottagers* (Dublin, 1814), 134.
[28] Mary Leadbeater, *The Pedlars* (Dublin, 1826), 26.

disliked ... loud laughter, which, he said, was not proof of good temper or happiness, for he had known those who seemed all spirits, and full of jokes at some times, at others sink into dejection or peevishness ready enough to hang up their fiddles at home: a saying applied to those who are not so pleasant in their own families as elsewhere.[29]

The need to avoid any kind of emotional extreme—be it joy or sorrow—was emphasized; a balanced temperament was presented as the ideal psychological state, suggesting harmony and order rather than turmoil and chaos. Excessive emotion suggested instability, the presence of high spirits too readily implied the opposing condition of despondency. Those extremes of elation and depression were exemplary of the very same conditions that gave rise to aestheticism and political dissatisfaction, which could, in turn, combine (producing disastrous consequences). The need to move beyond rigid oppositions and inhabit a linguistic and emotional middle ground was deemed essential for economic progress and the avoidance of political discontent, as though extremism and difference could be obliterated by liberal moderation.

Many of the pamphlets sought to illustrate the immense benefits to be gained from a close relationship between landlords and tenants. A shared commitment to improvement would erase many of the differences that had separated these two classes in Irish society, unifying by means of a common language (English), shared values, economic interests, and even farming practices. Landowners could reassert their power in the community by redefining their role in terms of education and commerce. The ideal landlord would be educated in agricultural theory and pass on relevant knowledge to his tenants. This educational role was central to the identity of the improving landlord. As Richard Drayton describes it, 'the virtuous landlords could preside over the perfection of learning and landscape as well as manuring and draining.'[30] Leadbeater tried to promote this practice in the extended 1814 edition of *Cottage Dialogues* by representing the ideal landlord–tenant relationship through the exemplary characters, Barney and Mr Seymour. Barney himself describes the benefits of his relationship with his landlord in the following manner:

'I am entirely obliged to your honour. Gentlemen have no notion what good they might do to poor people, by considering for them, and advising them; for gentlemen have such opportunities of seeing how work is done in different

[29] Ibid. 18–19.
[30] Richard Drayton, *Nature's Government: Science, Imperial Britain, and the 'Improvement' of the World* (Oxford: Oxford University Press, 1997), 60.

places, and of reading in books about the nature of land, and corn, and cattle, that when they give their mind to the like, and live among their tenants, and put them on good methods, they are a blessing to their country.'[31]

In this dialogue, the ideal nature of the landlord–tenant relationship is described: a peasant can rely on the landlord's agricultural knowledge and educated insight, which in turn allows the landlord to redefine his role in the community from that of despised absentee to respected paternalistic figurehead. In this imagined economy, both landlord and tenant benefit significantly from a mutually advantageous social and, indeed, economic relationship. Landlords can successfully and easily convey commercial values to their tenantry through these conversations and exchanges. Communication of this nature should resolve traditional suspicions, removing all cause of agrarian unrest as landlord and tenant discover themselves to be equally committed to abundant harvests and efficient farming techniques. Improvement discourse presented itself as a solution to the seemingly endemic divisions in Irish society by depicting (indeed, imagining) how social life would appear in the absence of religious and political tensions. In the process, it sought to provide a model for this social relationship by positing the existence of a supposedly neutral language and public discourse of information and economics. The neutral language of these discourses would, of course, reliably function in a direct, mimetic manner. In this linguistic economy, ambiguity would recede and, in the process, a form of unmediated communication would be brought into existence.

In Doyle's work of short fiction, *Irish Cottagers*, the exchanges between Mick Kinshella and Mr Bruce are presented as an example of effective communication across class and religious divides. Mick Kinshella is an improving tenant who receives advice and direction from Mr Bruce, the resident and improving landlord:

While Mick was engaged in throwing down these mouldering banks, Mr. Bruce rode into the field, for this gentleman was constantly encouraging and directing the rural improvements in his estate, as well as promoting the household comforts of his tenants; and seemed highly pleased with Mick's economy of his land.[32]

Following the advice of Arthur Young, Mr Bruce awards prizes to his more progressive and improved tenants. The knowledge passed from landlord to tenant is shown to strengthen the bond between these two

---

[31] Leadbeater, *Cottage Dialogues*, pt 2, 71.   [32] Doyle, *Irish Cottagers*, 7.

social groups. The narrative recounts how this tenant 'acquired much solid knowledge from his benevolent landlord, which he immediately applied to practice, to the surprise of his neighbours, who could not be persuaded that he was not making a fool of himself by changing the *ould method'*.[33] This tenant never fails to follow his landlord's advice and inevitably achieves increased fertility and production on his farm. In this dialogue, there is no ambiguity or confusion in the relation and subsequent reception of instruction and advice. The benefits of these transparent exchanges are always embodied unambiguously in an abundance of crops and the inevitable success of various farming ventures. The dialogues attempt to demonstrate that language can be plain, that signifier can be fixed to the signified. The fruits of such linguistic unity are always evident in palpable empirical terms from increased yields to greater domestic comfort and contentment. In this instance, Mick Kinshella is shown to have more in common with his landlord than his immediate, disdainful neighbours: the common ground between landlord and tenant exemplifies the possibility of a new social, linguistic, and political order in the countryside, which will displace older, barbaric, and regressive alliances.

Doyle tries to assure the reader that his representation of the relationship between Mr Bruce and Mick Kinshella was not purely fictional and was already established, in practice, on estates throughout the country. However, such assurances only confirm the prevalence of anxiety regarding the possibility of rural modernization in the terms established by improvement writers (while calling attention to the fictionality of the representation):

the gentry in many parts of this kingdom are very actively at work as improvers of the soil, and of the people; and I really believe, in spite of the vulgar prejudice in favour of good old times, that we are much better educated, and more usefully disposed, than our forefathers were. The squireens have nearly become extinct, and gentlemen of rank and property are beginning to estimate aright the advantages of improving their properties by *personal effort* — as to myself, I perceive very clearly the beneficial effects of my residence here both to myself and to others.[34]

Doyle seeks to banish nostalgia for the mindless leisure of the ascendancy past in favour of the expediency of attending to the practical duties of the present. According to Doyle, more Irish landlords were 'beginning

---

[33] Ibid. 10.   [34] Ibid. 55.

to estimate' the practicality and, indeed, morality of improvement and residence. However, such realization was only ever about to begin or occur without ever being put into practice in a truly significant manner. In other words, improvement stubbornly endured in its fictional state without ever achieving comprehensive application in practice. Significantly, the continual postponement of this modernized society is characteristic of all improvement writing. The very existence of improvement fiction and discourse is itself an indication of the absence of such a culture in the Irish countryside. Despite Doyle's effort to attend to the requirements of the present and future, his own writing represents, by its very nature, the continual postponement of such a society on the terms stipulated.

The perpetual failure of the landlord class to reform their estates in the manner of a Mr Bruce or Mr Seymour is emphasized in Doyle's *Address to the Landlords of Ireland on Subjects Connected with the Melioration of the Lower Classes* (1831). In this pamphlet, Irish landlords are accused of a dangerous neglect of economic and social responsibility, no doubt contributing to the widespread agrarian unrest in Ireland. Doyle was troubled by the appalling condition of many estates:

The want of enterprise is another distinguishing mark to which many of you, my lords and gentlemen ... must plead guilty. The embarrassed circumstances of numerous estates, resulting in many cases, from dissipation and extravagance; the mortgages, the judgments, the strictness of life tenantry, and the absence of capital prevent the enterprising improvements which British proprietors so munificently undertake and efficiently execute.[35]

Many Irish estates were presided over by dissipated, extravagant proprietors, and were excessively encumbered by debt. A commercial, enterprising ethos was evidently absent in rural Ireland within the broader context of the industrialization of agriculture that was occurring on English and Scottish estates. Doyle urges Irish landlords to become resident and modernize their properties, like their counterparts in England and Scotland. According to Doyle, Scotland had been, like Ireland, 'once infested with a petty gentry, which pressed against the moral energies of the people'. Over time, the Scottish gentry reformed, becoming 'an altered class in every respect' and, naturally reflecting their social superiors, the lower orders consequently arose 'from their comparable debasement'.[36] Scotland is repeatedly cited as a model for

---

[35] Doyle, *An Address to the Landlords of Ireland*, 16–17.   [36] Ibid. 24.

Ireland, and Scottish characters occasionally make appearances in Irish improvement pamphlets to personify modernization and progress. In Leadbeater's and Shackleton's *Tales for Cottagers* (1814), the local land-lord employs a Scottish ploughman, named Andrew, who discovers that 'the warm and generous Irish heart was open to advice when it was given in a gentle, kind manner, without assuming a superiority.'[37] Andrew eventually marries a local woman, demonstrating how the supposed warmth of the Irish can be successfully united with the rationality of the Scottish. This particular Scottish rationality is defined by the ploughman when he claims that 'in my country ... the same hand can guide the plough and the pen. We can cultivate our fields and calculate the expenses of cultivation.'[38] Scotland is presented as the standard which Ireland can and should attain after embarking on agricultural and moral improvement.

Doyle's improvement was expressed in terms of an attempt to rein-state an order believed to be both lost and threatened despite having never existed. Improvement was a means of preserving a rhetoric of the rural within a context of increased urbanization and industrializa-tion. Paradoxically, the countryside, it seems, could only be preserved in all its pastoral (and non-political) simplicity by modernizing and industrializing it.

The project for improvement as expressed by writers such as Lead-beater, Doyle, and Bardin worked to depoliticize the countryside by rewriting public discourse in Ireland within the terms of modernization and progress. The rhetoric of these texts belies the belief that politics and, indeed, history, could be subsumed into cultivated gardens, clean kitchens, and competing for a prize when the landlord's wife came to inspect the cottage and garden every month. An image of pastoral, rus-tic life—pervaded by tidy, busy peasants, and the 'pleasant' sounds of rural industry rather than the noise of political activity—informed these practical instructional dialogues. Implicit in this representation is a desire to reinvigorate a threatened rural aesthetic which never actually existed in the first place. Leadbeater's improvement writing was com-mitted to the restoration of a 'traditional' concept of rural life, though 'improved' by technology and the depoliticization of the rural popula-tion. In a sense, improved agriculture was the only means by which a particular representation of country life could be preserved. Leadbeater's

---

[37] Leadbeater and Shackleton, *Tales for Cottagers*, 158.
[38] Ibid. 156.

representation of a stable, fertile, and productive rural culture was rooted in a literary and visual expectation of the countryside rather than in a particular historical memory. The countryside at the heart of improvement discourse was both nostalgic and modern; nostalgia, in this instance, impelling modernization. Irish improvement writers were concerned with the preservation of a particular representation of rural life, seen to be threatened by both politics and the development of 'modern' genres such as the novel, not permitted—as discussed in Chapter 1—into the library on Lady Seraphina's estate in *The Landlord's Friend*. As that chapter demonstrated improvement fiction was itself clearly novelistic both in its desire to cultivate a middle-class culture and in assertion of a particular form and order. In Leadbeater's representation, improvement rendered an implicit 'natural' unity explicit, modernization restoring the countryside to an 'original' harmonious order. In *The Landlord's Friend*, the presence of decorative features in estate cottages prompts Lady Seraphina to comment that 'when the poor attempt at taste, it is evident that they are not discontented or oppressed.' This implies, in turn, that political discontent was an artificial imposition on the natural order of things.[39] In the fictional world of improvement discourse, political tensions vanish within a retrieved natural order. Improvement would ensure that the peasantry became generally uninterested in politics as they committed themselves to the demands of work and the market. These pamphlets seek to show how the basis of agrarian unrest is eradicated by means of modernization and the ease of communication between landlord and tenant, which was made possible by homogenization of language, morality, and public debate. Improvement would eliminate the endemic fixation on local issues, neighbourly disputes, and resentments that supposedly sustained the culture of secret societies. The inwardness and narrowness of locality would be translated into the broad, outward reach of the market.

In *Common Sense for Common People* (1834), Doyle depicts a particular secret society ('Whitefeet'), which is entirely immersed in local disputes and caters to all the petty jealousies and resentments of its membership:

The Whitefoot system of desperate nocturnal outrages commenced about this time, and unhappily afforded to every unprincipled fellow (who had a grudge against a more successful neighbour, or wished to prevent any one, against

---

[39] Leadbeater, *The Landlord's Friend*, 76.

whom he might have conceived a wanton antipathy, from occupying any particular farm) the means of gratifying his malignity, or of attaining his selfish objects, and this generally without personal risk to himself, but at the hazard of life ... to obey the orders of some demon in human shape, to burn houses, murder their helpless inmates, hough and otherwise torture unoffending and defenceless cattle, and terrify from occupying their fairly acquired land an industrious family, merely because it was the pleasure of some worthless and ejected tenant to glut his inhuman revenge.[40]

This passage clearly echoes Carleton's famous secret-society story 'Wild-goose Lodge', which was first published under the title 'Confessions of a Reformed Ribbonman' in the *Dublin Literary Gazette* in 1830.[41] Doyle notes that the secretary to the group was, unsurprisingly, 'a very ignorant, and at the same time, a very presuming, self-sufficient, and pompous blockhead, who had been occasionally an itinerant school-master in the parish'.[42] The 'Captain' in Carleton's 'Wildgoose Lodge' is the local schoolmaster, as, indeed, are most administrators of secret societies in his fiction. As we will see, even the details of secret-society activity described by Doyle are indebted to Carleton's story. The order of proceedings outlined in this passage summarizes precisely the sequence of events as recounted in the gothic 'Wildgoose Lodge', itself based on an incident the aftermath of which Carleton himself claims to have witnessed in County Louth in 1817.[43]

Doyle's rewriting of 'Wildgoose Lodge' demonstrates the value of Carleton's writing as source material for improvement discourse (as well as vice versa). At this point, it was impossible for Doyle to disclaim knowledge of Carleton's *Traits and Stories* as *Common Sense for Common People* was published in 1834, a year after both the first and second series of Carleton's stories had been published by William Curry. Regardless, most of the stories collected in both volumes of the *Traits and Stories* were originally published in periodicals such as the *Christian Examiner*

---

[40] Martin Doyle, *Common Sense for Common People* (Dublin, 1834), 35.

[41] Doyle, of course, could have read the story in its original manifestation as 'Confessions of a Reformed Ribbonman', in the *Dublin Literary Gazette, or Weekly Chronicle of Criticism, Belles Lettres and Fine Arts*, 1/4 (23 Jan. 1830), 49–51 and continued in 1/5 (30 Jan. 1830), 66–8.

[42] Doyle, *Common Sense for Common People*, 36.

[43] For background to Carleton's story, see T. G. F. Patterson, *The Burning of Wildgoose Lodge* (Dundalk: County Louth Archaeological Journal, 1972). Patterson's essay—printed as a pamphlet—examines the actual historical event from contemporary accounts and newspapers. On Carleton's alleged experience of the incidents recounted in the story, see his *Autobiography*, 115–18.

and the *Dublin Literary Gazette* between 1828 and 1832 and it is likely that Doyle would have encountered them in these publications before they were collected into book form.

In 'Wildgoose Lodge', the members of the local Ribbonmen are all individually summoned to appear in the local church on a particular time and date. The narrator describes the demeanour of the Captain of the Ribbonmen at the meeting: 'a dark shade come over his countenance, that contracted his brow into a deep furrow, and it was then for the first time, that I saw the satanic expression of which his face, by a very slight motion of its muscles, was capable' (*TSIP*, ii. 353). Hence Doyle's 'demon in human shape' dispensing orders to the Whitefeet under his command. In 'Wildgoose Lodge', the objective of the evening was to burn the farmhouse of an informer, who reported a previous attack on the property. The men responsible for the first attack were convicted and their relatives then sought retribution. Their vengeance, however, was not to be satisfied by the burning of the house alone, but also, as stated in 'Wildgoose Lodge', the 'unhappy inmates'—described above by Doyle as 'helpless inmates'—imprisoned within the burning house.

Carleton's own story depicts what was, for the improvement mind, the particularly disconcerting mix of oral and literate modes: the Ribbonmen are called to the meeting in the local church by a written summons and the meeting is directed by the local schoolmaster, who reads names from a list and forces all present to swear on a 'missal'. The meeting itself, however, is characterized by an intense orality allegedly 'beyond all power of description' despite the fact that it is then portrayed by the narrator in a written form:

peals of wild, fiend-like yells rang through the chapel, as the party which stood on the altar and that which had crouched in the darkness met; wringing of hands, leaping in triumph, striking of sticks and fire-arms against the ground and the altar itself, dancing and cracking of fingers marked the triumph of some hellish determination. (*TSIP*, ii. 355)

Carleton emphasizes the orality of the proceedings, which rarely progress beyond 'wild, fiend-like yells' to actual speech. In this story, the orality of Ribbonmen is embedded in gothic tropes, such as barbaric violence, murkiness, Catholicism, and a burning house. The violence of secret societies is gothicized in order to call attention to its complicity with a pre-modern social order. Carleton's fiction repeatedly demonstrates how the attempt to represent the Irish peasant invariably produced an extreme rhetoric, the moderation of improvement necessarily subsumed by fictional convention.

These descriptions of Ribbon meetings must have compounded pre-existing conceptions of lower-class politics amongst Carleton's improving contemporaries.[44] Carleton concludes his story by stating that the body of Paddy Devaun, the leader of these Ribbonmen

> hung for some months in chains ... his mother could neither go into nor out of her cabin, without seeing his body swinging from the gibbet. Upon seeing him, she always remarked 'God be good to the sowl of my poor marthyr!' The peasantry, too, frequently exclaimed, on seeing him, 'Poor Paddy!' A gloomy fact that speaks volumes. (*TSIP*, ii. p. 362)

Carleton calls attention to the strongly moral objective of his story by appending this note at the end and thereby stressing the latent morality of his gothic fiction. Carleton's story is strongly present in Doyle's improvement narrative and, indeed, throughout *Common Sense for Common People* as a whole. Doyle seems to reverse a perceived trend in literary history by translating Carleton's fiction into the improvement tract. In this case, literary fiction clearly shaped Doyle's improvement pamphlet much as Edgeworth's novels stimulated Leadbeater's instructive dialogues. As noted in Chapter 1, a particular literary-historical consensus is that the conduct or guide book shaped the ideology and 'rise' of the novel.[45] However, I would suggest that the strongly literary, novelistic context of improvement should call into question the professed plain realism of that discourse.

In order to associate his work with discourses of progress, Carleton was always eager to distinguish his writing from the culture that gave rise to secret societies. In his 'General Introduction' to the *Traits and Stories*, he emphasizes that secret-society violence was not a national trait.

> It is not just to the general character of our people, however, to speak of these crimes as national, for, in fact, they are not so. If Tipperary and some of the adjoining parts of Munster were blotted out of the moral map of the country,

---

[44] For a discussion of illiteracy and lower-class politics within the context of Scottish culture, see Penny Fielding, *Writing and Orality: Nationality, Culture and Nineteenth-Century Scottish Fiction* (Oxford: Clarendon Press, 1996), 31–42.

[45] See e.g. Nancy Armstrong, *Desire and Domestic Fiction: A Political History of the Novel* (Oxford: Oxford University Press, 1987), and J. Paul Hunter, *Before Novels: Cultural Contexts of Eighteenth-Century English Fiction* (London: Norton, 1992). Both writers discuss the impact of guide and conduct literature on the development of the English novel, but do not mention instances of the reverse.

we could stand as a nation in a far higher position than that which we occupy in the opinion of our neighbours. This is a distinction which, in justice to us, ought to be made, for it is surely unfair to charge the whole kingdom with the crimes which disgrace only a single county of it, together with a few adjacent districts—allowing, of course, for some melancholy exceptions in other parts. (*TSIP*, i. p. xxi)

In claiming that secret-society violence lacked a national basis—isolated to a few counties in Munster—Carleton declares it to be marginal and unrepresentative of national character. However, as noted earlier in this chapter, Beames has shown that Tipperary was particularly affected by secret-society activity because it contained the most fertile agricultural land and an improving ethos amongst the county's landowners. In this respect, Tipperary exemplified the reality of an improved future in its peculiar mix of cultivation with crime and modernization with disorder. For Carleton, however, agrarian unrest had to be dissociated from his fiction and the form of national life he was in the process of creating through his writing. However, agrarian unrest was a product of the exact same tensions as produced Carleton's own writing.

The barbarity of group behaviour is always opposed to the virtuousness of individualism in Carleton's writing, the former manifested in secret societies and the crowded, communal culture of pre-Famine Ireland and the latter characteristic of reading and writing. 'Setting aside their religious and political prejudices', the Irish, he claims in 'The Hedge School', 'are grateful, affectionate, honourable, faithful, generous, and even magnanimous'. Under the influence of secret societies, however—suffused by religious and political prejudices—these same people 'will murder, burn, and exterminate, not only without compunction, but with a satanic delight worthy of a savage' (*TSIP*, i. 312). Carleton's peasants thus shift readily from the extremes of domestic virtue to horrendous violence, slipping from the pages of an improving tale into the pages of a gothic fiction. His writing strives to balance representations of secret-society atrocities with depictions of a virtuous domestic sphere. In his 'General Introduction', for example, he notes that 'in domestic life there is no man so exquisitely affectionate and humanized as the Irishman. The national imagination is active and the national heart warm, and it follows very naturally that he should be, and is, tender and strong in all his domestic relations' (*TSIP*, i. p. xxii). And in *The Squanders of Castle Squander*, we are again reminded of this national characteristic:

There exists too among them a vast proportion of personal and domestic piety—which if it not be very enlightened—as in general it is not—is nevertheless a proof that they want nothing but education to raise this beautiful feeling from the wretched superstition, which, like a bad weed, too frequently overgrows it. (*Squanders of Castle Squander*, ii. 76)

Education would fully reveal this already innate civility by building upon core domestic virtues such as generosity, hospitality, and charity. In 'The Poor Scholar', the kind farmer who takes Jimmy M'Evoy into his home is, we are told, by no means the exception: 'the character of this excellent farmer is thoroughly that of our peasantry within the range of domestic life' (*TSIP*, ii. 285).

This natural domestic world was, however, forever threatened by economic depression, secret societies, and the neglect of landlords. That particular threat is explored in characteristic improvement terms in 'The Landlord and Tenant', originally published in *the National Magazine* and later retitled 'Tubber Derg, or the Red Well' when reprinted in the second series of the *Traits and Stories* in 1832.[46] In its evocation of two social extremes, the original title—'The Landlord and Tenant'—betrays the improvement tract embedded within the story. In both versions, the story doubles as an improvement tale for both landlords and tenants, advising at once on estate management and the improvement of small farms. In the process, the story urges the small farmer to exercise restraint and discipline, offsetting the reliability of improvement against the 'uncertainty' of secret societies and lower-class politics.

The tenant at the centre of the story, an industrious small farmer, Owen M'Carthy, had led a 'useful life', exemplifying the virtues of an improving small farming class. However, even so successful a farmer was to experience difficulties at the end of the Napoleonic Wars, or, as the text has it, the 'peace of 1814', which resulted in a severe agricultural depression (*TSIP*, ii. 371). M'Carthy was then unable to proceed with various improvements on his farm owing to a lack of 'adequate capital'. M'Carthy's farm regresses into backward impoverishment, losing in the process all the 'taste and neatness' of an improved holding. The machinery of agricultural improvement—'cars', 'ploughs', and 'farming implements'—falls into disrepair. Circumstances for the M'Carthys become impossible: increasingly impoverished, they fall victim to the

---

[46] See William Carleton, 'The Landlord and Tenant', *National Magazine and Dublin Literary Gazette*, 2/4 (Apr. 1831), 383–401.

corrupt practices of the agent on the estate, exemplifying, the narrator reminds the reader, the exact conditions which draw many small tenant farmers into the ranks of the Ribbonmen. The landlord indicated by the title is absentee and is completely unacquainted 'with the distresses of his tenantry', not knowing their names or any of them 'in person' (*TSIP*, ii. 377). Carleton's story warns landlords that unless they personally manage their estates, setting 'rents according to the market for agricultural produce' then 'vague political speculations, founded upon idle hopes of a general transfer of property, will spread over and convulse the kingdom' (*TSIP*, ii. 382). Like the fiction of Doyle and Leadbeater, the story warns that secret societies and political conspiracies thrive in the context of absenteeism and poverty. Landlords had to work to ensure that the truths of improvement could succeed in displacing the vagueness and 'idle hopes' of secret societies. Otherwise, 'falsehood' and 'materials of outrage' will filter 'into the bosom of peaceable families ... who would otherwise, never become connected with a system which is calculated to bring ruin and destruction upon those who permit themselves to join it' (*TSIP*, ii. 388). The story warns that secret societies exploit virtuous families such as the M'Carthys who have been recently evicted or unjustly treated by agents and landlords.

Carleton's story is an attempt to demonstrate that improvement rhetoric can ultimately triumph over secret societies despite the immense pressures of pre-Famine life. Owen M'Carthy rejects secret societies and, by internalizing the truths of improvement discourse, gradually and carefully works his way out of pauperism and, in time, a hand-to-mouth existence as well. It was improvement, not politics, that liberated the M'Carthys from poverty. Carleton's fiction attempts to exemplify the virtues of improvement and individualism as alternatives to political polemic. As this story indicates, Carleton's writing tried to imagine an improved and stable society rather than preserve a poor, oral, and turbulent backwardness.

Ribbonism is described as containing 'the most ignorant description of the people' and as being infused by ideas which purport to 'prepare them for some great change in their favour, arising from the discomfiture of heresy, the overthrow of their enemies, and the exaltation of themselves and their religion' (*TSIP*, ii. 386). Carleton emphasizes the extremism of this political rhetoric, which is supposedly shaped by the chapbooks and pamphlets in popular circulation, such as *Pastorini*:

Scarcely had the public mind subsided after the Rebellion of Ninety-eight, when the success of Buonaparte directed the eyes and the hopes of the Irish people towards him, as the person designed to be their deliverer. Many a fine fiction has the author of this work heard about that great man's escapes, concerning the bullets that conveniently turned aside from his person, and the sabres that civilly declined to cut him down. Many prophecies too were related, in which the glory of this country under his reign was touched off in the happiest colours. Pastorini also gave such notions an impulse. Eighteen twenty-five was to be the year of their deliverance; George the fourth was never to fill the British throne; and the mill of Lowth was to be turned three times with human blood. (*TSIP*, ii. 387)

The apocalyptic fictions of the rural poor are derided by Carleton for their factual distortions and irrationality. James S. Donnelly notes that *Pastorini*, the abbreviated interpretation of the Book of Revelation by Bishop Charles Walmesley, was a central text in the anti-tithe Rockite disturbances of the early 1820s despite the fact that it was reprinted in the 1790s as a counter-revolutionary tract.[47] According to Niall Ó Ciosáin, *Pastorini* was absorbed within 'a culture so strongly permeated by expectation of deliverance' that it contributed seamlessly to pre-existing 'messianic elements in Irish-language culture'.[48] Those passages which prophesied the overthrow of Protestantism in 1825 were extracted and printed separately, rapidly entering into the channels of popular literature.[49] In Carleton's writing, pamphlets such as *Pastorini* are shown to fit comfortably within an oral and semi-literate tradition and to be easily adaptable for oral transmission. The perception was that this printed material actually deepened existing oral modes. Penny Fielding notes that in Scottish culture 'popular literacy' was 'generally thought of as illiteracy', becoming such 'partly for its political content, but also because of its exposure to the dangerous scenes of popular orality'.[50]

---

[47] James S. Donnelly, Jr., 'Pastorini and Captain Rock: Millenarianism and Sectarianism in the Rockite Movement of 1821–4', in Samuel Clark and J. S. Donnelly, Jr. (eds.), *Irish Peasants: Violence and Political Unrest 1780–1914* (Manchester: Manchester University Press, 1983), 102–43.

[48] See Niall Ó Ciosáin, *Print and Popular Culture in Ireland, 1750–1850* (Basingstoke: Macmillan, 1997), 194. Ó Ciosáin provides a detailed account of the history of the circulation of *Pastorini* in rural Ireland, pp. 192–7. See also Donnelly, 'Pastorini and Captain Rock'.

[49] Ó Ciosáin, *Print and Popular Culture in Ireland, 1750–1850*, 196.

[50] Fielding, *Writing and Orality*, 34.

The frame of reference of Carleton's secret societies embraced a whole range of supposedly seditious texts from *Pastorini* to rebellious ballads, all of which, Carleton claims in his story 'The Hedge School', were standard reading material in these institutions:

Their education, indeed, was truly barbarous; they were trained and habituated to cruelty, revenge, and personal hatred, in their schools. Their knowledge was directed to evil purposes—disloyal principles were industriously insinuated into their minds by their teachers, most of whom were leaders of illegal associations. The matter placed in their hands was of a most inflammatory and pernicious nature, as regarded politics: and as far as religion and morality were concerned, nothing could be more gross and superstitious than the books which circulated among them. Eulogiums on murder, robbery and theft, were read with delight in the histories of Freney the Robber, and the Irish Rogues and Rapparees; ridicule of the Word of God, and hatred to the Protestant religion, in a book called Ward's Cantos, written in Hudibrastic verse; the downfall of the Protestant establishment, and the exaltation of the Romish church, in Columbkill's Prophecy, and latterly in that of Pastorini. Gross superstition, political and religious ballads of the vilest doggerel, miraculous legends of the holy friars persecuted by Protestants, and of signal vengeance inflicted by their divine power on those who persecuted them, were in the mouths of young and old, and of course firmly fixed in their credulity. (*TSIP*, i. 313)

The hedge school stands at the centre of popular and political culture and the schoolmasters are actively involved in the promotion of political extremism. According to this account, the reading material in the schools enforced this illiterate, political, and criminal culture as well as crude sectarianism. Like Hannah More, Carleton emphasizes the particular efficiency of print as a corrupting and politicizing force: print can fix ideas in the minds of the poor in a manner not possible by oral means alone. It seems that for Carleton—as well as for his improvement contemporaries—the orality of secret societies and hedge schools was abetted by writing and print to a truly alarming extent. Carleton's attempt to distinguish between speech and writing, to mark orality as definitively pre-modern and backward and literacy as modern and progressive, was disrupted by his own fiction.

Carleton strives to present his writing as a stabilizing, English-language discourse within a context of 'transition' from orality to literacy, Irish to English, and superstition to reason. As I argued in the previous chapter, this notion of a transitional culture is itself a convenient convention employed to explain unwanted elements. This 'transitional' state is described repeatedly throughout Carleton's writing; in *The Tithe Proctor*, he claims that the situation in Ireland is not particularly unusual as

In every country whose political, commercial, or social relations, are not properly settled, or in which there exists a struggle between the principles at variance with civil order and those of enlightened progress, there will always be found a considerable portion of the population ripe and ready for violence and crime. (*The Tithe Proctor*, 130)

The struggle between 'civil order' and secret-society crime is exacerbated by the unsettled nature of a society supposedly in transition between languages and tradition and modernization.[51] These pressures are continually expressed in the fraught prose of the writing itself and through the speech of schoolmasters. Carleton tries to demonstrate how secret societies always thrive in the space between civil order and anarchy or, in other words, the domain of the semi-literate, encapsulated by the 'low, vulgar fluency of language' spoken by the Ribbonmen and schoolmasters of his fiction (*The Tithe Proctor*, 4). It is supposedly the chaos of transition that makes for these peculiarly violent conditions even though the fiction itself repeatedly—if despite itself—shows the extent to which modernization and violence are intertwined.

The tension between improvement and violence is manifest in Carleton's anti-Ribbon tract *Rody the Rover* (1845), 'written', the Preface states, 'with the same anxious wish to benefit my countrymen that influenced me in the composition of *Art Maguire*' (the temperance narrative published that same year).[52] This tract was published in the Young Ireland Library of Ireland series (along with *Art Maguire* and *Parra Sastha*) and would have been commissioned by Charles Gavan Duffy. Improvement anxiety determined the composition of *Rody the Rover* as it had many others, compelling the act of writing and the production of texts. The setting for *Rody the Rover* is a standard village in rural Ireland which previously had no school and where the children had been 'half-wild, half-naked and half-fed, idle, lazy, and mischievous' (*Rody the*

---

[51] For a discussion of representation and violence in the novel in the nineteenth century, see David Lloyd, 'Violence and the Constitution of the Novel', in *Anomalous States* (Dublin: Lilliput Press, 1993), 125–62.

[52] *Rody the Rover* is itself a revision of an earlier story, 'Richard the Rake: In Three Snatches', published in *Dublin University Magazine*, 11/63 (Mar. 1838). The principal difference between these versions is that improvement was introduced by cultivation in 'Richard the Rake' and not as the result of mining.

Rover, 4). In time, however, improvement arrived in the form of a mine, discovered by an English company, which provided gainful employment for all the villagers. The arrival of the English company is undoubtedly a metaphor for both empire and improvement discourse. Domestic and social improvement were steadily achieved: a school was built, 'gardens were enclosed and patches of land cultivated' (p. 11). Improvement ensured that people became 'happy and peaceful ... neither mischievous, nor anxious to embroil themselves in the mad and senseless feuds of either faction or party' (p. 11). There were no secret societies as the people achieved proper contentment through work and discipline. Indeed, they were instructed by 'books'—which were read to them by their children—'to have nothing to do with these secret societies, or Ribbonism in any shape' (p. 19), optimistically demonstrating how improvement discourse can succeed in encouraging conformity to a preferred and more desirable mode of behaviour.

The arrival of Rody the Ribbonman, however, soon reversed the town's fortunes: the residents were gradually lured back into the idleness and politics of the past. The books which had successfully kept people away from secret societies were themselves pushed out by the orality of 'banter'. The prosperity of the town was quickly reversed by the disaffection instilled by Ribbonism, achieved by Rody's 'evident relish for banter with the people' which 'had sharpened and improved his wit, and gave to his humour all the zest which is communicated by a varied vocabulary of standard aphorism, which, while they seem to be the result of invention, are in reality only an act of memory' (*Rody the Rover*, 55). Carleton characterizes Ribbonism as an artificial discourse which is learnt by rote and specially attuned to the orality of peasant politics. In the story itself, Ribbonism is presented as an anti-Catholic conspiracy based in Dublin Castle and constructed to make Ireland appear 'unfit to be trusted with civil privileges or political power' (p. 132). The pamphlet claims that secret societies merely enforce prejudices against Irish Catholics by providing 'their enemies with a standing argument against their fitness for civil or religious liberty' (p. 74). In embracing Ribbonism, the town reverts to illiteracy and poverty: the mine closes and the people themselves regress to their previous barbaric state. Carleton's intentions are strongly propagandistic: in depicting Ribbonism as a conspiracy directed against both Catholicism and nationalism, he attempts to persuade his readers that secret societies only intensify existing prejudices against the Irish peasantry. In the process, the continued existence of secret societies

ensures that rural Ireland remains confined within a backward, primitive state, confirming suspicions that Irish character was incapable of
bearing the forces of modernization. At the same time, the tract implies
the vulnerability of improvement to secret societies. As such, Carleton
inadvertently represents improvement as merely rhetorical, much like
the 'orality' of Ribbonmen. In the dangerous 'transitional' environment
represented in Carleton's fiction, it seems that the achievement of
progress (or civility) could be reversed and subsumed by the barbarity
of secret societies. One convention or discourse could, it seems, easily
give way to the force of another. Carleton's parable of Ribbonism in
this tract is, as will be evident below, characteristic of Young Ireland
nationalism.

Carleton's Young Irelandism is likewise evident in *Parra Sastha*,
another Library of Ireland tract, written, he claims, in a mere six days.
It was hastily produced to replace Thomas Davis's planned volume on
Wolf Tone after the Young Irelander's sudden death. In his Preface,
Carleton describes Davis's particular commitment to the Library of
Ireland:

I know how deeply he felt interested in the success of the Irish Library—how
hopeful and ample were the expectations he had formed of its utility to our rising
literature, and with what enthusiasm he anticipated its power to awaken the
general intellect of the country, and to make Irishmen a thinking, enlightened
and independent country. (*Parra Sastha*, p. vii)

The essential connections between writing, 'thinking', and enlightenment forced Davis and Gavan Duffy to establish the Library of
Ireland series in the first place. Producing improvement and national
narratives that exemplified the supposedly unambiguous relationship
between literacy and enlightenment had to proceed without delay in
order to create a properly national culture. The assumption is clearly
that modernization would not be possible in oral culture and that 'the
general intellect of the country' could only be awakened by means of
writing and the material presence of 'national' books and print. These
volumes would presumably benefit the country's 'rising literature' by
becoming a written frame of reference which would be at once national
and nationalizing. The Library of Ireland would work to improve the
peasantry and form the foundation of a national literary tradition. Such
publications would also, of course, create 'civilized' (national) reading
habits rather than indulging the mindless consumption of texts such as
Pastorini and *Freney the Robber*.

As an improving tract, *Parra Sastha* would itself perform such an exemplary role and conform exactly to Davis's prescription for the series:

> Moved by his [Davis's] example, I have endeavoured to make the following sketch useful to my countrymen. If the perusal of it shall succeed in banishing from among them, and from among many of my countrywomen also, such habits of indolence and want of cleanliness as I have satirized, I shall feel that I have been the humble means of rendering an important service to my country. (*Parra Sastha*, pp. xiii–iv)

The national rhetoric of Davis is thus replicated with ease within the genre of the improving tract. The theme of agricultural improvement at the centre of the tract was not only appropriate for the Library of Ireland series but was of its essence. The Library of Ireland worked to encourage seemingly mundane and banal developments from hygienic practices in the home to the most recent agricultural innovations as well as establishing a national literary culture. Irish society had to be brought to a properly improved condition before the objectives of nationalism could be achieved. The intention of the Library of Ireland was to create a unified national consciousness and frame of reference which would, by definition, displace all other, mostly oral, discourses. Oral memory—represented by traditions of prophecy and chapbooks such as *Pastorini*—had to be replaced by a written history. It could be argued that memory—equated by Davis and Carleton with orality—had to be substituted by an authoritative (written) tradition. The assumption was that popular memory necessarily fictionalized the past while written history instinctively rationalized it (which presumes, of course, that Carleton's writing is truthful). A centralized, written frame of reference and history were to replace memory in all the oral senses of the term, rendered authoritative by means of representation in the chronological, linear format of a literate, printed account.

Like the improvement pamphlets of Leadbeater and Doyle, *Parra Sastha* tries to demonstrate how modernization of farming practice leads directly, and always unambiguously, to a prosperous rural economy. In his Preface, Carleton claims that in writing the tract, his 'object was to inculcate habits of industry, punctuality, cleanliness, comfort, intelligence, and that principle of social progress', all of which would help to form the national culture imagined in his fiction. In many respects, the ability to write a national literature would signal the culmination of the improvement project. The very existence of a national literature would indicate that the necessary preparation was complete and that writing proper could, so to speak, begin. Improvement for Carleton, on even the most mundane of levels such as clean kitchens and tidy gardens, was the means by which the act of writing itself could become meaningful. However, the very formlessness of Carleton's fiction signifies the endless postponement of an improved national society. As in the pamphlets of Doyle and Leadbeater, improvement is here seen to provide the necessary social organization for society to come into existence and develop.

Carleton declares that *Parra Sastha* was not written 'in conformity with the laws of romantic fiction, but according to those of truth and public utility'. In so doing, he was attempting to associate his writing with 'truth' rather than the fictionality of literature. Carleton tells us that it is his 'duty'

after having shown him [Paddy] as an impersonation of the indolent and negligent spirit peculiar to a large class of our countrymen, to let our readers see how far the recuperative principle may be developed in him by an individual who represents our national activity, and the awkward tendencies to progress and improvement. (*Parra Sastha*, 75)

Carleton tries to imply that the story is plotted and structured in accordance with truth and utility rather than with romance or the novel. The pamphlet is structured to demonstrate how improvement could be brought to bear on a seemingly 'indolent and negligent' culture by means of truthful representations rather than inherently fictional and novelistic depictions. Carleton is also warning that the seriousness of the story means that it cannot be read as fiction. In other words, fiction—however paradoxically—had to become literal for progress or social change to be achieved. In addition, the development of a national literature relied upon the veracity of contemporary 'fiction'.

Given the improving ambitions of the Library of Ireland, it is unsurprising that the nationalist writings of Thomas Davis should be pervaded by improvement discourse. Davis clearly drew upon improvement discourse in order to articulate his concept of the nation state, the creation of which depended upon the achievement of the modernization espoused by Leadbeater, Doyle, and Carleton. Benedict Anderson describes how the articulation of nationalist discourse was the consequence of, in part, the passing of 'a conception of temporality in which cosmology and temporality were indistinguishable', giving way to a concept of time which 'rooted human lives firmly in the very nature of things, giving certain meaning to the everyday fatalities of existence (above all death, loss and servitude) and offering, in various ways, redemption from them'.[53] I have noted throughout this study how improvement discourse sought to emphasize the material over the metaphysical and the linearity of time over 'cosmology' (as expressed in the superstitions and millenarianism of the rural poor). The readers of improvement pamphlets were urged to comprehend existence in the material, linear terms of natural history, realistic narratives, and the market. The discipline of the clock (as seen in Chapter 1) had to displace the chaotic patterns of the past, as manifest in oral storytelling, superstition, and the hand-to-mouth economy of the poor. It might be argued that the nationalist state envisaged in Davis's writing depended upon the creation of the coherent and stable rural community of improvement discourse.

Davis denounced secret societies in his writing, declaring them an affront to the various improving and nationalizing projects in progress throughout the country. Carleton's writing was embraced by Davis in the early 1840s, who recognized the improving, 'national' tendencies of stories such as 'The Landlord and Tenant' despite Carleton's professed anti-Repeal and anti-nationalist sentiments. According to Davis, Carleton's writing manifested a particular and necessary 'national' tradition, which had, he claims, a precedent in Scottish culture:

Far healthier with all its defects, was the idea of those who saw in Scotland a perfect model—who longed for a literary and artistic nationality—who prized the oratory of Grattan and Curran, the novels of Griffin and Carleton, the pictures of Maclise and Burton, the ancient music as much as any, and far more than most of the political nationalists, but who regarded political independence as a dangerous dream. Unknowingly they fostered it. Their writings, their patronage, their talk was of Ireland; yet it hardly occurred to them that the ideal would flow into the practical, or that they with their dread of agitation were forwarding a revolution.[54]

The 'perfect model' that many 'saw in Scotland' was the supposed achievement of a modern and enlightened culture from one originally deemed primitive and backward. This process was, Davis claims, now manifest in Ireland within a particular nationalizing aesthetic present in Irish fiction, music, and even political rhetoric (such as Young Ireland,

[53] Benedict Anderson, *Imagined Communities: Reflections on the Origin and Spread of Nationalism* (London: Verso, 1983), 40.
[54] Thomas Davis, 'Ballad Poetry of Ireland', in *Literary and Historical Essays*, ed. Charles Gavan Duffy (Dublin, 1862), 221–2.

of course). For Davis, this tradition conveys best the existence of shared themes and idioms across varying genres and forms and, presumably, class and religion as well. The rhetoric of nationality was, in Davis's thinking, a unifying and centralizing discourse, a homogenizing of form and content and, therefore, essential preparation for nationalism.

The national revival of the 1830s and early 1840s was continually undermined by the existence of secret societies, which exemplified an extremism that could not be accommodated within a 'national' culture. As a discourse, 'nationality' united many diverse groups and constituencies from the correspondents in *Dublin University Magazine* to the writers of the *Nation*. This unity was, however, always threatened by the activities of secret societies in rural Ireland. In Davis's article 'Munster Outrages', which strongly condemns the agrarian unrest in Tipperary in the early 1840s, he lists all those who were opposed to secret societies:

Let the men of Munster read the last Act of the Repeal Association, and they will find Daniel O'Connell, William Smith O'Brien, and the entire Repeal League confederated to proclaim and trample down the assassins. Let them enter their chapels, and from every altar they will hear their beloved priests solemnly warning them that the forms of the church are as fiery coals on the heads of the blood-stained. Let them look upon the government, and they will find a potent code and vast police—a disciplined army—all just citizens combined to quell the assassin; and then let them with their conscience approach their God, and learn that their murder is dark before them.[55]

Secret societies did not belong within the consensus which supposedly existed between such disparate institutions as the government, Young Ireland, and the Catholic Church. Ribbonmen were not part of the tacit understanding—literate, improved, 'national'—that pertained between these institutions and, indeed, writers of the period, such as Carleton.[56] These groups were all equally embarrassed by the existence of secret societies, believing them to be extreme and primitive within the context of the administrative, bureaucratic, and militaristic structures of the modern state. It seems that the very existence of secret societies somehow suggested the fragility of 'nationality' as a unifying discourse between such diverse constituencies as well as the impossibility of

[55] Thomas Davis, 'Munster Outrages', in *Prose Writings: Essays on Ireland*, ed. T. W. Rolleston (London: W. Scott, 1890), 260–1.
[56] On clerical opposition to secret societies see S. J. Connolly, *Priests and People in Pre-Famine Ireland* (Dublin: Four Courts Press, 1987; repr. 2001), 208–44.

ever achieving the organic community of improvement fiction. Secret societies were seen to threaten the feasibility of any nationalizing project, be it economic improvement, Repeal of the Union, or the ambition, as exemplified by Carleton's writing, to create a national literature.

Both Young Ireland and Repeal organizations were characterized by a particular discipline, rooted in improvement concepts of 'self-reliance', literacy, and sobriety, which was intent on the dislodging of the illiterate ideology of the Irish peasantry. For Davis, this ideology, propagated by secret societies and represented in detail in Carleton's writing, was embodied in the belief of many peasants 'that they were highly educated, nobly represented ... and that ... their misery was a mysterious fate, for which there was no remedy in human means.'[57] Such a deluded ideology had to be replaced by a materialist Young Ireland rhetoric of 'deliberate temperance', 'organized abstinence from crime', and increased 'political discipline'.[58] An improved population would of course conform more precisely to the coherence required of Young Ireland nationalism.

In Davis's mind, the methods of secret societies were redundant and utterly ineffective as political tools, superseded by written propaganda (such as Davis's own) in tracts and newspapers. It seems that the efficiency of 'information' would accelerate the nationalizing process in a manner which would not have been possible by the antiquated oral means of fireside storytelling or 'word of mouth'. However, Davis worried that the disorganized and chaotic methods of secret societies were threatening the 'moral force' he was trying to inculcate through the various channels of Young Ireland such as Repeal reading rooms. Additionally, the modernized methods of Repeal, exemplified by the use of print, were in a sense undermined by the 'oral' tactics of secret societies:

Will they wait till violence and suspicion are the only principles retaining power among them? Will they look on while the Repeal movement—the educating, the ennobling, the sacred effort for liberty—is superseded by the buzz of assassination and vengeance? Or will they now join O'Connell or O'Brien—the association, the law and the priesthood; and whenever they hear a breath of outrage, denounce it as they would atheism—whenever they see an attempt at crime, intervene with brave strong hand, and, in Mr. O'Brien's word, 'Leave the guilty no chance of life but in hasty flight from the land they have stained with their crime'.[59]

57 Davis, 'A Second Year's Work', *Prose Writings*, 266.   58 Ibid.
59 Davis, 'Munster Outrages', *Prose Writings*, 263–4.

The orality of secret societies, as expressed in 'the buzz of assassination and vengeance', is forever threatening to subsume the literacy of both national and nationalist discourses. In another *Nation* article, 'Moral Force', Davis states clearly that 'there are two ways of success for the Irish—arms and persuasion.' He asserts that the latter has been chosen by Repeal, for which the people 'learn history and forget quarrels', instead studying 'resources, and how to increase them'. All disputes are subsumed in the activity of practical education and improvement, traditional quarrels vanishing in the nationalizing and modernizing impetus of organizations such as Young Ireland. In order for moral rather than physical force to work, Davis claims, 'internal union is essential', itself dependent upon a shared discourse uniting Protestant and Catholic and rich and poor.[60]

The *Nation* newspaper had already, according to Davis, partly demonstrated the feasibility of such a project, as it 'canvassed' all classes 'incessantly and not in vain', contributing to the development of 'unanimity' in Irish life.[61] Physical force, it seems, only operated in the chaotic, oral, and anachronistic world of secret societies whereas 'moral force' was organized, literate, and modern. Carleton espouses a similar morality in his writing, the project of creating a national literature depending upon a coherent 'moral map' of the country (as described in his own Davisite 'General Introduction' to the 1842–4 edition of the *Traits and Stories* quoted above).

The particular advantages which 'modern' institutions such as Repeal and the *Nation* newspaper maintained over other, more old-fashioned modes of organization were described by Davis:

The Repeal organisation enables people to act together. It is the bark of the tree, guarding it and binding it. It is the cause of our unanimity; for where else has a party, so large as the Irish Repealers, worked without internal squabbles? It is the secret of our discipline. How else, but by the instant action of the Association on the whole mass of the people, through the Repeal press and the Repeal wardens, could our huge meetings have been assembled or been brought together? How else could the people have been induced to continue their subscriptions month after month and year after year?[62]

The Repeal movement, which was bound by discipline and meticulous organization, 'enables people to act together' on a national basis

---

[60] Davis, 'Moral Force', *Prose Writings*, 250.
[61] Davis, 'A Second Year's Work', 267.
[62] Davis, 'The Right Road', *Prose Writings*, 242–3.

rather than on the overly local and fragmented level of secret societies. Such success owes much to the activities of Repeal Wardens, busily 'collecting money, distributing cards, tracts and newspapers' in almost every parish. It is not clear exactly what tracts were distributed, but one wonders if they included the tracts of Leadbeater and Doyle: *Cottage Dialogues* was reprinted in 1841 and Martin Doyle had produced an agricultural text book for use in the new National Schools.[63] Like improvement, the official nature of the Repeal organization was reliant on printed information and technology, essential, Davis claims, as 'an ignorant and unorganized people would soon have tired of the subscriptions and meetings, and have broken into disorder or sunk into apathy.'[64] These methods of organization suggest the administrative, bureaucratic nature of Repeal over the supposedly random, casual structures of secret societies. Much like Leadbeater and Carleton, Davis is seeking to differentiate his particular nationalist writing and politics from secret societies by emphasizing the public, open, and centralized nature of his methods. Young Ireland politics are civilized, fully immersed in modern institutions, as compared with the barbarity of secret societies.

Davis is impatient to witness the emergence of an improved, national Ireland populated by Irish 'citizens', all of whom would be appropriately clean, sober, and literate:

Is there any town or district which has not a temperance band and reading room? If there be, let that town or district meet at once, and subscribe for instruments, music, and a teacher. Let the members meet, and read, and discuss, and qualify themselves by union, study, and political information to act as citizens, whether their duty lead them to the public assembly, the hustings or the hill-side. By acting thus, and not by listening for news about trials, the people have advanced from mouldering slaves into a threatening and united people; continuing to act thus, they will become a triumphant nation.[65]

All areas of the country had to be infused rapidly with this discourse, centred on instruction, reading, and discussion rather than alcohol and violence. Repeal reading rooms would educate in citizenship, creating a literate and enlightened population in preparation for nationhood. Davis

---

[63] See Doyle, *Agricultural Classbook, or How Best to Cultivate a Small Farm and Garden, together with Hints on Domestic Economy* (Commissioners of National Education in Ireland, 1856). This is perhaps the fifth reprint of an earlier edition and the place of publication is not noted in the text.

[64] Davis, 'The Right Road', *Prose Writings*, 243.   [65] ibid. 244.

claims that the Repeal movement had already succeeded in displacing much of the crass popular culture of the period—such as 'listening for news about trials'—with 'union, study, and political information'. The establishment of social institutions, which would create and shape modern citizenship, was essential for Davis's nationalism. These institutions were intended as an alternative to the public house and traditional oral fireside, signalling the clarity and efficiency of 'information' over older, more obscure modes of organization. The strategies of Davis and Young Ireland were modernizing in form, betraying an eagerness to bring Irish society into line with England and Europe (exemplified by Davis's desire to witness the 'green flag ... saluted' by other European states).[66] This modernizing nationalism required an orderly and unified population—sober, literate, and disciplined—as had been imagined previously in improvement discourse. While the assertive utilitarianism of Thomas Davis was noted by Malcolm Brown in his 1971 book, *The Politics of Irish Writing,* Young Ireland nationalism is more commonly linked to Romanticism.[67] However, it would appear that the intellectual roots of Young Ireland are probably best understood in the tradition of improvement discourse in Ireland, itself an early expression of a liberal utilitarianism which was counter-revolutionary and, indeed, counter-Romantic in origin. This is not, of course, a Bemthamite Utilitarianism, but one of a different order, which was produced in the particularly fraught conditions of post-Union Ireland and was expressed at an earlier period in both the novels and educational theory of Edgeworth and in the improvement fiction and tracts of writers such as Leadbeater, Bardin, Doyle, and Carelton. It is, however, no less utilitarian for that.

For Davis, the extremism represented by both secret societies and the coercive, oppressive structures of the traditional state had to be displaced by the moderation of a more enlightened politics, be it manifest in the harmonious cottage of Leadbeater's improvement fiction or the reading room of the Repeal organization. In a sense, Davis's nationalism is imbued with the liberalism of Leadbeater and Doyle, the nationalist

---

[66] On this issue, see Seamus Deane, 'The Famine and *Young Ireland*', in Seamus Deane (ed.), *The Field Day Anthology* (Derry: Field Day Company, 1991), ii. 115–21.

[67] For a discussion of Young Ireland as 'Romantic', see Joep Leerssen, *Remembrance and Imagination: Patterns in the Historical and Literary Representation of Ireland in the Nineteenth Century* (Cork: Field Day/Cork University Press, 1996), 22–4, 62, 147–52, and 224; see also Malcolm Brown, *The Politics of Irish Literature: From Thomas Davis to W. B. Yeats* (Seattle: University of Washington Press, 1971).

discourse of Young Ireland mediated by the improvement tracts and pamphlets of the early nineteenth century.[68]

Although Carleton admonished secret societies as they threatened the feasibility of both improvement and nationality, his writing was nonetheless the result of those same forces of modernization that had produced agrarian unrest. He represented secret societies as extreme, embodying the excesses of the pre-modern. These excesses of language, alcohol, and political expression had to be curbed and restrained by the moderation of improvement. By its very existence, a moderate language was to instil the conditions and terms in which modernization and progress could take effect. In this context, representation often meant subsuming difference and attempting to fix a standard of literacy and morality. It was as though representation should in and of itself eliminate difference: violence, once domesticated, would become civility; cabins, once improved, would be transformed into tasteful cottages; and nature, once cultivated, would be assimilated into culture. However, in castigating the backwardness of the rural poor, improvement writers adopted an extreme rhetoric of their own. This extremism is manifest in their sensational representations of the Irish peasantry as excessively drunken, oral, and superstitious. In a sense, the professed moderation of improvement discourse stands in ironic relation to the extremity of its own response to the (perceived) life of the rural peasant.

[68] For a related discussion of Young Ireland nationalism, see David Lloyd, *Nationalism and Minor Literature: James Clarence Mangan and the Emergence of Irish Cultural Nationalism* (Berkeley: University of California Press, 1987).

5

The Aesthetics of Excess: Improvement and Revivalism

LIKE improvement, the project of Young Ireland was concerned with rooting out misery and instilling comfort and respectability. For Young Irelanders such as Davis and Gavan Duffy, a disciplined and rationalized existence protected from a broken past and was the only means of achieving the modernized nationhood that ensured satisfaction. Implicit in improvement discourse is the assumption that progress was by definition unifying—all traditional antagonisms dissolved in the common ground of a modernized social order. In keeping with this tradition, Young Ireland nationalism was intolerant of a perceived oral backwardness, aspiring to rid Irish life of those residues of difference and peculiarity that set the country apart from the modernized mainstream. Improvement writers and Young Irelanders alike worked within those traditions of liberal utilitarianism that were a product of counter-revolutionary reaction in Britain and Ireland.[1] That discourse had also been responsible for determining the literary mainstream of nineteenth-century Ireland. The liberal utilitarianism of improvement repudiated the alleged aesthetic excesses of Romanticism in favour of what was deemed to be a tightly controlled rhetorical environment. In this tradition, the incoherent mutterings of the oral, hungry peasant were equated with the overly speculative and obscure literature of high culture, both removed from the material realities of everyday life. Fittingly, the literary fiction of nineteenth-century Ireland was primarily counter-Romantic, insisting upon the plain truths of realism over those delusional, convoluted fictions that were taken to characterize Romanticism and the oral culture

---

[1] For an analysis of the roots of liberal utilitarianism in counter-revolutionary discourse, see Philip Pettit, 'The Tree of Liberty', *Field Day Review*, 1 (2005), 29–43, and *Republicanism: A Theory of Freedom and Government* (Oxford: Clarendon Press, 1997), 17–50.

of the rural poor. For Yeats, a poet broadly working within the tradition of English Romanticism and French symbolism, this situation was all too evident both when he surveyed the literature of the nineteenth century and assessed that being produced in the 1880s and 1890s. As defined by Yeats, the Revival was to set itself the task of overwhelming the very improving and didactic traditions that have been surveyed in this book. In so doing, the 'high' revivalism of Yeats was opposed to the plain realism of improvement writers, mainstream nationalism, and the literary fiction of nineteenth-century Ireland.

Yeats's first published poem, 'A Dawn-Song', appeared in the *Irish Fireside*, a supplement with the nationalist *Weekly Freeman* in the 1880s. Both title and masthead—which promised readers 'entertainment', 'fiction', and 'instruction'—demonstrate the extent to which mainstream nationalist and improvement tropes were fully intertwined in the textual culture of the late nineteenth century. The *Irish Fireside* anticipates particular Revival preoccupations while being clearly rooted in earlier discourses, such as improvement fiction and Young Ireland. One of the most striking features of the *Irish Fireside* is its nostalgia for Young Ireland nationalism. A small column in the second issue laments the fact that 'the writing of ballad poetry, such as filled the pages of Irish journals in the stirring times of forty years ago, seems to be a lost art in Ireland at present', regretting the absence of 'successors' to the Young Irelandism of Thomas Davis and Charles Gavan Duffy.[2] From that point on, the supplement published ballads and folklore submitted by readers alongside practical advice on the treatment of pigs in summer. Echoing Young Ireland, the journal worked to fulfil a commitment to instruction as well as to a nationalist reawakening.[3] The *Irish Fireside* articulates a particular formula for national revival, comprising nationalism, economic improvement, balladry, and, in the issue of 2 January 1886, language revival.[4] In 1886 and 1887, it began to publish poems by Katherine Tynan, Yeats, and Douglas Hyde. Though the *Irish Fireside* was the first publisher of Yeats's work, he was soon to embark on a project to displace such literary institutions from Irish life. Those institutions were to be personified for Yeats in the early 1890s by Charles Gavan Duffy. Indeed, his famous quarrel in 1892 with Gavan Duffy over the contents of the New

    [2] *Irish Fireside*, 1/2, 9 July 1883, 23.
    [3] This would suggest that the *Irish Fireside* was a clear precursor for the *Irish Homestead* while itself being a successor to Martin Doyle's *Irish Farmer's and Gardener's Magazine*.
    [4] John Fleming, 'The Revival of the Irish Language', *Irish Fireside*, 6/133, 12–14.

Irish Library brought to light yet again those tensions—between didacticism and literariness, realism and idealism, utility and inutility, liberalism and republicanism—with which this study began. Accordingly, this dispute encapsulates the manner in which nineteenth-century Irish fiction, mainstream nationalism, and popular revivalism remained beholden to the counter-revolutionary and imperial discourse of improvement. This chapter demonstrates how the revival writings of Yeats, Hyde, and Synge express a disenchantment with that inheritance, seeking to transcend these particular intellectual and aesthetic constraints.

After his dispute with Gavan Duffy, Yeats committed himself to the creation of an Irish literature that was opposed to the Young Irelandism espoused by institutions such as the *Irish Fireside*. For Yeats, Irish cultural life had to be lured away from its devotion to these traditions (the legacy of improvement and Young Ireland) which were, in his mind, directly opposed to the 'nationality' that ought to be the basis of revivalist art. In 1891 and 1892, both before and after the death of Parnell, Yeats was involved in an attempt to 'nationalize' the Young Ireland Leagues throughout the country and expand the Southwark Irish Literary Club into a larger 'national' society. As noted in the previous chapter, Repeal and Young Ireland established a network of reading rooms and societies throughout Ireland in the 1840s that were then resurrected in the 1880s and which Yeats now wanted to place in the service of his revivalist ambitions. These ambitions found expression in plans for a series of lectures, performances, and, most ambitiously of all, the publication and distribution of 'national' books. At this point, Yeats was embarking on negotiations with the publisher Fisher Unwin for a series of books 'as neucleuses of lending libraries',[5] which could be distributed 'when our organization was complete'.[6] These books were to be circulated through the reading rooms and societies of Young Ireland and, according to W. P. Ryan's memoir of this period, directly to the Irish community in particular parts of Britain.[7] In October 1891, Yeats wrote what Roy Foster has termed 'a manifesto' in *United Ireland*,[8] which

[5] W. B. Yeats, Letter to Edward Garnett [early Aug. 1892], *Collected Letters of W. B. Yeats*, i. *1865–1895*, ed. John Kelly and Eric Domville (Oxford: Clarendon Press, 1986), 308 [hereafter cited as *CL*].

[6] W. B. Yeats, *Autobiographies* (London, Macmillan, 1955), 200.

[7] W. P. Ryan, *The Irish Literary Revival: Its History, Pioneers and Possibilities* (London: W. P. Ryan, 1894), 62.

[8] Roy Foster, *W. B. Yeats: A Life, i. The Apprentice Mage* (Oxford: Oxford University Press, 1997), 115.

declared that books would be distributed to these societies 'that feed the imagination'[9]. In later years, Yeats claimed that he had been determined that 'there ... be a popular imaginative literature' to distribute through the Young Ireland reading rooms, one which—because imaginative and national (rather than didactic)—would prepare the ground for the proper reception of his literary project.[10] However, Yeats must not have realized that imagination and popularity were, in fact, at odds with each other in Ireland in the late nineteenth century.

One component of that project was already in the final stages of composition, his play *The Countess Kathleen*, which he envisaged would in time meet its audience through the 'country branches' of the literary society. The later acrimonious reception at the first performance of *The Countess Kathleen* is sufficient indication of the depth of Yeats's faith in the early 1890s that a popular revivalism was possible. This play had been enormously controversial years before its first performance in 1899. A printed text of the play was published in 1892, which contained a scene in which a statue of the Virgin Mary is smashed. The public was quickly outraged and Yeats deleted the offensive scene prior to the play's inaugural performance. However, that did not ward off the protesters, who were enraged by this perceived attack on national piety. It is striking that Yeats was hoping to launch a popular revivalism with this particular play in mind. The play was published in a collection in 1892 under the title, *The Countess Kathleen and Various Legends and Lyrics*, which Foster states, 'handed weapons to the enemy'. The tone of the collection was exemplified by the poem entitled 'Apologia addressed to Ireland in the coming days' (later to be known as 'To Ireland in the Coming Times'). Foster claims that this poem brought together 'occultism and advanced nationalism' in a manner that could only have irritated the very mainstream nationalism he was seeking to dissolve.[11]

Yeats's publication scheme was, of course, modelled on the Young Ireland Library of Ireland of the 1840s, but with the crucial difference that his books were to be directed at the instilling of nationality rather than plain instruction or nationalist propaganda. By nationality, Yeats meant a force that could successfully rebuke the scourge of liberalism in the Western world and form the conditions in which the production of art might be once again possible. This nationality was not conventionally

---

[9] W. B. Yeats, 'The Young Ireland League', *United Ireland*, 3 Oct. 1891, repr. in *Uncollected Prose by W. B. Yeats*, ed. J. P. Frayne (London: Macmillan, 1970), i. 208

[10] Yeats, *Autobiographies*, 200.   [11] Foster, *W. B. Yeats*, 122.

nationalist and, despite (but also because of) its celebration of folklore and 'orality', sought to transcend the narrow provincialism of Young Ireland nationalism. Yeatsian nationality would achieve expression in particular works of art—his poetry and drama, Hyde's translations from the Irish language, the plays of Synge, and Augusta Gregory's *Cuchulainn of Muirthemne*—but also in the superstitions and folklore of the poor rural peasantry. Yeats wanted to infiltrate the Young Ireland reading rooms and societies with an art that was national in these terms and thereby displace the propaganda that passed itself off as literature in Ireland. However, at this stage (though later as well) the young Yeats appears not to have realized how difficult it would be to take control of 'culture' in Ireland. He was probably confident that he could readily subsume Young Irelandism within his own grander literary project and did not feel unduly bothered by mainstream nationalism. Yeats's experience of Gavan Duffy in 1892 would dispel a portion of that faith, but he would make yet more attempts to instil his 'popular' revival.

In early 1892 Yeats declared to John O'Leary his desire to be the editor of the publishing scheme, so that nobody 'could hamper my action'.[12] Exercising caution, he also suggested that there be three directors of the series to counter any suspicion that the publications were tainted by 'party' politics. Evidently, he wanted to retain complete control over the proceedings while appearing to be entirely fair. At this stage, Yeats was making arrangements for the following publications:

> Rolleston promises to do for the first volume a history of Fenianism of a popular nature & to fill it with sound national doctrine. I would myself do 'a ballad chronicle of Ireland'—a Davis idia—selected from all the ballad writers & piece the poems to gether with short historical notes. For later volumes I have been offered 'the Ossianic Stories' by York Powell and Education in Ireland by Lionel Johnston. O'Grady would probably do a book also & I myself have a wish to write a manual of Irish literature in the present century.[13]

If it had seen the light of day, that manual of Irish literature might have sought to shift literary modes away from didactic realism and propaganda. However, it is the only volume in the list that might have marked a departure from the prevailing orthodoxies of the period. From the outset, Yeats was keen to emphasize the literariness of his publication project, but these books are for the most part rooted in those very traditions he was hoping to jettison. Yeats's position appears to be fundamentally

[12] Yeats, Letter to John O'Leary, [after 17 Feb. 1892], *CL* 286.   [13] Ibid. 285.

contradictory and even confused: at a meeting of the Irish Literary Society in Dublin on 8 August 1892—at which Gavan Duffy spoke (see below)—Yeats called for books for the New Irish Library that would 'appeal to ... such interests as were universal—heroism, the love of true manhood, and so on'.[14] These 'interests' would not be served by either 'a ballad chronicle of Ireland' or a book on Irish education. At this time, he was attempting to make a distinction between his revivalism and previous attempts to instil culture in Ireland, such as those embarked upon by both improvement and Young Ireland. His idea of culture was supposed to be distinct from that implicit in the discourses of improvement and Young Ireland in which culture signified the attainment of domestic comfort, relative prosperity, and respectability. However, the books he was planning to publish were at odds with his core ideals of culture.

At a practical level, Yeats was probably forced to rely on a Young Ireland model to get the series off the ground as there was little else available from which to construct a series of Irish books. As noted previously, he was still in the throes of defining his own literary project and did not, at this point, think of Young Ireland as a significant threat to his revivalist ambitions. That would come later. Roy Foster has suggested that Yeats was in part to blame for Gavan Duffy's editorial decisions as, in a letter to the *Daily Express*, 'he gave hostages to fortune in his hastily compiled model for the Library of Ireland'. The 'model' he presented to the readers of the *Daily Express* included Gavan Duffy's *The Spirit of the Nation* and the same titles he had mentioned in his letter to O'Leary.[15] It would appear that Young Irelandism did not become a literary and political obstacle, indeed impasse, for Yeats until Gavan Duffy, backed by J. F. Taylor and T. W. Rolleston, assumed full control of the New Irish Library. Yeats only then realized that Young Ireland did not simply represent a range of innocuous conventions that would easily fall prey to his literary project, but was, in fact, solidly institutionalized in Irish culture. Is it possible, however, that the manner of Yeats's organization of the New Irish Library was an early manifestation of what Joyce—referring directly to his management of the Irish Literary Theatre—described in 1901 as 'Mr. Yeats's treacherous instinct of adaptability'.[16] This was, in Joyce's mind, Yeats's greatest limitation in

---

[14] Yeats, quoted in *CL* 312 n.   [15] Foster, *W. B. Yeats*, 120.
[16] James Joyce, 'The Day of the Rabblement', *United Irishman*, 2 Nov. 1901, repr. in James Joyce, *Occasional Critical and Political Writing*, ed. Kevin Barry (Oxford: Oxford University Press, 2000), 51.

his administration of the theatre, but it would appear to have also been his principal shortcoming as early as 1892 in his arrangements for the New Irish Library when he succumbed to the 'rabblement' in order to be accepted by mainstream nationalism.[17]

Yeats felt the need to cultivate support for his editorship of the Library in the mainstream nationalist community in Dublin and London. By any standards, he was not an obvious representative of that community. In the early 1890s, Yeats, whose stance on most matters tended to be uncompromising, was associated with political extremism by the more moderate constituencies in those cities, who did not welcome any rhetoric that suggested either Fenian or Parnellite sympathies.[18] At this point, Yeats was drawn to O'Learyite Fenianism, and his friendship with the elderly republican would have been sufficient grounds for suspicion. In a letter of 2 June 1892 to the *Daily Express*, he stated that 'these books and lectures will be national but not political in any narrow sense of the word.'[19] Aware of the suspicion surrounding his motives, Yeats publicly declared that his project was not in the control of any faction or party. In part, this was probably true: his ambitions were deeply political, but not in the particular terms of any existing political group or institution in the 1890s. Primarily, he wanted to keep the didactic, propagandizing constituency—and, by implication, those traditions of liberalism and utilitarianism—far away from his publication scheme. However, his mistake had been to pander to those interests in the first place by invoking the traditions of Thomas Davis and Charles Gavan Duffy.

At the invitation of the Irish Literary Society in London, Gavan Duffy arrived in June 1892 to take up the presidency and to speak at its inaugural meeting. Gavan Duffy was not content to be a mere figurehead of the Literary Society and was especially eager to take an active role in the publication scheme. The Young Irelander had already expressed a desire to relaunch the Library of Ireland of the 1840s, as though he felt a need to bring that particular Young Ireland project to a conclusion. Prior to the inaugural meeting, Yeats mentioned his plans for the first three volumes in a letter to Gavan Duffy, enquiring if he considered 'this a good selection or if you have anything to say in opposition or in modifaction'.[20] Gavan Duffy could not have

[17] Ibid. 50.   [18] See the analysis in Foster, *W. B. Yeats*, 119–20.
[19] Yeats, Letter to the *Daily Express*, 2 June 1892, *CL* 299.
[20] Yeats, Letter to Sir Charles Gavan Duffy [week ending 23 July 1892], *CL* 305.

been unhappy with any of the books mentioned by Yeats as they were precisely the kind of thing he eventually published, but his speech expressed implicit disapproval of any kind of aesthetic revival. His library project was most certainly opposed to Yeats's vision of a nation enraptured by a popular 'imaginative literature'. The nation was, in Gavan Duffy's mind, far too imaginative already and was in urgent need of being made fully aware of the desperate material conditions of the nineteenth century. In his memoir, Ryan notes that Gavan Duffy 'had pondered for years upon Irish legislative and industrial problems. Nor was literature entirely forgotten in his plans, though very often it was literature of the didactic and ethical kind.'[21] Gavan Duffy brought the entirety of his Young Ireland pragmatism and strong utilitarian instincts to bear on his plans for the New Irish Library. After Gavan Duffy's speech—conducted, Ryan records, in the auspicious setting of Oak Tree House, Hampstead, 'amidst trees, idyllic scenery, and artistic associations'—the establishment of a publishing company, which would administer the New Irish Library, was embarked upon, though not without controversies.[22]

Gavan Duffy clearly outlined the instructional, practical programme of his New Irish Library in his speech to the Irish Literary Society in London. He asserted the need for 'books of a practical character' as, he argued, 'the condition of the country was now too serious for madrigals.' The 'madrigals' he had in mind were clearly anything of a 'high' literary or speculative bent. Gavan Duffy insisted on the need for instructional literature because 'the business of education is not for ornament merely, but for practical use.'[23] It was not simply that aesthetic considerations were to be entirely subordinate to a modernizing propaganda and didacticism, but that they were not to interfere with these plans on any level. Yeats would soon be excluded from the publication scheme in order to guarantee that literary and aesthetic matters would not at all impinge upon whatever plans Gavan Duffy had for the Library. The Young Irelander professed impatience with such concerns whereas in fact he was profoundly disconcerted by literariness—all too vividly expressed by the young Yeats—associated by him with idleness, inertia, and politics. Even in the 1840s, he had been in reaction against an alleged

---

[21] Ryan, *The Irish Literary Revival*, 62.   [22] Ibid.
[23] Charles Gavan Duffy, 'What Irishmen May Do for Irish Literature', 23 July 1892, printed in *The Revival of Irish Literature, Addresses by Sir Charles Gavan Duffy, Dr. George Sigerson and Dr. Douglas Hyde* (London: Fisher Unwin, 1894), 18.

aestheticism, which he associated with a regressive tendency that was by its very nature at variance with the necessary work of modernization. That was borne out by his publication of improvement tracts in the Library of Ireland. In the figure of Gavan Duffy, Yeats was forced to confront directly nineteenth-century traditions of liberal utilitarianism. Particularly worrying for Yeats was the attempt to repeat those very same botched experiments in the 1890s. As an idea, the 'nation' meant entirely different things to Yeats and Gavan Duffy; for the former, it was a literary construct which by definition had to exist in opposition to liberal progress whereas, for the latter, it was a modernizing ideology.[24] Gavan Duffy wanted to complete the nineteenth-century programme of utilitarian improvement in Ireland and then call that place a nation. For Yeats, however, the nation could only be achieved by extricating itself fully from those traditions.

Malcolm Brown argues that the dispute between the two came down to a contest between poetry and history, that 'one of Duffy's contentions was that Irishmen could best employ their time in the study of the Irish past than in the reading of contemporary poetry.'[25] In his speech, Gavan Duffy claims that there were numerous texts written by Young Irelanders as well as reams of Gaelic literature which 'still lies buried in untranslated MSS'.[26] A series of books could be immediately constructed from all of this extant material. Gavan Duffy was keen for Thomas Davis's *The Patriot Parliament of 1689* to be the first volume in the New Irish Library, declaring the historical emphasis and tone of the Library from the very outset. Clearly, historical writing (of a very particular variety) was for Gavan Duffy practical in that it both stabilized the past and contained the present. In this respect, history was distinct from literature, which threatened to disturb historical narratives rather than finalizing and closing them off. Gavan Duffy expressed an uncompromising loyalty to his Young Ireland roots: as the previous chapter demonstrated, Young Ireland used the writing of history in order to distinguish historical fact from oral memory, making a nationalist historical narrative acceptable by domesticating (and thereby conventionalizing) it within the tropes

[24] For discussions of this theme in general terms, see David Lloyd, 'The Poetics of Politics: Yeats and the Founding of the State', *Anomalous States: Irish Writing and the Post-Colonial Moment* (Dublin: Lilliput Press, 1993), 59–88, and Marjorie Howes, *Yeats's Nations: Gender, Class and Irishness* (Cambridge: Cambridge University Press, 1996).
[25] Malcolm Brown, *The Politics of Irish Literature: From Thomas Davis to W. B. Yeats* (Seattle: University of Washington Press, 1971), 361.
[26] Gavan Duffy, 'What Irishmen May Do for Irish Literature', 16.

of a middle-class textual culture. Gavan Duffy was seeking to bring Irish history in from the wild, disassociating talk of conquest and colonization from a primitive, oral backwardness and regional fragmentation. As with Young Ireland projects such as the *Nation* and the Library of Ireland, Gavan Duffy's New Irish Library was supposed to embed a nationalist story within a narrative order of improved domesticity. Gavan Duffy's historicizing was intended to unify historical experience and memory into a nationalist (because unifying) narrative. As a project, this was both desperate and impossible, destined to fail in the 1890s just as it had failed in the 1840s despite the persistent existence of an audience that appeared to be willing to lend it credence.

For Gavan Duffy, historical narratives disciplined the people into a proper nationalist community. He explained that

Liberty will do much for a nation, but it will not do everything. Among a people who do not know and reverence their own ancestors, who do not submit cheerfully to lawful authority, and do not love the eternal principles of justice, it will do little. But moral sentiments, generous impulses, religious feelings still survive in the Irish race, and they give assurance that in that mystic clime on the verge of the Western Ocean, where the most debasing currents of European civilization only reach it at high tide, there is place for a great experiment for humanity.[27]

Gavan Duffy's experiment was directed at instilling a nationalism that was, of course, distinct from republicanism and was, in essence, counter-revolutionary. A Young Ireland historicism would be central to this project or 'experiment' as it would narrativize historical experience and, in so doing, would ward off the threat of extremism. Ireland appeared to offer the possibility of realizing this kind of nationalist state as, unlike in pre-Revolutionary France, there did not exist a class of 'artisans ... who were so often Godless scoffers'.[28] The deep religiosity of the Irish people should offer a natural protection against the atheism and cold rationality of Republicanism, allowing instead for a fully practical programme of nationalist economic reform.

Gavan Duffy insisted that education (like literature) should be strongly utilitarian, transforming Ireland from peasant backwardness into middle-class respectability. He even credits the National Schools—later much criticized in the Revival period as denationalizing institutions—with having assisted in this process, commenting that, by

[27] Gavan Duffy, 'What Irishmen May Do for Irish Literature', 20–1.
[28] Ibid. 22.

their means, 'the boy who emerged from a smoky and squalid cabin, shared with a pig, is turned into a clean and shapely youth.'[29] All institutions that instilled discipline—National Schools, the army, the police force—were especially commended for civilizing a pre-modern slovenly mass into fully modern citizens. Gavan Duffy even goes so far as to claim that 'the decent uniform and the punctual system soon make a new man of the peasant.'[30] Echoing writers such as Edgeworth and Leadbeater, Gavan Duffy insists that 'the deficiencies in national character may be repaired by discipline.' In this analysis, Irish character could only be redeemed by the institutions of modernization. National progress would require the Irish masses 'to be prudent and temperate in action, and to regard the whole nation as members of a common household'.[31] Metaphorically, the household as nation was to indicate unity and coherence, the achievement of the common ground and domestication necessary for modernization. Indeed, Leadbeater's clean, orderly cottage—itself an emblem of the modernized, rationalized state—made Gavan Duffy's nationalism possible. His programme of nationalism was reliant on what he terms a 'strenuous self-discipline', each citizen fully embodying the (disciplined) truths of the nation state. In this rhetoric, the individual citizen represents the family and the family in turn represents the state (and vice versa), each serving as an analogy for the other. These analogies seek to enforce and authenticate particular political and literary forms of representation. Improvement writers and mainstream nationalists (such as Gavan Duffy) were eager to organize Irish writing (and institutions) in accordance with this system.

To other writers of this period, such a system was detrimental to the creation of literature and they laboured to write beyond it. For these writers, aesthetic possibility could exist only in the impoverished conditions of the dishevelled Irish cabin or in the desolation of a bleak, unimproved landscape. In the Preface to his collection of peasant folklore, *Beside the Fire*, Hyde describes 'the antiquity of these tales, as told today by a half-starving peasant in a smoky Connaught cabin'.[32] The attempts of improvement writers to reform fireside orality are clearly rebuked by the title of Hyde's collection, which asserts the innate civility of the chimney corners in the squalid cabins of the west of

---

[29] Ibid.   [30] Ibid.   [31] Ibid. 20.
[32] Douglas Hyde, Preface, *Beside the Fire: A Collection of Irish Gaelic Folk Stories* (London: D. Nutt, 1890), p. xli.

Ireland. By a variety of means, the entire collection strives to counteract the assumptions of improvement. Hyde seeks to emphasize the
authenticity of the material in his collection, which is, in his thinking,
guaranteed by the impoverishment of his narrators and the absence
of any improvement whatsoever. The narrators of the stories collected in *Beside the Fire* are, he claims, 'the oldest, most neglected, and
poorest of the Irish-speaking population'.[33] This remoteness—indeed
hunger—supposedly guaranteed authenticity, the purity of origins and
indeed civilization, preserved in the mouths of hungry peasants in
the west of Ireland. The peasantry embodied civilization as they had
not been modernized (modernization, for Hyde, was really barbarism).
Poverty, folktales, and the Irish language were supposed to provide a
rhetorical defence against an ever-encroaching materialism and ruthless
practicality as expressed by modernizers such as Gavan Duffy. In its
proper and supposedly authentic typeface, the Irish language symbolized, in Hyde's mind, a revivalist resistance to modernization. The
language had to be protected from modernization by being encoded
and, therefore, preserved within its own, ancient typeface, estranged
and removed from the material world by inhabiting a script that could
not accommodate the representational forms of modernization.[34] The
obscurity signified by Irish-language culture was, for Hyde, in the process of being comprehensively replaced by the transparency of progress.
The appearance of Irish in roman type in newspapers such as *United
Ireland* irritated him as it normalized the language and made it capable
of representing the very modernization he was seeking to prevent. The
language had to appear useless: if Irish could be brought within the
modern marketplace and thus made representational, it would no longer
be of value to a cultural revival. It may appear odd to cast Hyde as
a figure who was ambivalent towards the actual revival of the Irish
language, but his literary work of the 1890s was profoundly antagonistic
to modernization, including the tendency of mainstream nationalists
to 'modernize' the Irish language. The comprehensive revival of Irish
would have entailed a corruption of the language. Additionally, Hyde's
appreciation of the language was profoundly textual, indeed, aesthetic.

[33] Douglas Hyde, Preface, *Beside the Fire: A Collection of Irish Gaelic Folk Stories*.
[34] On this topic in a broader historical context, see Seamus Deane, *Strange Country:
Modernity and Nationhood in Irish Writing, 1700–1900* (Oxford: Clarendon Press,
1997), 100–44, and Joep Leerssen, *Remembrance and Imagination: Patterns in the
Historical and Literary Representation of Ireland in the Nineteenth Century* (Cork: Field
Day/Cork University Press 1996), 195–8.

Beside the Fire purports to document the raw artefacts of an Irish-language culture which are distinguished precisely because they have not been translated into the conventions of literary realism. Instead, the stories are supposedly transcribed directly from the mouths of peasants and are then literally translated into English. Some of the stories are also accompanied by the Irish-language original in its apparently appropriate type face. In this mode, Hyde's volume estranges the stories and the Irish language from the prevailing norms and conventions of English-language writing. In so doing, he aestheticizes both the Irish language of the stories and the hungry storytellers. As such, Hyde's collection opposes itself to the rationalizing modes of previous collections of folk material and to former representations of the oral and savage peasant which had been propounded in the improving tracts of the nineteenth century (while, of course, creating another, equally troubling, range of stereotypes).

Gavan Duffy cites an unnamed book—in fact this is Elizabeth Hamilton's *Cottagers of Glenburnie*—as an example of the kind of publication he has in mind for the New Irish Library. He claims that he has been assured by 'the critics' that Hamilton's tract had 'routed filth and laziness out of the farmhouses of Scotland'.[35] If allowed to roam free in Ireland, Hamilton's text would, it is implied, quickly eradicate the subject matter of Hyde's *Beside the Fire*, Yeats's poetry and fiction, and, at a later date, Synge's drama as well. Hamilton's improving tract had itself been one of the most successful of its kind in the nineteenth century and had been widely distributed throughout Ireland. It is notable, indeed striking, that Hamilton's Scotland—one symbolized by a Highland cabin which is eventually purged of all regional idiosyncrasy and brought into the British mainstream—should become a model for an Irish nationalist. Implicit in Hamilton's text is a claim that improvement is entirely feasible in Scottish conditions, that the movement from a Celtic barbarity into a civil Britishness can be unambiguously achieved. It was undoubtedly this assurance that appealed to Gavan Duffy. However, the absence of improvement (and thus distance from the British mainstream) was what made Ireland valuable as literary subject matter for many Revival writers.

This was as true for Hyde and Yeats in the early 1890s as it would also be for Synge in the final years of the century when he began to publish

---

[35] Gavan Duffy, 'What Irishmen May Do for Irish Literature', 32.

his accounts of life on the Aran Islands.[36] It was the orality of the Aran Islands (and the fact that Hamilton's text had not yet brought them in from the wild) that served as their appeal to Synge. The Aran Islands do not evoke for Synge a pre-modern backwardness but an aesthetic modernity. Synge claims that the storytelling of the Aran Islander Pat Dirane gave him 'a strange feeling of wonder' at hearing an 'illiterate native of a wet rock in the Atlantic telling a story that is so full of European associations'.[37] The life of the Aran Islands still retained those conditions that gave rise to both the aestheticism of a Synge and the modernizing ambitions of a Gavan Duffy:

On the low sheets of rock to the east I can see a number of red and grey figures hurrying about their work. The continual passing in this island between the misery of last night and the splendour of today, seems to create an affinity between the moods of these people and the moods of varying rapture and dismay that are frequent in artists and in certain forms of alienation.[38]

The physical conditions of life on the Aran Islands closely resemble the metaphysical conditions that give rise to 'art'. Extremes of mood—from despair to exhilaration—make Synge's peasants truly emblematic of modernity. Far from backward, the peasants on the Aran Islands are characteristically modern, though not in the terms of a modernizing nationalism. Synge's Aran Islands were, of course, the very kind of primitive remnant (or fragment) that Hamilton—along with all improvers and mainstream nationalists—sought to have thoroughly absorbed in a modernizing mainstream and narrative. It was the continued existence of such places in Ireland that provided the impetus for Gavan Duffy's modernizing nationalism. Given the fundamentally standardizing ambitions of Hamilton's text, it is unsurprising that it appealed to the sensibilities of a Gavan Duffy. Like the improvement writers of the early nineteenth century, Scotland was a significant point of reference for Gavan Duffy, a model of national improvement which 'for nearly two centuries ... had excellent parish schools where the children of the industrious population get a practical and religious education at the cost of the state'. The Scottish model had to be emulated; as

---

[36] Synge's first article on the Aran Islands was published in the *New Ireland Review* in 1898. He completed his book on the Islands in 1901, but it was not published until 1906.

[37] J. M. Synge, *The Aran Islands*, 1906, ed. Tim Robinson (London: Penguin, 1992), 20.

[38] Ibid. 30.

Gavan Duffy points out, 'the Scotch boy is taught mathematics and trained early in business' (and thus middle-classness) and is, therefore, appropriately equipped for survival (and use) in a modernizing economy rather than being needlessly educated in a range of subjects, such as Latin and Greek, that merely distract from the work at hand.[39] In part, Gavan Duffy—like so many improvement and nationalist writers in Ireland—was frustrated with the inability of Ireland to resemble Scotland and its failure to become exemplary of those traditions of liberal utilitarianism that contributed to the shaping of British identity from the 1790s.

Yeats was soon to encounter this improving, nationalist tradition in person when Gavan Duffy travelled to Ireland in August of 1892 'to propound his scheme to the metropolis at home' at a meeting of the Irish National Literary Society in Dublin. Yeats had not been present at the London meeting the previous July, but was very much in the audience in the Mansion House in August. Gavan Duffy's plans for the Publishing Company were to prove less welcome in Dublin, striking a more ambivalent chord with the Dublin audience. Ryan contends that 'the representatives of a new Irish generation, keenly conscious of intellectual wants and wishes' and 'with pronounced ideas on the subject of their fulfilment' dominated the Society in Dublin. This group was, Ryan claims, 'more disposed to criticize Sir Charles's scheme and its proposed working than their brethren in London'.[40] The most prominent member of this Irish group was Yeats, who was soon to articulate his immense dissatisfaction with Gavan Duffy's project. From that point on, it became difficult to reconcile the interests of the Dublin and London literary societies. By September, the argument was being aired in the newspapers, initiated by Yeats, who wrote to the *Freeman's Journal* to express his suspicion that Gavan Duffy was acquiring sole control of the publication scheme. That letter was to elicit responses from both Gavan Duffy and his supporter J. F. Taylor.

The dispute in the *Freeman's Journal* was sparked by Yeats's claim that Gavan Duffy was too elderly and detached from Ireland to be an effective editor of a series of national books. At another level, the quarrel arose because Yeats correctly sensed that he was being pushed

[39] Gavan Duffy, 'Books for the Irish People', 17 June 1893, printed in *The Revival of Irish Literature*, 44. This speech was also published under the title *The Prospects of Irish Literature for the People: An Address Before the Irish Literary Society London by its President, Sir Charles Gavan Duffy* (London: Gaskill, Jones and Co., 1893).

[40] Ryan, *The Irish Literary Revival*, 66.

out of all publication negotiations. On realizing that Gavan Duffy was taking over, Yeats was to become the most severe critic of the New Irish Library. Yeats concluded his letter by stating that 'if we fail now to interest the people of Ireland in intellectual matters by giving them books of the kind they seek for, if we fail to enlist the sympathy of the young men who will have the building up of the Ireland of tomorrow, we may throw back the intellectual development of this country for years.'[41] For Yeats, the New Irish Library was to be one of the necessary first steps in his revival project, cultivating both the conditions and the audience for his writing. However, that opportunity was now lost to the stringent conventionalism of Gavan Duffy. In order to dilute the influence of Gavan Duffy, Yeats suggested that an editorial committee be established which would comprise figures such as Douglas Hyde, George Sigerson, and John O'Leary.

In the very next issue of the *Freeman's Journal*, Taylor, Gavan Duffy's principal spokesman throughout the dispute, bluntly declared that no such editorial committee was to be created and that Gavan Duffy's editorship would ensure that 'the company will be worked on broad principles, and not in the interest of any coterie, however, precious.' That preciousness was undoubtedly a description of Yeats's supposedly impractical, ethereal interests. Taylor mocks the manner in which Irish literary life was then being conducted: 'it is not an edifying spectacle to see A reviewing B, and B in turn reviewing A, and both going into raptures of admiration', to which he adds, 'it will be gratifying to Mr. Yeats to know that Sir Charles, as editor, will be able to restrain such log-rolling and to work the enterprise in an earnest and honest way.'[42] In the hands of Gavan Duffy, the New Irish Library would not become a vehicle for the literary ambition of young writers such as Yeats. T. W. Rolleston soon reported that Gavan Duffy needed to be the sole editor of the Library as he had 'to protect the books from becoming imbecile, extravagant, or partisan'.[43] Perhaps Rolleston was implicitly equating Yeats's 'extravagant' literary project with the more extreme elements of Irish nationalism. Despite Yeats's own discomfort with extreme politics in later poems such as 'Easter 1916', his staunchness in the 1890s and friendship with John O'Leary ensured that he was to be associated with political extremism in the 1890s. Cleary, Taylor, Rolleston, and

---

[41] W. B. Yeats, Letter to the *Freeman's Journal*, 6 Sept. 1892.
[42] J. F. Taylor, Letter to the *Freeman's Journal*, 7 Sept. 1892.
[43] Quoted in *CL* 315 n.

Duffy were eager to protect against the literary and political interests of 'extremists'. Neither could result in the achievement of social, linguistic, or political harmony, forever disrupting the possibility of a stable middle ground.

The grounds for shutting Yeats out of the New Irish Library were made fully clear by another missive from J. F. Taylor to the *Freeman's Journal* on 9 September:

[The Library] is a commercial undertaking which must reckon upon merely average men, not upon men of supreme gifts. Its work must be done by careful, painstaking literary workmen, who may do something to spread knowledge and cultivated opinion as well as to develop thought among the people, thus supplying a most crying need. It is not the work of Richelieu or Queen Christina or the Empress Catherine that is to be done by the Company. It can neither seek out nor patronize men of genius. If such men there be in Ireland (as God grants there may!) I think they will keep far away from all local committees, working in grim seclusion, going through the great preparatory silence needful for all memorable things, and then patiently, modestly, but inflexibly scaling the steep, slippery ascent which leads to immortality. Our work is on a lower level than this.[44]

Taylor is adamant that the New Irish Library was not supposed to be a literary or aesthetic project but was directed at solidly practical, vocational ends. The commercialism of the Library (which was synonymous with practicality) excluded by definition any consideration of literary matters, which could only antagonize and disturb the objectives of the scheme. For Taylor, the literary and the commercial were fully opposed, the one effectively destroying the possibility of the other. The demands of commerce, conducted in a busy marketplace and prey to all kinds of pressures and constraints, could not accommodate 'men of genius'. Taylor declares that the Library would fail if it did not commission the most ordinary and prosaic of material. The 'lower level' at which the New Irish Library was being organized was exactly what Yeats had hoped to avoid. That level also encapsulated a tradition of writing in Ireland that Yeats was striving to transcend. For his revival, Yeats was, in fact, thinking along the grand, aesthetic lines of a Richelieu or Empress Catherine or—as expressed at a later point—Byzantium.

Gavan Duffy had clearly accumulated sufficient support in the Irish literary community to shut Yeats out of all library negotiations. The New Irish Library was nonetheless beset by a range of practical and

---

[44] J. F. Taylor, Letter to the *Freeman's Journal*, 9 Sept. 1892.

financial problems, though it finally managed to procure a contract with Fisher Unwin. Gavan Duffy's Library was suggested to Unwin by T. W. Rolleston, who made known the details of Yeats's earlier negotiations with the publisher. On hearing a rumour that Rolleston and Gavan Duffy had acquired a contract with Unwin, Yeats wrote to Edward Garnett to enquire if he really had been betrayed and to plead for caution in handing the series over to Gavan Duffy. Striking a defiant note, Yeats declared that 'at any rate as I practically planned and started this whole Irish literary movement I do not think that anything should be done behind my back.'[45] However, Yeats had lost the New Irish Library and with it the opportunity to instil an imaginative literature within an affordable, 'popular' medium.

In Gavan Duffy's hands, the New Irish Library was to be firmly conducted in the spirit of Young Ireland. He was eager that the Library volumes should work at the preservation of a range of supposedly national characteristics which were then—as they had been continually from the late eighteenth century onwards—seriously threatened by the many foreign books in circulation in Ireland. Gavan Duffy explains that these books were corrupting those virtues 'for which our people were distinguished, purity, piety and simplicity'.[46] Those very traits were themselves produced by nineteenth-century literary and nationalist discourses in an attempt to ward off 'French' influence. As such, they were to be the foundation of the nation state and, in the case of Carleton's fiction, of a national literature. These virtues (or nationalist clichés) were, Gavan Duffy warned, about to be swapped for a set of foreign and corrupt (because mostly French) traits. One of the purposes of the New Irish Library would be to cleanse Irish reading habits and drive out this 'defective' and 'sensational' fiction that arrived from America and England—all 'vile translations from the French of vile originals'—which then comprised the 'intellectual diet' of the people. This 'impure and atheistical' literature had to be replaced by nationalizing and improving texts, instilling a Catholic respectability while pushing out a particularly worrisome influence, comprising republicanism, atheism, political discontent, and 'theory'.[47]

In his *Autobiographies*, Yeats recounts that Gavan Duffy joined forces with Archbishop Walsh, who was eager to protect against a

---

[45] Yeats, Letter to Edward Garnett [*c*.9 Nov. 1892], *CL* 330.
[46] Gavan Duffy, 'What Irishmen May Do for Irish Literature', 12–13.
[47] Gavan Duffy, 'Books for the Irish People', 49.

dreaded infiltration of French literature into the Irish mainstream.[48] The Catholic Church would instinctively have welcomed the efforts of Gavan Duffy over those of a Yeats whose veneration of peasant pagan belief would have been an immense irritation to the Catholic hierarchy. Both improvement and modernizing nationalism would have been broadly welcomed by the Catholic Church, which also sought to root out popular superstition and backwardness. In however complicated a manner, both Gavan Duffy and the Catholic Church were modernizing forces in Irish society and, to them, Yeats would have been a nuisance. In addition, Yeats was at this point steeped in Romanticism, French symbolism, and English aestheticism. These traditions would have been an affront to the sensibilities of both Walsh and Gavan Duffy. Yeats himself noted in his *Memoirs* that those

who believed perhaps—as indeed thousands did—that The Spirit of the Nation was as great lyric poetry as any in the world would then say that I disliked it because I was under English influence—the influence of English decadent poets perhaps—and I would reply that it was them, whose lives were an argument over wrongs and rights, who could not escape from England even in their dreams.[49]

In Yeats's mind, mainstream nationalism was rooted in the imperial discourses it professed to be repudiating. This book has demonstrated that Young Ireland nationalism was firmly grounded in the imperial discourse of improvement. Indeed, mainstream nationalism in Ireland would never resolve this fundamental tension. For Yeats, this nationalism was to be forever limited by its inability to 'escape from' those discourses which were also tied to a counter-Romanticism. Consequently, Yeats's revivalism could never have won the approval of mainstream nationalists despite his various attempts to accommodate their rhetoric. Yeats claimed that he and Taylor were profoundly irreconcilable as he worked within a tradition (Blake, Shelley, and Keats) despised by Taylor and did not read his favoured writers (Locke, Swift, and Grattan). To make matters worse, Yeats knew nothing of the history that was of such importance to Taylor and, clearly, to Gavan Duffy as well.[50]

---

[48] For Yeats's account of Gavan Duffy's alliance with Archbishop Walsh, see *Autobiographies*, 227.

[49] W. B. Yeats, *Memoirs*, 1962, ed. Denis Donoghue (Dublin: Gill and Macmillan, 1972), 69.

[50] For Yeats's account of his poor relations with Taylor, ibid. 69.

Gavan Duffy gave a second speech to the Irish Literary Society in London after he had acquired complete control of the Library. In that speech, he presented a strongly didactic account of his publication plans. That didacticism was central to his modernizing and nationalizing ambitions. Gavan Duffy insists that fiery patriotism is necessary for modernization because a love of country 'burns up the grosser sentiments in young men, and teaches them that life has happier as well as nobler pursuits than self-indulgence'.[51] Nationalism was thus a regulating force, fostering a necessary postponement of gratification and a reining in of excess (both literary and political). Interestingly, Gavan Duffy opposes modernization to what he calls 'self-indulgence': undoubtedly that brooding on the self that then seeks outlets in aesthetics and politics. Like his improvement precursors, Gavan Duffy expresses irritation with this 'self-indulgence', which is seen to impede and retard progress rather than fostering an ethic of physical work and 'moving on'. 'Love of country', Gavan Duffy claims, leads one 'to abjure sensual and slavish vices', and thus break with oral and primitive patterns.[52] (In this rhetoric, both Catholic and nationalist tropes are inextricable.) By such means, the organic, realist narrative of nationalism effectively displaces the diffuse, oral fragments of the pre-modern. The orality of peasant backwardness was as unacceptable to nationalists as it had been to improvers and, in Young Ireland rhetoric, nationalism was to credit itself with being particularly effective in Irish conditions in dissolving that supposedly 'pre-modern' past. For Yeats, however, peasant orality had to be preserved as it was exemplary of aesthetic possibility. The similarities—or perceived identification—between orality and aestheticism had, as Chapter 1 argued, already been a source of anxiety for improvement writers, their project directed at the disruption of an identification which they had themselves constructed. In keeping with this, Yeats was to associate the work of art with the illiterate peasant at every opportunity (which suggests both his liberation from the rhetorical modes of improvement discourse and his continued confinement within them). In his Introduction to Lady Gregory's *Cuchulainn of Muirthemne*, he described how for the peasant 'his art ... is often at its greatest when it is most extravagant ... He understands as well as Blake that the ruins of time build mansions in eternity.'[53] Hence, the

---

[51] Gavan Duffy, 'Books for the Irish People' 42.   [52] Ibid. 42.

[53] Yeats, Introduction to Lady Gregory, *Cuchulainn of Muirthemne* (London, 1902), 14.

impoverishment and immaterialism of the peasant is equated with the production of an art that is itself abundant and lavishly material.

For Gavan Duffy the New Irish Library had to be strongly didactic because in Ireland, he declared, the people 'learn little thoroughly, and little of a useful and reproductive character, and we commonly pay the penalty in a lower place in the world'.[54] That lower place in the world was in part the result of an absence of industrial reproduction in Ireland. Gavan Duffy implies that production in Ireland is centred on single objects (fragments perhaps), such as crafts. All that is required to elevate Ireland into a higher place in the world is the discipline and unity of 'modern' work and industrial modes of production, which would be reproductive and unifying by comparison with the fragmentation and disunity of the pre-modern and aesthetic artefact. Yeats was of course drawn to this fragmentation, which for him epitomized the condition of art in the modern world while suggesting the only ground in which aesthetic production was possible. To make this claim is not to reiterate the argument that 'high' Revival writers sought in the peasant culture of Ireland a recourse from industrial reproduction. Peasant culture did not provide a sanctuary from materialism, but rather epitomized a 'truth' which was distorted by narratives of modernization.

Irish education lacked, in Gavan Duffy's mind, a properly vocational component, neglecting instruction in the very technical areas that were essential for industrial development. He claimed that Ireland had not 'made even a beginning in the practical education which makes industry possible'.[55] To compensate for this, he suggested a scheme for the distribution of the New Irish Library volumes, which would convey this practicality, through a 'system of canvassing agents by which books are brought to the remotest farmhouses and the canvassers paid a reasonable compensation'.[56] Gavan Duffy claims that such schemes were in existence in America, but, as this book has shown, there were more local models to hand for this project, from the distribution of Leadbeater's *Cottage Dialogues* and the Kildare Place pamphlets to Young Ireland's own Library of Ireland series.

By these means of distribution, Gavan Duffy's practical books would infiltrate the remotest of regions, such as those toured by Synge in the early twentieth century. Indeed, the kind of economic improvement

---

[54] Gavan Duffy, 'Books for the Irish People', 43.
[55] Gavan Duffy, 'What Irishmen May Do for Irish Literature', 22.
[56] Ibid. 27.

advocated by Gavan Duffy would, it was assumed, fully incorporate Ireland within the modern mainstream and purge those peculiarities that were to become the focus and concentration of Synge's writing. Interestingly, Synge was himself anxious that the source of his art was simultaneously the source of misery for the rural poor. In his travel writings for the *Manchester Guardian*, Synge, reflecting upon the people in Connemara, notes this exact problem:

One's first feeling as one comes back among these people and takes a place, so to speak, in this noisy procession of fishermen, farmers and women, where nearly everyone is interesting and attractive, is a dread of any reform that would tend to lessen their individuality rather than any very real hope of improving their well-being. One feels then, perhaps a little later, that it is part of the misfortune of Ireland that nearly all the characteristics which give colour and attractiveness to Irish life are bound up with a social condition that is near to penury.[57]

In part, Synge's own drama fed off the impoverished misery of the people and these peasants were only colourful and individual so long as they were poor and deprived. It was this eccentricity and peculiarity that impelled his dramatic project, but which would also, in Synge's mind, have made it universal by calling attention to those fundamental 'truths' of human existence which were being concealed by the rhetoric of modernization. Synge's travel writings are laden with the contradiction of his position: he expresses both empathy for the impoverishment of the people and anxiety that their condition will be improved (which would destroy the oddity his work dwelt upon). Synge himself reports that in those 'improved' areas of Connemara and Mayo conditions are undoubtedly better: the incidence of typhus is rare and there are cheaper sources of flour and meal than previously. In west Kerry, he describes how a 'little group of blue-coated men lying on the grass, and the group of girls further off, had a singular effect in this solitude of rocks and sea; and in spite of their high spirits it gave me a sort of grief to feel that utter loneliness and desolation of the place that has given these people their finest qualities.'[58] Synge suspected that those improvements in roads, agriculture, and education that were then sweeping the west of Ireland would obliterate this singularity. It is evident that the desolation that marked life in the west of Ireland was akin to the alienation that is such a preoccupation of Synge's own writing. It is not just that the

[57] Synge, *Travels in Wicklow, West Kerry and Connemara*, 1911 (London: Serif Books, 2005), 145.
[58] Ibid. 98.

work of art is signified by the peasant or that those conditions that produce poverty are also conducive to art, but that the precariousness of the peasant both in these desolate regions and in the broader context of improvement modernization signifies the discomfort and alienation that produces art.[59] In his travel writings, Synge does not depict an organic community in which production and consumption are devoid of alienation. Synge's peasants are deeply alienated. Improvement writers commented endlessly on the alienation of the rural poor, to them a worrisome phenomenon that had to be addressed as a matter of urgency. (Like Synge, these writers were, of course, themselves alienated.) For improvement writers, this alienation was of serious concern because it so readily expressed itself in politics, idleness, and drunkenness. Their solution to this alienation—for themselves as well as for the rural poor—was to promote a firm focus on the material conditions of life. Improvement writers sought to 'restore' to rural life the kind of organic community that would eradicate this alienation, itself a product of modernization. Improvers would, of course, have argued that the desolation that surrounds these Kerry peasants was a result of the very sitting and lying around described in this passage. In an improved economy, there would be no time for this kind of idleness. What Synge clearly apprehends as interesting and, in fact, beautiful, a Leadbeater or Doyle would castigate as backward and primitive. Indeed, improvers would quickly point out that the 'high spirits' of these people in a Kerry field were typical of those who simultaneously inhabit squalid homes and live from hand to mouth. As the previous chapter demonstrated, improvement tracts warned that 'high spirits' invariably connoted a corresponding proclivity to violence and chronic despondency. Writing in a Romantic tradition, Synge expresses the disaffection of a divided self and community, which refuses to be lured by those versions of either individualism or 'community' asserted in both improvement modernization and mainstream nationalism.

Like the improvers discussed in this book, Gavan Duffy was keen to 'humanize' Ireland in the wake of the colonial past and erase all of that 'aesthetic' bleakness. He describes how 'hard laws and hard taskmasters' had combined with 'twenty years of agitation' ('the fever of a tempestuous time') to blunt the 'moral sensibility' of the people.[60]

---

[59] On this topic, see Seamus Deane, 'Synge and Heroism', *Celtic Revivals: Essays in Modern Irish Literature 1880–1980* (London: Faber and Faber, 1985), 51–63.

[60] Gavan Duffy, 'Books for the Irish People', 46.

For Gavan Duffy, the problem with Ireland was that it persisted in being political and politics were for him—as for all modernizers—an obstacle to progress. The political obsessiveness in Ireland was, in his mind, partly understandable, but all of that could now be resolved by means of modernization. Contentment would, it seems, unambiguously follow on from a strict focus on practical matters. Gavan Duffy's ambition for the Library of Ireland was that it would assist in the humanizing of post-Famine Ireland, a humanization that could only be achieved by practical, didactic means. In place of the instability of the past, Gavan Duffy sought a 'contented and fruitful' people, who were at once productive and satisfied rather than idle and dissatisfied.[61] This transition, which would, it was assumed, effectively depoliticize the countryside, could be embarked upon by instruction in rural industry and, accordingly, he suggested that a book be produced for the New Irish Library which chronicled 'the localized industries of the continent and the honest outdoor enjoyments which help to make life happy'.[62] Such a volume would, it seems, clarify the connections between material gain (or modernization) and satisfaction, thereby highlighting the disappointments that follow on from a commitment to political idealism. The achievement of prosperity would erase any lingering (and antagonizing) memory of the despotic past, alienation, and thus all inclination towards political extremism. Gavan Duffy's revived Ireland was to be a culmination of the utilitarian, humanizing work of writers such as Edgeworth and Leadbeater, without either need or desire for politics and, for that matter, art. This position brings to light the reactionary nature of improvement liberalism, particularly when embodied in the Catholic nationalism of a Charles Gavan Duffy.

Figures such as Gavan Duffy had nothing but contempt for the peasant 'orality' venerated by Yeats and was eager for it to be replaced without delay by a literate English-language civility. Gavan Duffy embodied that nineteenth-century tradition of liberal counter-revolution (and counter-Romanticism), which was, of course, more immediately striking and troubling to Yeats at a literary level than at a political one. That they would disagree was, of course, to be expected and, predictably, their disagreement centred on those very debates that had determined the improvement project in Ireland in the early nineteenth century. At the first opportunity, Yeats was going to lash out at the intellectual and aesthetic inadequacies of Gavan Duffy's editorship. In an 1894

---

[61] Gavan Duffy, 'Books for the Irish People', 47.   [62] Ibid. 48.

Bookman review of the Library of Ireland volumes, he did precisely this. The first volume of the series to be published was *The Patriot Parliament of 1689*—in keeping with Gavan Duffy's wishes—which Yeats describes as

an historical tractate which, if modified a little, had done well among the transactions of a learned society, but it bored beyond measure the unfortunate persons who bought some thousands of copies in a few days, persuaded by the energy of the two societies, and deluded by the names of Sir Charles Gavan Duffy and Thomas Davis upon the cover. Pages upon pages of Acts of Parliament may be popular literature on the planet Neptune, or chillier Uranus, but our quick-blooded globe has altogether different needs.[63]

Yeats was convinced that the series fully misunderstood the literary needs and desires of the people by publishing dull historical material, which, he claims, resulted in 'the vehement refusal of numbers of the peasantry to take anything from a series which had already beguiled them so outrageously'. Yeats's imaginative peasants had, it seems, been waiting for some properly literary books to read and were appropriately dismayed by what the New Irish Library was providing. Nothing, Yeats claimed, could persuade the Irish peasantry to purchase *The New Spirit of the Nation* or *The Parish Providence*—two of the early New Irish Library volumes—both produced in the very worst traditions of crude Young Ireland propaganda and improvement didacticism. *The New Spirit of the Nation* was modelled on Young Ireland's earlier *The Spirit of the Nation* and contained, according to Yeats, the most deplorable writing imaginable. He describes the verse as 'jigging doggrel' [*sic*], claiming that such a publication would impede Revival and deter the educated classes from participation in any 'national' movement. Yeats was infuriated by the kind of audience implied by this collection of poetry and ballads:

You may persuade the half-educated country clerk or farmer's son that 'Come richest and rarest, come purest and fairest' is noble rhythm and shining poetry, but the wholly uneducated peasant of the mountains and the wholly educated professional man of the cities will have none of it, for the one has his beautiful Gaelic ballads and his tumultuous world-old legends, while the gleaming city of English literature flings its wide doors to the other.[64]

---

[63] Yeats, 'Some Irish National Books', *Bookman* (Aug. 1894), reprinted in ed. *Uncollected Prose*, ed. Frayne, i. 333.

[64] Ibid. 334.

The implication is that Gavan Duffy's New Irish Library was established to encourage the very worst elements in Irish society by appealing to the likes of clerks and middling farmers. In pandering to the values of that social group, Gavan Duffy was accommodating the vulgarity of middle-class Ireland over the imaginative depths of both oral culture and Yeatsian high Revivalism. Quite unlike the audience for *The New Spirit of the Nation*, Yeats's Revival readership was ideally to consist of the impoverished and the well-educated and certainly not the dreaded middle classes. As construed by Yeats, Revival was supposed to rid Ireland of that social group, eliminating those conditions in which the middle classes thrive and prosper. Yeats clearly saw Gavan Duffy's New Irish Library as an obstruction to his project of Revivalism; what he perceived to be his territory was now encroached upon and impeded by Gavan Duffy's publications.

In producing these volumes, Gavan Duffy had, Yeats claimed, 'let that old delusion, didacticism, get the better of his judgment'.[65] The dispelling of delusion was, in part, the point of improvement didacticism, which set itself the task of rooting out fictionality and fantasy and demonstrating the satisfaction that inhered in a rigid concentration on ordinary, productive life. As Yeats characterizes it, Gavan Duffy 'has always been an influence making for didacticism, rather than literature—for his great qualities are essentially practical'.[66] (This was, in Yeats's mind, the Young Irelander's greatest weakness.) Gavan Duffy's predilection for solid didacticism was made all too evident in the New Irish Library volumes and in his publication of Carleton's improving tracts of 1845. Carleton's abundant literary talent had, according to Yeats, been stifled by Gavan Duffy, who compelled him to produce tracts on agricultural improvement, agrarian unrest, and temperance. For Yeats, the poor writer's literary abilities never recovered from this immersion in the crass morality of improvement discourse. These tracts were, Yeats claims, intended 'to make some commonplace moral shine out with artificial distinctness' whereas, he went on to insist, 'a wiser age would do other than hold all such works for the creation of the Father of Lies.'[67] The tracts were commissioned by Gavan Duffy, but by 1845—as this book has shown—Carleton was already experienced in the production of didactic literature.[68] Gavan Duffy's shortcomings

---

[65] Yeats, 'Some Irish National Books', 335.   [66] Ibid. 335.   [67] Ibid.
[68] Both *Art Maguire* and *Parra Sastha* appear in an advertisement for a series of reprints of 'Duffy's Library of Ireland' in the *Freeman's Journal* on 10 Sept. 1892 at

as editor of the New Irish Library were all too evident in his plans to reprint Carleton's Library of Ireland tracts in the 1890s. Long before Carleton's direct associations with Young Ireland, he had worked hard on his own behalf to suppress whatever imaginative or literary tendencies that existed in his writing (not, of course, that he always succeeded). Carleton's Library of Ireland tracts were in part a laying bare of the improvement discourse and didacticism that lay at the core of so much of his fiction. That didactic mode sought to shape itself against literary writing, instilling clarity and organization in place of the obscurity and disorder associated with literariness. To Yeats, of course, didactic improvement—as articulated by an Edgeworth, Leadbeater, or Gavan Duffy—was the most delusional and mystified of all.

Carleton had been close to the principal figures of Young Ireland not just because he was himself torn between unionism and nationalism or that writing for money necessitated that he publish wherever he could, but because the differences between unionism and Young Ireland nationalism in the nineteenth century were not always entirely clear. His associations with supposedly diverse periodicals such as *Dublin University Magazine* and the *Nation* are by no means indicative of torn loyalties: Carleton was a modernizing 'national' writer and all of these periodicals were institutions of modernization. His politics were, like Gavan Duffy's, those of a modernizer who sought order and discipline in an attempt to represent a future that might resolve fully the differences that afflicted Irish life. In that respect, Carleton was as much an impeccable Young Irelander as he was a *Dublin University Magazine* Tory.

Yeats's anxiety was that the limitations of nineteenth-century Irish writing were about to be visited upon his Revival through the work of Charles Gavan Duffy. Yeats declared in a letter to *United Ireland* that the New Irish Library volumes were destined to alienate the 'educated classes', and erode those 'very qualities which make literature possible'. The unique—and necessary—conditions for Yeats's Revival were being destroyed by Duffy's publications: according to Yeats, 'the best opportunity ... these many decades' to produce an Irish literature was now in danger of 'ebbing out in a tide of irrelevant dullness'.[69] Yeats's

the height of the controversy between Yeats and Gavan Duffy. Carleton's tracts are also listed in the sales catalogue of the New Irish Library. See *Sales Catalogue for New Irish Library* [n.d.].

[69] Yeats, Letter to *United Ireland*, 1 Sept. 1894, *CL* 398.

Revival was supposed to overwhelm that dullness, but now his project was in danger of being engulfed by Duffyite mediocrity. It so happened that the New Irish Library volumes that were published sold relatively well, frequently entering into the best-seller lists of the *Bookman*.[70] However, Yeats needed to believe that the Irish reading public was still disappointingly awaiting the arrival of a national literature (which he would have to provide by other means) since Gavan Duffy had failed to deliver it through the New Irish Library. Yeats had to account for the relative commercial success of the New Irish Library volumes, having already decided that the series would be a failure in the hands of Gavan Duffy. In his letter to *United Ireland*, he states that 'it is perfectly well known that the first volume of any much-talked of series is certain of a large sale, quite independent of its merits, and the ten or fifteen thousand sold is not exceptional.'[71] Hence, the respectable sales of *The Patriot Parliament* were by no means owing to its literary merits, but should be attributed to the fact that the series as a whole had been the subject of considerable publicity. The New Irish Library did collapse soon after, but too late for Yeats to acquire it for his own particular interests and needs.

In a letter to John O'Leary, Yeats mentions that 'surely the world has not seen a more absurd "popular series" than this one', remarking to his delight that the books were no longer selling very well.[72] It is indeed impossible to imagine how E. M. Lynch's *A Parish Providence* could have held any appeal for an Irish readership. Yeats complained that Gavan Duffy had re-packaged an already weak Balzac novel by appending a didactic introduction on rural industry. To compound matters, he omitted the name of Balzac from the text and was attempting to pass 'this queer piece of "Irish literature" .... as an innocent "country tale" by E. M. Lynch'. Gavan Duffy's Introduction does mention the name of the original novel, *Medecin de Campagne* (a suggestive title for improvers?) but there is no reference to Balzac. The book is a mess: a confused mix of statistics, Balzac novel, and Duffyite didacticism which makes reference to nineteenth-century tract literature, but, unlike that genre, appears to be much less assured of its purpose. Gavan Duffy had to claim the narrative for didacticism, stating in his Introduction that 'our people are so destitute of practical and technical teaching, that a

[70] See the account in *CL* 501.
[71] Yeats, Letter to *United Ireland*, 1 Sept. 1894, *CL* 397.
[72] Yeats, Letter to John O'Leary, 26 June [1894], *CL* 392.

man here and there who acted in the spirit of the hero of this story, might in a brief time change the face of social Ireland to something brighter and better.'[73] Clearly anxious that readers might not know what to make of the text, Gavan Duffy's Introduction attempts to demonstrate how the narrative might provide guidance on the improvement of rural Ireland.

Gavan Duffy was eager that Lynch's tract be read as an example of what could supposedly be achieved in the material conditions of contemporary Ireland and how politics can be fully subordinate to the practical labour of modernization:

> Let no one fancy that I suppose this work will be a substitute for political action. I only insist that political action will be no adequate substitute for it. Such work occupies ground which political action only reaches slowly, or never reaches at all. I have lived in countries enjoying the most complete political liberty where large sections of the industrous classes were over-tasked and miserably poor. In some of the mountain communes of the French Republic I have seen the people work harder and live on scantier fare than the peasants of Connemara … Liberty has not made them prosperous because the resources of France are squandered by dishonest politicians.[74]

Republican liberty is therefore an entirely separate project from modernization and, it would appear, can even be at odds with it. Perhaps this is an attempt to distinguish modernization (or 'work') from republicanism (and, indeed, from all political discourse). The project of improvement was an attempt to define itself as a discourse of modernization that was distinct from republicanism (much like realism sought to mark itself off from Romanticism) and all 'political action'. For improvers and for Young Irelanders, it was as though work could provide redemption from politics and, for that matter, literature. The kind of modernizing reform implicit in these discourses is supposed to be an entirely separate process of rationalization from that which marked the revolution in France. The reformation achieved by modernization, directed at the transformation of material conditions, rather than seeking a revolution in ideas or institutions, is of greater benefit than 'political action'. Like all liberal improvers, Gavan Duffy was convinced that politics, particularly of a republican variety, were a dangerous distraction from the work of modernized progress. As previous chapters have demonstrated,

---

[73] Gavan Duffy, Introduction, *A Parish Providence* by E. M. Lynch (London: Fisher Unwin, 1894), p. x.
[74] Ibid. p. xxxix.

republicanism was seen to foster unrealistic expectations that could never be fulfilled, instilling a continual idleness or hanging around, time consumed in some long wait for a political redemption that was so impractical to begin with it could never possibly be achieved. When so-called liberty was achieved, the results were, as Gavan Duffy explains above, disappointing and even disastrous. This was to be expected as, according to this counter-revolutionary discourse, republicanism was divorced from the material world, existing only in a speculative realm removed from practical action or work. In this respect, republican-ism would worsen 'the inertness of the Irish peasant' whereas liberal improvement was seeking to dissolve that inertia.[75] In the liberal critique of republicanism which Gavan Duffy articulates, republican discourse was believed to encourage a postponement of any practical engagement with present conditions until such time as 'liberty' was achieved. This was one particular aspect of republican discourse—as it was perceived to play itself out in Irish conditions—that disconcerted improvement writers and those representatives of nationalist Ireland such as Thomas Davis and Charles Gavan Duffy.

An antidote to republicanism, or idealism of any form, is supposed to be provided by the harmonious and satisfying ordinariness of the fictional community depicted in *A Parish Providence*. One of the principal characters in Lynch's peculiar adaptation of Balzac's novel is described as being 'unpretending, unpoetic, commonplace'. Such a character would have been an outrage to Yeats and he would not have wanted him anywhere near his Revival. Lynch's fictional French mayor—and the hero of the tract—appropriately declares that he is far too grounded in practical matters to idealize the peasantry around him:

I never idealized my peasants; I took them for poor fellows who are neither perfectly good, nor absolutely wicked. They are too hard-worked to be highly strung. But they can feel acutely on occasion. One thing, I know for certain: you won't influence an agricultural population much, unless you can enlist self-interest, and give people something quickly for their pains.[76]

It is evident that any kind of idealization is at odds with rationalization and progress, leading only to some kind of dreamy backwardness (especially the 'idealizing'—Yeatsian-style—of the peasantry or the poor). In a realistic social order, free of idealization, the peasantry themselves fully inhabit the material world and, as a consequence, are

---

[75] Gavan Duffy, Introduction, p. xliii.   [76] Lynch, *A Parish Providence*, 42.

not either 'highly strung' (and therefore given to excess) or devoid of all feeling (and therefore coldly rational, revolutionary types). The perfect balance of both rationality and emotion is thereby achieved by a refusal to indulge any idealizing impulse whatsoever. These points are emphasized repeatedly throughout the tract: the fictional parish of the title is a place where everything 'ought to be strictly practical' and whose mayor claims that he doesn't 'generally deal ... in empty theories'.[77] Another character is praised because 'he did not trouble himself with theory, having enough to do with the practical side of things.'[78] Hence, theory and idealization exist in opposition to modernization and will fully disrupt the work of progress. In an Edgeworthian, counter-Romantic mode, speculation and, indeed, aestheticism are here seen to be regressive forces which impede improvement.

The reverse was to be the case for Yeats's Revival, which set itself the objective of overturning the work of progress. In the pamphlets and tracts produced in early nineteenth-century Ireland, the peasant served as a fictional point of origin for the creation of society from barbarity. In keeping with this, the peasantry becomes a mainstay of nineteenth-century Irish writing as either anarchic and violent or sentimental and endearing, the latter easily contained within the narratives of the modern nation state. Revival writers were afraid of merely reproducing this range of stereotypes, fearing that it might prevent them from producing a literature at all. Yeats spent the early years of the 1890s pronouncing endlessly on the need to transcend this tradition. As such, his Revival project—and that of Hyde and Synge—depended in part upon a re-imagining of the peasant primitivism of improvement discourse.[79] The peasantry had to be re-imagined, so that the prevailing conventions of nineteenth-century Irish writing could be transcended. Yeats partly defined his theatrical project against the example of Boucicault, whose dramas were banned by him from the stage of the Abbey.[80] Clearly, Yeats feared that such writing would corrupt his uncompromising aesthetic project. Yeats's literary theatre was not to be associated with the crude stereotypes of the nineteenth-century tradition (though its success in this particular quest is debatable). Therefore, in place of an unproductive and political peasantry, Revival writers produce a peasant who is imaginative,

---

[77] Ibid. 29.   [78] Ibid. 38–9.

[79] On Revival primitivism in a broader context, see Sinéad Garrigan Mattar, *Primitivism, Science, and the Irish Revival* (Oxford: Oxford University Press, 2004).

[80] On this policy, see Christopher Morash, *A History of Irish Theatre 1601–2000* (Cambridge: Cambridge University Press, 2002), 117.

productive, and conventionally apolitical. Re-imagining both the Irish peasantry and language as productive was embedded in a project which, at a certain level, sought to be unproductive. In this mode, Revivalism appears to be at odds with purposeful action in the world, confirming those fears of aestheticism that were expressed in improvement discourse, modernizing nationalism, and the literary realism of the nineteenth century. Yeats's work was, of course, a response, indeed, rebuke, to these traditions. As such, Yeatsian Revival was not a matter of plain realism in either political or literary terms. Recent accounts of the Revival tend to emphasize its more practical and material components, focusing on the intricate administration and alliances that existed across a range of political and cultural divides (including popular and aesthetic Revivalist tendencies). However, the Revival was beset by an irresolvable tension between popular, mainstream Revivalism—as expressed by a Gavan Duffy—and the work of writers such as Yeats and Synge. The fact that Yeats did paperwork and served on committees should not indicate that he was engaged in a pragmatic programme of reform or 'alternative modernization'. [81] Yeats's work was directed against the entrenched and, in his mind, debilitating, pragmatism of late Victorian society which was itself enmeshed in those longer traditions of liberal utilitarianism, improvement, and literary realism. For Yeats, those traditions were entirely delusional and his project was supposed to expose them as such.

If the Irish peasant had to be re-imagined in the Revival period, so too had the Irish language and so-called Hiberno-English. The depiction of the Irish language as unproductive in improvement discourse prepares the way for its representation as redundant in the melodramatic and sentimental tropes of Irish Victorianism ('asthore', 'machree'), particularly in the writing of Carleton and then, in a histrionic vein, in the melodramas of Boucicault. In these texts, the Irish language is so heavily conventionalized that it becomes paralytic. Hyde is desperate to release the language from this paralysis, but his Revivalism deepens rather than resolves the problem. What holds for the Irish language was also, in part, true for Hiberno-English. Yeats sought to liberate Hiberno-English (or literary language in Ireland) from the range of stereotypes—of backwardness, unproductivity, and barbarity—that constituted nineteenth-century writing so that he might be able to

---

[81] For the most recent analysis of the Revival in these terms, see P. J. Mathews, *Revival: The Abbey Theatre, Sinn Féin, The Gaelic League and the Co-operative Movement* (Cork: Cork University Press/Field Day, 2003).

produce rather than reproduce (or plagiarize like a Boucicault). For Yeats, the Irish language was symbolic of a broader cultural condition, one which he believed himself capable of experiencing despite having no direct knowledge of the language. This was certainly the theme of his response to Hyde's famous speech as President of the Irish Literary Society, 'On the Necessity for De-Anglicising Ireland'.[82] The rehabilitation of Hiberno-English would also be a form of redemption for the Irish language even if the actual existence of the language was severely threatened. Yeats insisted that the world evoked by the Irish language could be kept alive in Hiberno-English and could provide as strong a barrier to modernization. His early poetry and prose were supposed to exemplify this possibility. Yeats's Hiberno-English defined itself against the standard English of nineteenth-century Irish prose as well as the Victorian literary tradition while Hyde's Irish language was opposed to any attempt to standardize or homogenize language. The effort of writers such as Edgeworth, Leadbeater, and Carleton to standardize language was shunned by Yeats, Hyde, and Synge even though their work was, at the same time, made possible by those earlier standardizing modes. What had been cast off as anachronistic, backward, and primitive could be reclaimed by Revival writers as more truthful and civilized than that which was taking its place. In doing so, the Revival remained rooted in the terms it was supposed to be replacing. That was to be its greatest limitation. In the Revival period, modernization came to be seen as an impediment to writing and associated with conditions that were antagonistic to aesthetic production (but which were also stimulating that very production). Hence, Revivalism laboured to oppose itself to those processes of modernization that in part produced it. Out of the failures of the project of both improvement and Young Ireland emerged the 'high' Revivalism of writers such as Yeats, Hyde, and Synge.

At the same time, Yeats's Revivalism was not seeking to transcend social and political conditions by losing itself in some heightened transcendental reverie or fantasy of peasant supernaturalism. Yeats was not pitting art against politics, nor was he at this point representing Anglo-Irishness versus Irish nationalism. His failure to take control of the New Irish Library forced him to revise the terms upon which he had originally formulated his literary Revivalism. In literary terms, the Library debacle compelled Yeats to distinguish his Revival project from

[82] W. B. Yeats, 'The De-Anglicising of Ireland', *United Ireland*, 17 Dec. 1892, repr. in *Uncollected Prose*, ed. Frayne, i. 254.

previous literary or cultural 'experiments' in Ireland, especially those of improvement writers, Young Ireland, and the mainstream nationalism of the 1890s. It is clear that at the time of the Library controversy, Yeats did not understand the implications of those traditions in Ireland and the extent to which they were not in his interest. Hence, in 1892, he could flippantly recommend books for the New Irish Library which, two years later, he would condemn as detrimental to the work of Revivalism. His quarrel with Gavan Duffy forced him into an understanding of the liberal utilitarianism that underpinned both mainstream nationalism and the literary tradition of nineteenth-century Ireland. His own writing had always been working against that tradition, but after his loss of the New Irish Library he would self-consciously seek to counteract the liberal mainstream of both Irish writing and political life. However, his career was to be continually marked by tension between—in Joyce's terms—the will of 'the rabblement' and that of the artist. Yeats attempted to instil popular Revivalism with both the New Irish Library and the Irish Literary Theatre. The latter project made Joyce aware of the perils of seeking to cultivate a popular audience. In Joyce's mind, Yeats's theatre—so soon after its encouraging start in artistic terms—was surrendering to the power of the very same mainstream nationalism that had shut Yeats out of the New Irish Library in 1892. That same constituency had protested at the production of Yeats's play *The Countess Kathleen* in 1899, on the grounds that it caused profound offence to Irish national self-understanding. Joyce's particular retort to those 'mean influences' was, of course, delivered in both *Dubliners* and *A Portrait of the Artist as a Young Man*.[83]

Malcolm Brown comments that in the dispute over the Library, Gavan Duffy may have won the battle, but that Yeats won the war, literary greatness triumphing over provincial mediocrity.[84] Despite the fact that the New Irish Library experiment was cut short, did Gavan Duffy not win both battle and war? Is this not borne out by post-Revival literary and cultural history in which literary realism and narrow provincialism dominate? Yeats was repeatedly forced to confront a Duffyite nationalism in the 'philistines' who rioted at Abbey productions and refused to find a gallery to house the Hugh Lane collection of paintings. Yeats's 'Revival' was disrupted on numerous occasions by that literary and political mainstream. It is quite possible that 'the people' of Ireland

83 Joyce, 'The Day of the Rabblement', 51.
84 Brown, *The Politics of Irish Literature*, 359

did not really want to indulge in imaginative literature, but found fulfilment instead in 'rhetoric', didacticism, and fact. Yeats clearly came to suspect that it was didacticism, not literature, that was the reality of 'modern' Ireland. Hence, 'September 1913', which declares the loss of literary Ireland to the materialistic middle classes. After all, post-Famine Ireland was probably more drawn to Duffyite pragmatism than Yeatsian aestheticism. The Irish Free State was clearly more of a fulfilment of Gavan Duffy's ambitions than Yeats's Revival project: its conservatism in keeping with the narrow (and Catholic) conventionalism of Gavan Duffy's modernizing nationalism. Additionally, the literary mainstream of the period was itself strongly realist, dismissing literary experimentation and enquiry as foolish and extravagant in a context of pressing material need.[85] As such, the Irish Free State was more comfortable with the rhetorical (anti-intellectual) legacy of improvement discourse than with the thoughtfulness of a Stephen Dedalus, his stream of consciousness antagonizing the possibility of modernized progress.[86]

[85] On this topic, see Emer Nolan, 'Modernism and the Irish Revival', in Joe Cleary and Claire Connolly (eds.), *The Cambridge Companion to Modern Irish Culture* (Cambridge: Cambridge University Press, 2005), 157–73.

[86] On this topic, see Seamus Deane, 'Joyce and Stephen: The Provincial Intellectual', *Celtic Revivals: Essays in Modern Irish Literature, 1880–1980* (London: Faber and Faber, 1985), 75–92.

Conclusion

IMPROVEMENT discourse is central to an understanding of both nine-teenth-century and Revival-period Ireland. The writers examined in this book were instrumental in an attempt to articulate a realism that would distinguish their fictions from the fictionality of the novel and other literary discourses. That project had a lasting impact on Irish writing and was inseparable from improvement preoccupations with education, agricultural modernization, the standardization of language, the reform of traditional landlordism, and the eradication of agrarian unrest. Social institutions were supposed to conform to the representational modes of these tracts, which repeatedly sought to demonstrate the possibility of a transparent and harmonious political order. Later, these issues would become definitive of the mainstream nationalism of Young Ireland and popular Revivalism.

Improvement writers implied that there were two social and political possibilities: liberal reform or radical revolution, the former associated with rational modernization (supposedly the essence of contentment), making reference to John Locke, Adam Smith, and the novels of Edge-worth and the latter linked to violent revolution and equated with Jean-Jacques Rousseau and Romantic writing in general. This study has shown how nineteenth-century Irish writing acutely manifests a counter-revolutionary and counter-Romantic tradition, registering a fear of what 'liberty' might entail while partaking of the rhetoric of its possibility (which is especially evident in, for example, the work of women writers such as Edgeworth and Leadbeater).

This study began with Hannah More's anxious reaction to the French Revolution, the novel, and Romanticism. The Cheap Repository Tracts were essentially the result of her fraught engagement with Romanti-cism (which connoted for her revolution and republicanism). More's plain, rigidly realistic, and evangelical narratives were pitted against her perception of 'literary' discourse. While the Cheap Repository Tracts were enormously influential for Irish writers, their evangelicalism was deemed unsuitable in post-Union Ireland. Writers in Ireland such as Edgeworth, Leadbeater, and Doyle claimed that evangelical rhetoric was destined to inflame religious passions and sensitivities. Hence, these writers sought a liberal public sphere which was by definition free of the religious, political (and, surely, gender) differences that had obstructed progress in the past. As such, these writers articulated a liberalism which laboured to express its opposition to the republicanism of the French Revolution. It did so by formulating that liberalism in a strongly utilitarian mode, eschewing all inclination towards 'grand' political or literary statement while espousing an ideology of progress and modernization. Improvement emphasizes the ordinary and the material, demonstrating how freedom can be experienced through conditions of our own making, such as the rationalization (and, therefore, betterment) of work, 'belief', and daily practice. Improvement writers declared that freedom could be achieved and experienced by means of progress, that taking responsibility for the conditions one inhabits—making things better—would allow for control over one's own self as well as external forces such as economic and political realities.

This project was of course fraught with contradiction. The writings of both Edgeworth and Leadbeater implicitly express desire for freedom from specific forms of oppression, that of the traditional state, patriarchy, and religious authority. In addition, as women writers of novelistic prose, they were also seeking liberation from the perceived oppressiveness of the literary tradition (equated with a male poetic inheritance). At the same time, both Edgeworth and Leadbeater were made nervous by the possibility that the Irish rural masses would be similarly drawn to this notion of 'freedom' and seek emancipation from those forces that had kept them oppressed: the state, landlords, the Church of Ireland, and indeed, the class to which most improvement writers in Ireland belonged. Hence, their improvement tracts attempted to contain the potential excessiveness of those ideas of freedom that, in part, made their writing possible. Their work, therefore, needed to define a liberalism that would not disturb existing social structures, such as the landlord –tenant relationship or the Act of Union of Great Britain and Ireland. The solution forwarded by these writers was for comprehensive reform, in fact, modernization, of social institutions. Modernization was to provide the solution to those endemic problems of Irish life, creating, in Irish conditions, the organic community that had never before been possible. This community would be relieved of the difficulty and stress that had plagued Irish life, characterizing itself as liberated from those archaic fixations on religion and politics.

These tracts all prescribe the same strategy for improvement: landowners must be resident and must educate themselves in agricultural science and contemporary educational methods. In addition, this class must take on an educational role themselves by disseminating information on agricultural improvement to their tenantry, establishing vocational schools, and becoming committed, busy administrators of their properties. Likewise, the Irish peasantry could discover ample fulfilment—liberation, in fact—in the ordinary, pleasant life that awaited them if they cleaned out their houses, adopted modernized agricultural methods, and forsook the debilitating orality of peasant life in rural Ireland. In their unimproved state, the Irish peasantry embodied for improvers a terrifying lack of culture and civilization, vividly signifying a savage, raw state of nature that had to be subsumed into the civilizing tropes of modernized progress.

Improvement writers emphasized the necessity of work in the form of both physical labour and writing as the means by which civil society could be created and stabilized. In the process, these writers constructed distinctions between speculation and work, idealism and realism, and poetry and prose. Improvement tracts were supposed to demonstrate how ambiguity and confusion could be avoided by means of a rigorous plainness. In the course of this book, I have argued that a fear of fiction or the literary becomes one of the dominant themes in nineteenth-century Irish writing. This writing proclaimed itself free of all mystification because it was rooted in the ordinary world rather than in the 'high' literary tradition. However, improvement tracts repeatedly demonstrate their origins in literary discourse, continually invoking the tropes of the domestic novel for the representation of an improved domestic and political economy. In so doing, improvement confirms itself as resolutely literary rather than strictly practical.

The realistic fiction of writers such as Edgeworth, Leadbeater, and Carleton charged itself with the creation of a stable social order in the assumption that the processes of representation would both reflect and perpetuate the possibility of rational stability. That project was entirely at odds with the Revivalism of Yeats. In this respect, it is misleading to think of Edgeworth and Yeats as comprising one particular ('big house' ascendancy) tradition in Irish literary history while Sydney Owenson

and Thomas Davis characterize another (nationalist and 'Gaelic').[1]
Explicitly working within the tradition of Blake, Shelley, and French
symbolism, Yeats's work was fully at odds with Edgeworth's counter-
Romantic project. In fact, Yeats tried to undo all of Edgeworth's literary
and administrative labour. Revival writers such as Yeats, Synge, and
Hyde attempt to resist the assumptions of liberal improvement as well
as the conventions of mainstream nationalism, even if their work does
not provide a viable or even appealing alternative. Despite the prevalent
categorization of Sydney Owenson as a Romantic writer—prompted
by her fondness for an 'exotic' Gaelic culture—her work is better
understood in the terms of a counter-revolutionary tradition. It is true
that her novels do anticipate components of Young Ireland nationalism,
but more in the terms of a practical utilitarianism than Romanticism.[2]

An improving, 'national' writer, Carleton's work mediates between
the work of writers such as Leadbeater, Bardin, and Doyle and that of
Young Ireland. In this respect, it exemplifies the continuities between
improvement discourse and Young Ireland nationalism. Carleton's fiction, which relentlessly sought a rationalizing mode of representation,
belongs within both nineteenth-century traditions of imperial improvement and mainstream nationalism. The ambitions of Young Irelanders
were to attain the integrated, modernized state articulated in improvement discourse. As such, these modernizing nationalists were more
engaged with a counter-revolutionary tradition of liberal utilitarianism
than a European Romantic project. Mainstream nationalism in Ireland
has never extricated itself from those rhetorical and cultural roots.

Recent scholarship on nineteenth-century Ireland has tended to cat-
egorize the writing of the period as a component of a larger, European
Romantic project. This book is a reaction against this critical roman-
ticization of nineteenth-century Irish writing. Much of the writing
categorized as 'Romantic' in contemporary scholarship was, in fact,

---

[1] See Joep Leerssen, *Remembrance and Imagination: Patterns in the Historical and
Literary Representation of Ireland in the Nineteenth Century* (Cork: Field Day/Cork
University Press, 1996), 61-2; Terry Eagleton, *Heathcliff and the Great Hunger: Studies in
Irish Culture* (London: Verso, 1995), 145–225; Ina Ferris, *The Romantic National Tale
and the Question of Ireland* (Cambridge: Cambridge University Press, 2002); Marilyn
Butler, 'Edgeworth, The United Irishmen, and "More Intelligent Treason" ', in *An
Uncomfortable Authority: Maria Edgeworth and Her Contexts*, Chris Fauske and Heidi
Kaufman (eds.) (Newark: University of Delaware Press, 2004), 23–62.

[2] For a discussion of Sydney Owenson as a precursor to Young Ireland, see Leerssen,
Remembrance and Imagination.

written in stern reaction to Romanticism. The work of both Maria Edgeworth and Thomas Davis exemplifies that reaction. Accordingly, the enormous impact of a particular counter-revolutionary discourse on Irish writing and culture has been emphasized in this study. That discourse was secularizing and liberal, but most certainly not in the terms of the Romanticism and republicanism that produced the revolution in France and that supposedly threatened the possibility of social and political stability in Ireland. The secular liberalism of improvement discourse was a discourse of modernization, but one which has remained firmly rooted in, and limited by, the paternalist modes of imperialism. Improvement liberalism was not significantly questioned until the Revival period. It was, however, the persistent questioning of those orthodoxies of modernization and nationalism which produced the literature of the Revival period, culminating in the modernism of writers as diverse as W. B. Yeats, J. M. Synge, James Joyce, Samuel Beckett, and Elizabeth Bowen.

Bibliography

The bibliography is divided into three sections:

A. Works by William Carleton: (i) books; (ii) newspaper and periodical contributions; and (iii) manuscripts.
B. Primary sources: (i) archival material; (ii) newspapers and periodicals; (iii) pamphlets and other literature, mainly from the nineteenth century.
C. Critical studies.

A. WORKS BY WILLIAM CARLETON

(i) Books

Father Butler/The Lough Dearg Pilgrim (Dublin, 1829).
Traits and Stories of the Irish Peasantry, First Series (Dublin, 1830).
Traits and Stories of the Irish Peasantry, Second Series (Dublin, 1833).
Fardorougha the Miser, or The Convicts of Lisnamona (Dublin, 1839).
Traits and Stories of the Irish Peasantry, 2 vols. (Dublin, 1842–4).
Rody the Rover, or The Ribbonman (Dublin, 1845).
Art Maguire, or The Broken Pledge (Dublin, 1845).
Parra Sastha, or The History of Paddy Go-Easy and his Wife Nancy (Dublin, 1845).
Tales and Sketches, Illustrating the Character, Usages, Traditions, Sports and Pastimes of the Irish Peasantry (Dublin, 1845).
Valentine M'Clutchy, the Irish Agent, or The Chronicles of Castle Cumber (Dublin, 1845).
The Black Prophet: A Tale of Irish Famine (Belfast, 1847).
The Emigrants of Ahadarra: A Tale of Irish life (London and Belfast, 1848).
The Tithe Proctor: A Novel, Being a Tale of the Tithe Rebellion in Ireland (Belfast, 1849).
The Squanders of Castle Squander (London, 1852).
Willy Reilly and His Dear Colleen Bawn: A Tale Founded upon Fact (London, 1855).
Alley Sheridan and Other Stories (Dublin, 1857).
The Double Prophecy, or Trials of the Heart (London and Dublin, 1862).
Redmond Count O'Hanlon, the Irish Raparee (London and Dublin, 1862).
The Silver Acre and Other Tales (London, 1862).
The Red-Haired Man's Wife (Dublin and London, 1889).
The Life of William Carleton, 2 vols. completed by David O'Donoghue (London: Downey and Co., 1896).

Subsequent Reprints

The Works of William Carleton, 2 vols. First published New York: Collier, 1881 (repr. New York: Collier, 1970).

The Black Prophet: A Tale of Irish Famine. First Published Belfast, 1847; Introduction by Timothy Webb (Shannon: Irish University Press, 1972).

The Traits and Stories of the Irish Peasantry, 2 vols. First published Dublin, 1842–4; Preface by Barbara Hayley (repr. Gerrards Cross, Bucks.: Colin Smythe, 1990).

The Black Prophet First Published Belfast, 1847; Introduction by John Kelly (repr. Poole: Woodstock Books, 1996).

The Autobiography. Foreword by Benedict Kiely (Belfast: White Row Press, 1996).

(ii) Periodicals and Newpapers

'A Pilgrimage to Patrick's Purgatory', *Christian Examiner and Church of Ireland Gazette*, 6/34 (Apr. 1828), 268–86; 6/35 (May 1828), 323–62.

'The Broken Oath', *Christian Examiner*, 6/36 (June 1828), 425–39; 7/37 (July 1828), 27–39.

'Father Butler', *Christian Examiner*, 7/38 (Aug. 1828), 109–19; 7/39 (Sept. 1828), 192–202; 7/40 (Oct. 1828), 271–290; 7/41 (Nov. 1828), 355–65; 7/42 (Dec. 1828), 423–43.

'Retrospections', *Christian Examiner*, 7/39 (Sept. 1828), 233–4.

'The Midnight Hour', *Christian Examiner*, 7/41 (Nov. 1828), 390.

'The Station', *Christian Examiner*, 8/43 (Jan. 1829), 45–60; 8/44 (Feb. 1828), 250–69; 8/45 (Mar. 1829), 422–38.

'Dick M'Grath: A Sketch of Living Character', *Dublin Family Magazine*, 1/5 (Aug. 1829), 336–43.

'The Retrospect', *Dublin Family Magazine*, 1/5 (Aug. 1829), 293–4.

'The Death of a Devotee', *Christian Examiner*, 9/55 (Oct. 1829), 267–83.

'Confessions of a Reformed Ribbonman', *Dublin Literary Gazette, or Weekly Chronicle of Criticism, Belles Lettres, and Fine Arts*, 1/4 (23 Jan. 1830), 49–51; 1/5 (30 Jan. 1830), 66–8.

'The Priest's Funeral', *Christian Examiner*, 10/58 (Jan. 1830), 41–51; 10/59 (Feb. 1830), 128–42.

'The Brothers: A Narrative', *Christian Examiner*, 10/55 (Mar. 1830), 205–13; 10/61 (Apr. 1830), 287–96; 10/62 (May 1830), 365–77; 10/63 (June 1830), 440–52.

'Popular Romish Legends—no. 1: Lachlin Murray and the Blessed Candle', *Christian Examiner*, 10/65 (Aug. 1830), 598–610.

'The Lianhan Shee: An Irish Superstition', *Christian Examiner*, 10/68 (Nov. 1830), 845–61.

'Irish Legends. Sir Turlough; or, The Church-Yard Bride', *National Magazine*, 1/5 (Nov. 1830), 599–603.

[Wilton], 'The Illicit Distiller, or The Force of Conscience', *Christian Examiner*, 10/69 (Dec. 1830), 929–39.

'Laying a Ghost', *National Magazine*, 2/1 (Jan. 1831), 41–8.

'The Landlord and Tenant: An Authentic Story', *National Magazine and Dublin Literary Gazette*, 2/4 (Apr. 1831), 383–401.

'The History of a Chimney-Sweep', *Christian Examiner*, 11/70 (Apr. 1831), 276–91.

'The Materialist', *Christian Examiner*, 11/73 (July 1831), 512–32.

'The Resurrections of Barney Bradley', *Dublin University Magazine*, 3/14 (Feb. 1834), 177–93.

'Stories of Second Sight and Apparition', *Dublin University Magazine*, 3/17 (May 1834), 546–59.

'Richard the Rake: In Three Snatches', *Dublin University Magazine*, 11/63 (Mar. 1838), 364–83.

'Barney Brady's Goose, or Dark Doings at Slathbeg', *Dublin University Magazine*, 11/65 (May 1838), 604–24.

'The Irish Fiddler', *Irish Penny Journal*, 1/7 (15 Aug. 1840), 52–5.

'The Country Dancing-Master: An Irish Sketch', *Irish Penny Journal*, 1/9 (29 Aug. 1840), 69–72.

'The Irish Matchmaker', *Irish Penny Journal*, 1/14 (2 Oct. 1840), 116–20.

'Bob Pentland, or The Gauger Outwitted', *Irish Penny Journal*, 1/16 (17 Oct. 1840), 125–7.

'Irish Superstitions: Ghosts and Fairies', *Irish Penny Journal*, 1/21 (21 Nov. 1840), 164–6.

'Irish Superstitions: Ghosts and Fairies; The Rival Kempers', *Irish Penny Journal*, 1/24 (12 Dec. 1840), 188–91.

'The Irish Widwife', *Irish Penny Journal*, 1/26 (26 Dec. 1840), 202–4; 1/27 (2 Jan 1841), 209–13.

'Irish Superstitions—no. III: Ghosts and Fairies', *Irish Penny Journal*, 1/34 (20 Feb. 1841), 269–71.

'The Castle of Aughentain, or A Legend of the Brown Coat: A Tale of Tom Greissy the Shanahus', *Irish Penny Journal*, 1/40 (5 June 1841).

'O'Sullivan's Love: A Legend of Edenmore', *Dublin University Magazine*, 29/171 (Mar. 1847), 277–95; 29/172 (Apr. 1847), 428–46.

'An Irish Election in the Time of the Forties', *Dublin University Magazine*, 30/176 (Aug. 1847), 176–92; 30/177 (Sept. 1847), 287–97.

'Fair Gurtha; or The Hungry Grass. A Legend of the Dumb Hill', *Dublin University Magazine*, 47/280 (Apr. 1856), 414–35.

'Utrom Horum? Or the Revenge of Shane Roe Na Soggarth: A Legend of the Golden Fawn', *Dublin University Magazine*, 55/329 (May 1860), 653–74.

(iii) Manuscripts:

National Library of Ireland:
Copy Letter from William Carleton to Sir William Wilde, MS 27609 (1/4).
Letter from William Carleton to James Duffy Enquiring about Proofs, National
Library of Ireland, MS 27098.

B. OTHER PRIMARY SOURCES

(i) Archives

Representative Church Body Library
Minute Book, Association for Discountenancing Vice, 1818–20, MS 174.
Minute Book, Carlow Parish School, Oct. 1819—Mar. 1839, P 317–13.

National Library of Ireland
The Scrapbook of Mrs William Hickey, MS 407.
Ballitore Papers, Bundle E, 1–40: Letters of Maria Edgeworth on Literary
Matters, n.1008 p.1090.

Cambridge University
Catalogue to the Bradshaw Collection of Irish Books (Cambridge, 1916).

(ii) Newspapers and Periodicals

Irish Farmer's and Gardener's Magazine and Register of Rural Affairs, Dublin,
1833–40, eds. William Hickey and Edmund Murphy.
Irish Penny Journal, Dublin, 1840–1.
Freeman's Journal, 5–10 Sept. 1892.

(iii) Pamphlets and Other Literature

Alexander, Samuel, Logical Essay, on the Syntax of the English Language
(Omagh, 1822).
Bardin, Charles: see under Kildare Place Society.
Beddoes, Thomas: see under Kildare Place Society.
Burke, Edmund, *A Philosophical Enquiry into the Origin of our Ideas of the
Sublime and the Beautiful*, London, 1757; expanded 2nd edn. 1759 (repr.
Oxford: Oxford University Press, 1990).
——*Reflections on the Revolution in France*, 1790; ed. Conor Cruise O'Brien
(London: Penguin Books, 1986).
Constant Visitor, A, 'An Irish Hedge School', *Dublin University Magazine*, 40
(Nov. 1862), 600–16.
Croker, Crofton, *Researches in the South of Ireland* (London, 1824).
Curry, James, *A Catalogue of Books, Chiefly Modern* (Dublin, 1830).

Davis, Thomas, *Prose Writings: Essays on Ireland,* ed. T. W. Rolleston (London: W. Scott, 1890).

—— *Literary and Historical Essays,* ed. Charles Gavan Duffy (Dublin, 1862).

—— *The Patriot Parliament of 1689,* Introduction by Charles Gavan Duffy (London: Fisher Unwin, 1893).

Day, Angélique, and Patrick McWilliams (eds.), *Ordnance Survey Memoirs of Ireland, v. Parishes of Co. Tyrone I, 1821, 1823, 1831–6. North, West and South Tyrone* (Belfast: Institute of Irish Studies in association with the Royal Irish Academy, 1990).

———— *Ordnance Survey Memoirs of Ireland, xx. Parishes of Co. Tyrone II, 1825, 1833–5, 1840. Mid and East Tyrone* (Belfast: Institute of Irish Studies in association with the Royal Irish Academy, 1993).

Day, Thomas: see under Kildare Place Society.

Dorian, Hugh, *The Outer Edge of Ulster: A Memoir of Social Life in Nineteenth-Century Donegal,* ed. Breandán Mac Suibhne and David Dickson (Dublin: Lilliput Press, 2000).

Doyle, Martin [William Hickey], *The State of the Poor of Ireland Briefly Considered and Agricultural Education Recommended, to Check Redundant Population and to Promote National Improvement* (Carlow, 1820).

—— *Hints Addressed to the Smallholders and Peasantry of Ireland, on Road-making, Ventilation, &c, &c* (Dublin, 1830).

—— *Hints for the Small Farmers of Ireland* (Dublin, 1830).

—— *Hints Originally Intended for the Small Farmers of the County of Wexford, but suited to the Circumstances of Most Parts of Ireland* (Dublin, 1830).

—— *An Address to the Landlords of Ireland, on Subjects Connected with the Melioration of the Lower Classes* (Dublin, 1831).

—— *Hints on Emigration to Upper Canada: Especially Addressed to the Lower Classes* (Dublin, 1831).

—— *Irish Cottagers,* first published 1830 (Dublin, 1833).

—— *Hints Addressed to the Small Holders and Peasantry of Ireland on Subjects Connected with Health, Temperance, Morals* (Dublin, 1833).

—— *Practical Gardening for the Use of all Classes* (Dublin, 1833).

—— *Common Sense for Common People* (Dublin, 1835).

—— *The O'Mulliganiad, or The Views, Objects and Motives of O'Sullivan, Maghee and Todd Detected and Exposed in Three Cantos* (Wexford, 1836).

—— *The Works of Martin Doyle,* i–ii (Dublin, 1836).

—— *The Labouring Classes in Ireland: An Inquiry* (Dublin, 1845).

—— *Agricultural Classbook, or How Best to Cultivate a Small Farm and Garden, together with Hints on Domestic Economy* (Commissioners of National Education in Ireland, 1856).

Duffy, Charles Gavan, *The Spirit of the Nation* (Dublin, 1845).

—— *The Ballad Poetry of Ireland* (Dublin, 1845).

Duffy, Charles Gavan, *The Prospects of Irish Literature for the People: An Address before the Irish Literary Society, London*, 17 June 1893 (London: Gaskilll Jones and Co., 1893).

—— *The New Spirit of the Nation* (London: Fisher Unwin, 1894).

—— *The Revival of Irish Literature: Addresses by Sir Charles Gavan Duffy, Dr. George Sigerson and Dr. Douglas Hyde* (London: Fisher Unwin, 1894).

—— *Short Life of Thomas Davis 1800–1845* (London: Fisher Unwin, 1895).

—— *Young Ireland: A Fragment of Irish History* (London: Fisher Unwin, 1896).

Edgeworth, Maria, *Practical Education* (London, 1798).

—— *Castle Rackrent* (London, 1800).

—— *Moral Tales*, 3 vols. (London, 1802).

—— *Ennui* (London, 1809).

—— *The Absentee* (London, 1812).

—— *Ormond: A Tale* (London, 1817).

[Ferguson, Samuel], 'Irish Storyists—Lover and Carleton', *Dublin University Magazine*, 4/21 (Sept. 1834), 298–311.

—— 'The Didactic Irish Novelists: Carleton–Mrs. Hall', *Dublin University Magazine*, 26/156 (Dec. 1845), 737–52.

Freney, James, *Life and Adventures of James Freney*, 1754, ed. Frank McEvoy (Kilkenny: Hebron Books, 1988).

Gregory, Augusta, *Cuchulain of Muirthemne* (London, 1902).

Griffin, Gerald, *The Collegians*, first published London, 1829 (repr. Belfast: Appletree Press, 1992).

Hamilton, Elizabeth, *The Cottagers of Glenburnie, A Tale for the Ingle-Nook: An Instructive and Entertaining Lesson for Youth* (Edinburgh, 1808).

Hooper, Glenn (ed.), *The Tourist's Gaze: Travellers to Ireland 1800–2000* (Cork: Cork University Press, 2002).

Hyde, Douglas, *Beside the Fire: A Collection of Irish Gaelic Folk Stories* (London: D. Nutt, 1890).

Hyland, Áine, and Kenneth Milne (eds.), *Irish Educational Documents*, i (Dublin: Church of Ireland College of Education, 1987).

Joyce, James, *A Portrait of the Artist as a Young Man*, 1916; ed. Seamus Deane (London: Penguin, 1992).

—— *Occasional, Critical, and Political Writing*, ed. Kevin Barry (Oxford: Oxford University Press, 2000).

Kildare Place Society, *Irish-English Primer, or Spelling Book* (Dublin, 1820).

—— *The Brothers; or Consequences: A Story of What Happens Everyday* (Dublin, 1820).

—— *Amusing Stories: A Collection of Histories, Adventures and Anecdotes* (Dublin, 1820).

—— *The History of the Honest Widow Riley* (Dublin, 1820).

—— *Natural History of Domestic Animals* (Dublin, 1821).

—— *Natural History of Animals* (Dublin, 1822).

—— *The History of Prince Lee Boo, to which is added The Life of Paul Cuffee, also some account of Paul Sackhouse, The Esquimaux* (Dublin, 1822).

—— *The New Robinson Crusoe: An Instructive and Entertaining History* (Dublin, 1822).

—— *Mungo, or The Little Traveller, to which is annexed The Seven Wonders of the World* (Dublin, 1822).

—— *The Dangerous Voyage performed by Captain Bligh ... in the Year 1789* (Dublin, 1824).

—— *Discovery of America by Christopher Columbus* (Dublin, 1824).

—— *Animal Sagacity, Exemplified by Facts* (Dublin, 1824).

—— *James Talbot* (Dublin, 1825).

—— *The Entertaining Medley, Being a History of True Histories and Facts* (Dublin, 1826).

—— *Aesop's Fables* (Dublin, 1826).

—— [Charles Bardin] *The Cottage Fireside* (Dublin, 1826).

—— —— *Voyage of the Amber* (Dublin, 1831).

—— [Thomas Day], *The History of Little Jack, a Foundling, to which are added a Friendly Gift to Servants and Apprentices and 'The Brazier'* (Dublin, 1829).

—— —— *The Miscellany; or Evening's Occupation for the Youthful Peasantry of Ireland* (Dublin, 1830).

—— —— *The History of Richard MacReady, the Farmer Lad* (Dublin, 1830).

—— —— *Voyages in the Arctic Seas, from 1821 to 1825, for the Discovery of a North West Passage to the Pacific Ocean* (Dublin, 1830).

—— —— *The Voyage of the Arrow* (Dublin, 1831).

—— —— *Arctic Voyages; Being an Account of Discoveries of the North Polar Seas, 1818, 1819, and 1820* (Dublin, 1831).

—— [Thomas Beddoes], *History of Isaac Jenkins* (Dublin, 1831).

—— —— *Natural History of Domestic Beasts* (Dublin, 1832).

—— —— *The Schoolmistress* (Dublin, 1832).

Leadbeater, Mary, *Anecdotes Taken from Real Life, for the Improvement of Children, with Appropriate Engravings* (Dublin, 1809).

—— *Cottage Dialogues among the Irish Peasantry* (Dublin, 1811).

—— *Cottage Dialogues among the Irish Peasantry*, with Preface, Notes and Glossary by Maria Edgeworth (London, 1811).

—— *The Landlord's Friend: Intended as a Sequel to Cottage Dialogues* (Dublin, 1813).

—— *Short Stories for Cottagers Intended to Accompany Cottage Dialogues* (Dublin, 1813).

—— *Cottage Dialogues*, expanded edition (Dublin, 1814).

—— *Cottage Biography, Being a Collection of the Lives of the Irish Peasantry* (Dublin, 1822).

—— *The Pedlars* (Dublin, 1826).

Leadbeater, Mary, *Papers: The Annals of Ballitore with a Memoir of the Author; Letters from Edmund Burke heretofore unpublished and the Correspondence of Mrs. R. Trench and Rev. George Crabbe with Mary Leadbeater*, 2 vols. (London: Bell and Daldy, 1862).

—— and Elizabeth Shackleton, *Tales for Cottagers, Accommodated to the Present Condition of the Irish Peasantry* (Dublin, 1814)

Lynch, E. M., *A Parish Providence*. Introduction by Charles Gavan Duffy (London: Fisher Unwin, 1894).

Martineau, Harriet, *Letters from Ireland*, ed. Glenn Hooper (Dublin: Irish Academic Press, 2001).

Mason, William Shaw, *A Statistical Account or Parochial Survey of Ireland drawn up from the Communications of the Clergy*, 3 vols. (Dublin 1814–19).

Mill, John Stuart, *Collected Works*, vi. *Essays on England, Ireland, and the Empire* (London and Toronto: University of Toronto Press and Routledge & Kegan Paul, 1982).

More, Hannah, Cheap Repository for Religious and Moral Tracts printed in Ireland in 1798, 1803, and 1844 (Dublin, n.d.):
The History of Tom White, the Postillion.
The Shepherd of Salisbury Plain.
The Two Wealthy Farmers.
The Two Shoemakers.
The Brothers.
The Two Servants.
Path to Richness and Happiness.
The Wonderful Advantages of Adventuring in the Lottery.
The Beggarly Boy, a Parable.
The Two Soldiers.
The Good Mother's Legacy.
The History of Mary Wood, The Housemaid.
Sorrowful Sam, or the Two Blacksmiths.
The Gamester, to which is added The Story of Sinful Sally Told by Herself.
History of Charles Jones, the Footman.
Black Giles the Poacher, with some Account of a Family Who Would Rather Live by their Wits than Their Work.

Morgan, Lady [Sydney Owenson], *The Wild Irish Girl*, first published 1806 (repr. Oxford: Oxford University Press, 1999).

Newman, John Henry, *The Idea of a University*, ed. I. T. Kerr (Oxford: Clarendon Press, 1976).

O'Grady, Standish, *Selected Essays and Passages*, Introduction by Ernest Boyd (Dublin: Talbot Press, 1917).

Otway, Caesar, 'On the Lawfulness of Employing Fictitious Narrative as a Means of Recommending and Conveying Religious Instruction', *Christian Examiner*, 9/6 (Sept. 1829), 367–70.

—— Preface, *Christian Examiner*, 10/55 (Jan. 1831), p. iv.

—— *Sketches in Ireland: Descriptive of Interesting Portions of the Counties of Donegal, Cork and Kerry* (Dublin, 1827; 2nd edn. 1838).

—— 'Our Portrait Gallery, no. XV—William Carleton', *Dublin University Magazine*, 67/97 (Jan. 1841), 66–72.

Porter, J. L., *The Life and Times of Henry Cooke*, first published London 1871 (repr. Belfast: William Mullan, 1875).

Rousseau, Jean-Jacques, *Émile*, first published 1762; trans. Barbara Foxley (London: Dent, 1974).

—— *The Basic Political Writings*, trans. and ed. Donald A. Cress (Indianopolis: Hackett, 1988). Based on *Œuvres Complètes de Jean-Jacques Rousseau* (Paris: Pléiade, 1964), iii.

Ryan, W. P., *The Irish Literary Revival: Its History, Pioneers and Possibilities* (London: W. P. Ryan, 1894).

Synge, John Millington, *The Playboy of the Western World and Other Plays*, ed. Ann Saddlemyer (Oxford: Oxford University Press, 1995).

—— *The Aran Islands* 1906, ed. Tim Robinson (London: Penguin, 1992).

—— *Travels in Wicklow, West Kerry and Connemara*, 1911. Drawings by Jack. B. Yeats and Foreword by Paddy Woodworth (London: Serif, 2005).

[Unsigned], 'Our Portrait Gallery—Martin Doyle', *Dublin University Magazine*, 15/7 (Apr. 1840), 374–6.

Whitney, Harry, Philomath [Patrick Kennedy], *Legends of Mount Leinster: Tales and Sketches* (Dublin, 1855).

Wordsworth, William, *Lyrical Ballads* (1800), ed. W. J. B. Owen (Oxford: Oxford University Press, 1969).

Yeats, W. B., *Representative Irish Tales*, 1891 (repr. Gerrards Cross, Bucks.: Colin Smythe, 1991).

—— *The Celtic Twilight*, 1902 (Gerrards Cross, Bucks.: Colin Smythe, 1994).

—— *The Secret Rose* (London: Lawrence and Bullen, 1897).

—— *Autobiographies* (London: Macmillan, 1955).

—— *Essays and Introductions* (London: Macmillan, 1961).

—— *Uncollected Prose*, i, ed. John P. Frayne (London: Macmillan, 1970).

—— *Memoirs*, ed. Denis Donoghue (Dublin: Gill and Macmillan, 1972).

—— *Collected Letters of W. B. Yeats*, i. *1865–1895*, ed. John Kelly and Eric Domville (Oxford: Clarendon Press, 1986).

—— *The Major Works*, ed. Edward Larissey (Oxford: Oxford University Press, 1997).

Young, Arthur, *Arthur Young's Tour in Ireland 1776–1779* (London: George Bell, 1780; repr. 1892).

C. CRITICAL STUDIES

Adams, J. R. R., *The Printed Word and the Common Man: Popular Culture in Ulster 1700–1900* (Belfast: Institute of Irish Studies, 1987).

Akenson, Donald H., *The Irish Education Experiment: The National System of Education in the Nineteenth Century* (London: Routledge, 1970).

Albee, Ernest, *A History of English Utilitarianism* (London: George Allen and Unwin, 1957).

Anderson, Benedict, *Imagined Communities: Reflections on the Origin and Spread of Nationalism* (London: Verso, 1983).

Armstrong, Nancy, *Desire and Domestic Fiction: A Political History of the Novel* (Oxford: Oxford University Press, 1987).

Bakhtin, M. M., *The Dialogic Imagination*, ed. Michael Holquist, trans. Caryl Emerson and Michael Holquist (Austin: University of Texas Press, 1981; repr. 1990).

Barrell, John, *The Idea of Landscape and the Sense of Place, 1730–1840: An Approach to the Poetry of John Clare* (Cambridge: Cambridge University Press, 1972).

Benjamin, Walter, *Illuminations: Essays and Reflections*, ed. Hannah Arendt, trans. Harry Zohn (New York: Schocken Books, 1988).

——— *Reflections: Essays, Aphorisms, Autobiographical Writings*, ed. Peter Demetz, trans. Edmund Jephcott (New York: Schocken Books, 1989).

Benson, Charles, 'Printers and Booksellers in Dublin 1800–1850', in Robin Myers and Michael Harris (eds.), *Spreading the Word: The Distribution Network of Print, 1550–1850* (Winchester: St Paul's Bibliographies, 1990).

Bigelow, Gordon, *Fiction, Famine and the Rise of Economics in Victorian Britain and Ireland* (Cambridge: Cambridge University Press, 2003).

Boué, André, 'William Carleton and the Irish People', *Clogher Record*, 6/1 (1966), 66–70.

——— *William Carleton: Romancier Irlandais, 1794–1869*, Série Sorbonne, 6 (Paris: Publications de la Sorbonne, Imprimerie Nationale, 1978).

——— 'William Carleton as a Short Story Writer', in Terence Brown and Patrick Rafriodi (eds.), *The Irish Short Story* (London: Colin Smythe, 1979).

Bowen, Desmond, *The Protestant Crusade in Ireland 1800–70* (Dublin: Gill and Macmillan, 1978).

Brown, Malcolm, *The Politics of Irish Literature: From Thomas Davis to W. B. Yeats* (Seattle: University of Washington Press, 1971).

Brown, Terence, *The Life of W. B. Yeats: A Critical Biography* (Dublin: Gill and Macmillan, 1999).

Buchan, David, 'The Expressive Poetry of Nineteenth-Century Farm Servants', in T. M. Devine (ed.), *Farm Servants and Labour in Lowland Scotland, 1779–1914* (Edinburgh: John Donald, 1984).

Burke, Peter, *Popular Culture in Early Modern Europe* (London: Temple Smith, 1978).

Butler, Marilyn, *Maria Edgeworth: A Literary Biography* (Oxford: Clarendon Press, 1972).

—— 'Edgeworth, the United Irishmen, and "More Intelligent Treason" ', in Chris Fauske and Heidi Kaufman (eds.), *An Uncomfortable Authority: Maria Edgeworth and her Contexts* (Newark: University of Delaware Press, 2004), 33–61.

Cahalan, James M., *Great Hatred, Little Room: The Irish Historical Novel* (Dublin: Gill and Macmillan, 1983).

—— *The Irish Novel* (Dublin: Gill and Macmillan, 1998).

Canuel, Mark, *Religion, Toleration and British Writing, 1790–1830* (Cambridge: Cambridge University Press, 2002).

Casey, Daniel J., and Robert E. Rhodes (eds.), *Views of the Irish Peasantry 1800–1916* (Hamden, Conn.: Archon Books, 1977).

Clark, Samuel, and James S. Donnelly, Jr. (eds.), *Irish Peasants: Violence and Political Unrest, 1789–1914* (Manchester: Manchester University Press, 1983).

Connolly, S. J., *Priests and People in Pre-Famine Ireland, 1780–1845* (Dublin: Four Courts Press, 1982; repr. 2001).

Cronin, John, *The Anglo-Irish Novel: The Nineteenth Century* (Belfast: Appletree Press, 1980).

Cullen, Louis, *An Economic History of Ireland since 1660*, first published 1972 (London: Batsford, 1987).

—— *The Emergence of Modern Ireland, 1600–1900* (London: Hutchinson, 1981).

Cunningham, Bernadette, and Máire Kennedy (eds.), *The Experience of Reading: Irish Historical Perspectives* (Dublin: Rare Books Group of the Library Association of Ireland and Economic Social History of Ireland, 1999).

Daly, Mary, and David Dickson (eds.), *The Origins of Popular Literacy in Ireland: Language Change and Educational Development 1700–1920* (Dublin: Trinity College and University College, 1990).

Davie, Donald, *The Heyday of Sir Walter Scott* (London: Routledge, 1961).

Deane, Seamus, *Celtic Revivals: Essays in Modern Irish Literature, 1880–1980* (London: Faber and Faber, 1985).

—— *A Short History of Irish Literature* (London: Hutchinson, 1986).

—— 'Irish National Character, 1790–1900', in Tom Dunne (ed.), *The Writer as Witness: Literature as Historical Evidence* (Cork: Cork University Press, 1987), 90–113.

—— *The French Revolution and Enlightenment in England, 1789–1832* (Cambridge, Mass.: Harvard University Press, 1988).

—— 'National Character and National Audience: Races, Crowds and Readers', in Michael Allen and Angela Wilcox (eds.), *Critical Approaches to Anglo-Irish Literature* (Gerrards Cross, Bucks.: Colin Smythe, 1989), 40–52.

—— (ed.), *The Field Day Anthology of Irish Literature*, 3 vols. (Derry: Field Day Company, 1991).

Deane, Seamus, *Strange Country: Modernity and Nationhood in Irish Writing since 1790* (Oxford: the Clarendon Press, 1997).

—— *Foreign Affections: Essays on Edmund Burke* (Cork: Cork University Press/Field Day, 2005).

De Fréine, Seán, *The Great Silence: The Study of a Relationship between Language and Nationality* (Dublin: Foilseachán Naisiúnta Teoranta, 1965).

De Man, Paul, *Blindness and Insight: Essays in the Rhetoric of Contemporary Criticism*, first published 1971 (repr. London: Routledge, 1996).

—— *Allegories of Reading: Figural Language in Rousseau, Nietzsche, Rilke and Proust* (New Haven: Yale University Press, 1979).

—— *The Rhetoric of Romanticism* (New York: Columbia University Press, 1984).

—— *The Resistance to Theory* (Minneapolis: University of Minnesota Press, 1986).

—— *Aesthetic Ideology* (Minneapolis: University of Minnesota, 1996).

Derrida, Jacques, *Of Grammatology*, first published Paris, 1967; trans. Gayatri Chakravorty Spivak (Baltimore: Johns Hopkins University Press, 1976).

Dolan, Terence Patrick (ed.), *A Dictionary of Hiberno-English* (Dublin: Gill and Macmillan, 1998).

Donnelly, James S., and Kerby Miller (eds.), *Irish Popular Culture, 1650–1850* (Dublin: Irish Academic Press, 1998).

Douglas, Aileen, 'Maria Edgeworth's Writing Classes', *Eighteenth-Century Fiction*, 14/3–4 (Apr.–July 2002), 371–90.

Dowling, P. J., *The Hedge Schools of Ireland* (Cork: Mercier Press, 1968).

—— 'Patrick Lynch, Schoolmaster, 1754–1818', *Studies*, 20 (Sept. 1931), 461–72.

Doyle, O. S. A, Revd. P. A., 'Bannow School (1821–1826)', *The Past: The Organ of Uí Ceinnsealaigh Historical Society* (Nov. 1920), 122–9.

Drayton, Richard, *Nature's Government: Science, Imperial Britain, and the 'Improvement' of the World* (New Haven: Yale University Press, 2000).

Duffy, P. J., 'Carleton, Kavanagh and the South Ulster Landscape c.1800–1950', *Irish Geography*, 18 (1985), 25–37.

Dunne, Tom (ed.), *The Writer as Witness: Literature as Historical Evidence* (Cork: Cork University Press, 1987).

—— 'Haunted by History: Irish Romantic Writing', in Roy Porter and Mikulás Teich (eds.), *Romanticism in National Context* (Cambridge: Cambridge University Press, 1988).

Eagleton, Terry, *Heathcliff and the Great Hunger: Studies in Irish Culture* (London: Verso, 1995).

—— *Crazy John and the Bishop* (Cork: Field Day/Cork University Press, 1998).

—— *Scholars and Rebels in Nineteenth-Century Ireland* (Oxford: Blackwell, 1999).

Earls, Brian, 'A Note on Seanchas Amhlaoibh í Luinse', *Béaloideas: Journal of the Folklore Society of Ireland*, 52 (1984), 9–34.

—— 'Supernatural Legends in Nineteenth-Century Irish Writing', *Béaloideas: Journal of the Folklore Society of Ireland*, 60–1 (1992–3), 93–144.

—— 'The Carleton Canon', *Studia Hibernica*, 21 (1981), 95–125.

Ellmann, Richard, *Yeats: The Man and the Masks*, 2nd edn. (London: Penguin, 1979).

Ferguson, Paul, Patrick O'Flanagan, and Kevin Whelan (eds.), *Rural Ireland 1600–1900: Modernization and Change* (Cambridge: Cambridge University Press, 2000).

Ferris, Ina, *The Romantic National Tale and the Question of Ireland* (Cambridge: Cambridge University Press, 2002).

Fielding, Penny, *Writing and Orality: Nationality, Culture and Nineteenth-Century Scottish Fiction* (Oxford: Clarendon Press, 1996).

Finnegan, Ruth, *Literacy and Orality: Studies in the Technology of Communication* (Oxford: Blackwell, 1988).

Flanagan, Thomas, *The Irish Novelists, 1800–1850* (New York: Columbia University Press, 1959).

Foley, Tadgh, and Seán Ryder (eds.), *Ideology and Ireland in the Nineteenth Century* (Dublin: Four Courts Press, 1998).

Foster, John Wilson, *Forces and Themes in Ulster Fiction* (Dublin: Gill and Macmillan, 1974).

—— *Nature in Ireland: A Scientific and Cultural History* (Dublin: Lilliput Press, 1997).

Foster, R. F., *Paddy and Mr. Punch: Connections in Irish and English History* (London: Penguin, 1993).

—— *W. B. Yeats: A Life*, i. *The Apprentice Mage* (Oxford: Oxford University Press, 1997).

—— 'Square-Built Power and Fiery Shorthand: Yeats, Carleton and the Irish Nineteenth Century', in *The Irish Story: Telling Tales and Making It Up in Ireland* (London: Allen Lane, 2001).

—— *W. B. Yeats: A Life*, ii. *The Arch Poet* (Oxford: Oxford University Press, 2003).

Gellner, Ernest, *Nations and Nationalism* (Oxford: Blackwell, 1983).

Gibbons, Luke, *Transformations in Irish Culture* (Cork: Cork University Press/Field Day, 1996).

—— *Gaelic Gothic: Race, Colonization, and Irish Culture* (Centre for Irish Studies: Arlen House, 2004).

Goldstrom, J. M., *The Social Content of Education, 1808–1870: A Study of the Working-Class School Reader* (Shannon: Irish University Press, 1972).

Goody, Jack (ed.), *Literacy in Traditional Societies* (Cambridge: Cambridge University Press, 1968).

Grady, Clara I., 'The Condition and Character of the Irish Peasantry as Seen in the *Annals* and *Cottage Dialogues* of Mary Leadbeater', *Women and Literature*, 3/1 (1975), 28–38.

Habermas, Jürgen, *The Structural Transformation of the Public Sphere: An Enquiry into a Category of Bourgeois Society*, first published 1962; trans. Thomas Burger with the assistance of Frederick Lawrence (Cambridge: Polity Press, 1989).

—— *The Philosophical Discourse of Modernity: Twelve Lectures*, 1987 (Cambridge: Polity Press, 1990).

Hartman, Geoffrey, *The Unremarkable Wordsworth* (Minneapolis: University of Minnesota Press, 1973).

Hayley, Barbara, 'Irish Periodicals from the Union to the Nation', *Anglo Irish Studies*, 1/2 (1976).

—— *Carleton's Traits and Stories and the Nineteenth Century Anglo-Irish Tradition* (Gerrards Cross, Bucks.: Colin Smythe, 1983).

—— *A Bibliography of the Writings of William Carleton* (Gerrards Cross, Bucks.: Colin Smythe, 1985).

Hislop, Harold John, 'The Kildare Place Society 1811–1831: An Irish Experiment in Popular Education', Ph.D. thesis, University of Dublin, 1990.

Hollingworth, Brian, *Maria Edgeworth's Irish Writing: Language, History, Politics* (London: Macmillan, 1997).

Hooper, Glenn, *Travel Writing and Ireland 1760–1860: Culture, History, Politics* (Basingstoke and London: Palgrave, 2005).

—— and Leon Litvack (eds.), *Ireland in the Nineteenth Century: Regional Identity* (Dublin: Four Courts Press, 2000).

Hopkins, Mary Alden, *Hannah More and her Circle* (New York: Longmans, Green and Co., 1947).

Howes, Marjorie, *Yeats's Nations: Gender, Class and Irishness* (Cambridge: Cambridge University Press, 1996).

Hunter, J. Paul, *Before Novels: Cultural Contexts of Eighteenth-Century English Fiction* (London: Norton, 1992).

Hutchinson, John, *The Dynamics of Cultural Nationalism: The Gaelic Revival and the Creation of the Irish Nation State* (London: Allen and Unwin, 1987).

Hutton, Clare, 'Publishing the Irish Literary Revival: The Evoluation of Irish Textual Culture, 1886–1992', D.Phil. thesis, University of Oxford, 1999.

Ibarra, Eileen S., 'William Carleton: An Introduction', *Éire-Ireland*, 5/1 (Spring 1970), 81–6.

Jacobus, Mary, *Tradition and Experiment in Wordsworth's Lyrical Ballads* (Oxford: Oxford University Press, 1976).

Jones, M. G., *Hannah More* (Cambridge: Cambridge University Press, 1952).

Keane, Angela, *Women Writers and the English Nation in the 1790s* (Cambridge: Cambridge University Press, 2000).

Keane, Maureen, *Mrs. S. C. Hall: A Literary Biography* (Gerrards Cross, Bucks.: Colin Smythe, 1997).

Kelleher, Margaret, *The Feminization of Famine: Expressions of the Inexpressible?* (Cork: Cork University Press, 1997).

Keogh, Dáire, and Kevin Whelan (eds.), *Acts of Union: The Causes, Contexts and Consequences of the Union* (Dublin: Four Courts Press, 2001).

Kiberd, Declan, *Inventing Ireland: The Literature of the Modern Nation* (London: Jonathan Cape, 1995).

—— *Irish Classics* (London: Granta, 2000).

Kiely, Benedict, *Poor Scholar: A Study of William Carleton, 1794–1869*, first published 1948 (2nd edn. Dublin: Wolfhound, 1997).

Kilfeather, Siobhan, 'Terrific Register: The Gothicization of Atrocity in Irish Romanticism', *boundary 2*, 31/1 (Spring 2004), 49–71.

King, Jason, 'Emigration and the Anglo-Irish Novel: William Carleton, "Homesickness" and the Coherence of Gothic Conventions', *Canadian Journal of Irish Studies*, 26/2–27/1 (Fall 2000–Spring 2001), 104–19.

Krause, David, *William Carleton the Novelist: His Carnival and Pastoral World of TragiComedy* (Washington, DC: University Press of America, 2000).

Leerssen, Joep, *Remembrance and Imagination: Patterns in the Historical and Literary Representation of Ireland in the Nineteenth Century* (Cork: Field Day/Cork University Press, 1996).

Lloyd, David, *Nationalism and Minor Literature: James Clarence Mangan and the Emergence of Irish Cultural Nationalism* (Berkeley: University of California Press, 1987).

—— *Anomalous States: Irish Writing and the Post-Colonial Moment* (Dublin: Lilliput Press, 1993).

Long, Gerard (ed.), *Books beyond the Pale: Aspects of the Book Trade in Ireland before 1850* (Dublin: Rare Books Group of the Library Association of Ireland, 1996).

Lukács, Georg, *The Theory of the Novel: A Historico-Philosophical Essay on the Forms of Great Epic Literature*, first published 1920; trans. Anna Bostock (Cambridge, Mass.: MIT Press, 1990).

McCormack, William J., *Ascendancy and Tradition in Anglo-Irish Literary History, 1798–1939* (Oxford: Clarendon Press, 1985).

MacDonagh, Oliver, *Ireland: The Union and its Aftermath* (London: George Allen and Unwin, 1977).

McHugh, Roger J., 'The Artist as Propagandist', *Studies*, 27 (March 1938), 47–62.

McManus, Antonia, *The Irish Hedge School and its Books, 1695–1831* (Dublin: Four Courts Press, 2002).

Mathews, P. J., *Revival: The Abbey Theatre, Sinn Féin, The Gaelic League and the Co-operative Movement* (Cork: Field Day/Cork University Press, 2003).

Mattar, Sinéad Garrigan, *Primitivism, Science, and the Irish Revival* (Oxford: Oxford University Press, 2004).

Meir, Colin, 'Voice and Audience in the Early Carleton', *Études Irlandaises*, 4 (Dec. 1979), 271–86.

Milne, Kenneth, *The Irish Charter Schools, 1730–1830* (Dublin: Four Courts Press, 1997).

Morash, Christopher, *Writing the Famine* (Oxford: Clarendon Press, 1995).

—— 'Spectres of the Famine', *Irish Review*, 17–18 (Winter 1995), 74–80.

—— *A History of Irish Theatre* (Cambridge: Cambridge University Press, 2002).

Moretti, Franco, *Atlas of the European Novel* (London: Verso, 1998).

Nolan, Emer, 'The Irish Literary Revival', in Joe Cleary and Claire Connolly (eds.), *The Cambridge Companion to Modern Irish Culture* (Cambridge: Cambridge University Press, 2005).

O'Brien, H. J., 'The Poor Scholar: the Oral Style of William Carleton', *Aquarius*, 4 (1971), 74–81.

Ó'Ciosáin, Niall, *Print and Popular Culture in Ireland, 1750–1850* (Basingstoke: Macmillan, 1997).

O'Grady, Thomas B., 'The Parish and the Universe: A Comparative Study of Patrick Kavanagh and William Carleton', *Studies*, 85/337 (Spring 1996).

O'Hagan, Timothy, *Rousseau* (London: Routledge, 1999).

Ó Háinle, Cathal G., 'The Gaelic Background of Carleton's *Traits and Stories*', *Éire-Ireland*, 18/1 (Spring 1983), 6–20.

O'Neill, Kevin, 'Mary Shackleton Leadbeater: Peaceful Rebel', in Dáire Keogh and Nicholas Furlong (eds.), *Women of 1798* (Dublin: Four Courts Press, 1998).

ÓTuathaigh, Gearóid, *Ireland before the Famine, 1798–1848* (Dublin: Gill and Macmillan, 1990).

Ong, Walter J., *Orality and Literacy: The Technologizing of the Word* (London: Methuen, 1982).

Orel, Harold, 'Coloured Photographs: William Carleton's Contribution to the Short Story Tradition', *Éire-Ireland*, 19/2 (Summer 1984), 75–97.

Parkes, Susan, *Kildare Place: The History of the Church of Ireland Training College, 1811–1869* (Dublin: Church of Ireland College of Education, 1984).

Parry, Geraint, '*Émile*: Learning to be Men, Women and Children', in Patrick Riley (ed.), *The Cambridge Companion to Rousseau* (Cambridge: Cambridge University Press, 2001).

Patterson, T. G. F., *The Burning of Wildgoose Lodge* (Dundalk: County Louth Archaeological Journal, 1972).

Pederson, Susan, 'Hannah More Meets Simple Simon: Tracts, Chapbooks, and Popular Culture in Late Eighteenth-Century England', *Journal of British Studies*, 25/1 (Jan. 1986), 84–113.

Pettit, Philip, *Republicanism: A Theory of Freedom and Government* (Oxford: Clarendon Press, 1997).

—— 'The Tree of Liberty, Republicanism: American, French, and Irish', *Field Day Review*, 1 (2005).

Philpin, C. H. E. (ed.), *Nationalism and Popular Protest in Ireland* (Cambridge: Cambridge University Press, 1987).

Plunkett, Horace, *Ireland in the New Century*. Foreword by Trevor West, 1904 (Dublin: Irish Academic Press, 1983).

Porter, Roy, *Enlightenment: Britain and the Creation of the Modern World* (London: Allen Lane, 2000).

Rafferty, SJ, Oliver P., 'Carleton's Ecclesiastical Context: The Ulster Catholic Experience', *Bullán*, 4/2 (Winter 1999–Spring 2000), 105–24.

Regan, Stephen, 'W. B. Yeats and Irish Cutlural Politics in the 1890s', in Sally Ledger and Scott McCracken (eds.), *Cultural Politics at the* Fin de Siècle (Cambridge: Cambridge University Press, 1997).

Rena-Dozier, Emily, 'Hannah More and the Invention of Narrative Authority', *ELH*, 71/1 (Spring 2004), 209–27.

Richardson, Alan, *Literature, Education and Romanticism: Reading as Social Practice, 1780–1832* (Cambridge: Cambridge University Press, 1994).

Roche, Daniel, *The Culture of Clothing: Dress and Fashion in the Ancien Regime*, first published Paris: Fayard, 1989; trans. Jean Birrell (Cambridge: Cambridge University Press, 1994).

—— *A History of Everyday Things: The Birth of Consumption in France, 1600–1800*, first published Paris: Fayard, 1997; trans. Brian Pearce (Cambridge: Cambridge University Press, 2000).

Said, Edward, *Orientalism: Western Concepts of the Orient*, 1978 (London: Penguin, 1991).

—— *Nationalism, Colonialism and Literature: Yeats and Decolonization*, Field Day Pamphlet no. 15 (Derry: Field Day, 1988).

Shaw, Rose, *Carleton's Country* (Dublin: Talbot Press, 1930).

Slack, Paul, *From Reformation to Improvement: Public Welfare in Early Modern England* (Oxford: Clarendon Press, 1999).

Sloan, Barry, *The Pioneers of Anglo-Irish Fiction, 1800–1850* (Garrards Cross, Bucks.: Colin Smythe, 1986).

Stott, Anne, *Hannah More: The First Victorian* (Oxford: Oxford University Press, 2003).

Sullivan, Eileen, 'William Carleton, Artist of Reality', *Éire-Ireland*, 12/1 (Spring 1977), 130–40.

—— *William Carleton* (Boston: Twayne, 1983).

Thuente, Mary Helen, *The Harp Re-Strung: The United Irishmen and the Rise of Irish Literary Nationalism* (Syracuse, NY: Syracuse University Press, 1994).

Vance, Norman, *Irish Literature, A Social History: Tradition, Identity and Difference* (Oxford: Blackwell, 1990).

Waters, Maureen, 'William Carleton: A Divided Tradition', *Canadian Journal of Irish Studies*, 10/2, (Dec. 1984), 27–37.

—— 'Heaney, Carleton and Joyce on the Road to Lough Derg', *Canadian Journal of Irish Studies*, 14/1 (July 1988).

Watt, Ian, *The Rise of the Novel: Studies in Defoe, Richardson and Fielding* (London: Chatto and Windus, 1957).

Whelan, Kevin, *The Tree of Liberty: Radicalism, Catholicism and the Construction of Irish Identity, 1760–1830* (Cork: Cork University Press/Field Day, 1996).

Williams, Raymond, *Culture and Society, 1780–1950* (Harmondsworth: Penguin Books in association with Chatto and Windus, 1963).

—— *The Country and the City* (London: Chatto and Windus, 1973).

—— *Keywords: A Vocabulary of Culture and Society*, first published 1976 (revised and expanded London: Fontana, 1983).

Wilner, Joshua, *Feeding on Infinity: Readings in the Romantic Rhetoric of Internalization* (Baltimore: Johns Hopkins University Press, 2000).

Woolf, Robert Lee, *William Carleton: Irish Peasant Novelist: A Preface to his Fiction* (New York and London: Garland Publishing, 1979).

Journals

The Carleton Newsletter, 1/1 (July 1970)–5/2 (April 1975).

Index